BARRON'S
BUSINESS
LIBRARY

Marketing

Second Edition

Robert D. Hisrich
Mixon Chair and Professor
Weatherhead School of Management
Case Western Reserve University

BARRON'S

All inquiries should be addressed to:
Barron's Educational Series, Inc.
250 Wireless Boulevard
Hauppauge, New York 11788
http://www.barronseduc.com

Library of Congress Catalog Card No. 00-021669

International Standard Book No. 0-7641-1404-2

Library of Congress Cataloging-in-Publication Data

Hisrich, Robert D.
   Marketing / Robert D. Hisrich.—2nd ed.
      p.   cm.—(Barron's business library)
   Includes index.
   ISBN 0-7641-1404-2
   1. Marketing.   I. Title   II. Series.
HF5415.H5435   2000
658.8—dc21
                                                    00-021669
                                                        CIP

PRINTED IN THE UNITED STATES OF AMERICA
10 9 8 7 6 5 4 3 2 1

Preface

The importance of marketing in successfully starting and operating a business cannot be overstated. Statistics indicating the high failure rate of newly created ventures and newly introduced products focus on the importance of marketing for success in both areas. Even though marketing affects every aspect of our lives, it is one of the most difficult concepts to understand fully and even more difficult to apply successfully in a business situation.

This book provides an in-depth, understandable, and practical explanation of marketing and marketing management for today's businesspeople. Each of 19 chapters presents a picture of one aspect of marketing as a dynamic, creative activity that impacts business success on a regular basis. The theoretical concepts are presented and illustrated to indicate their practical value in properly managing the marketing function. To make the book as meaningful as possible, each chapter begins with an introduction and the main points, contains numerous examples throughout, and concludes with a chapter perspective—a summary of the key concepts covered.

Many individuals—students, marketing executives, professors, and publishing staff—have made this book possible. Particular thanks goes to Teresa Kabat, without whom the manuscript would not have been typed in a clear, timely manner, and to Branko Bucar, Bostjan Antoncic, and Jennifer Baker for providing research material and editorial assistance. Finally, special thanks goes to Wendy Sleppin, project editor, and Sara Black, copy editor.

I am deeply indebted to my spouse, Tina, and my daughters, Kelly, Kary, and Katy, whose patience, support, and understanding helped bring this effort to fruition. It is to Kelly, Kary, and Katy and to the generation they represent that this book is particularly dedicated.

Contents

The Role of Marketing and Marketing Management

INTRODUCTION AND MAIN POINTS

Marketing is a central aspect of every society, and to some extent affects the lives of everyone. This makes its analysis and understanding an important venture for all. In this chapter we will make sure you understand that marketing is not an isolated function within a firm, but rather begins and ends in the changing external hypercompetitive environment, starting with the idea for a product or service and finishing only when the consumer has had sufficient time for evaluation and hopefully purchase. We will focus on the fact that marketing is a process by which decisions are made in a totally interrelated business environment on all the activities that facilitate exchange so that targeted groups of customers are satisfied and the objectives of the organization are accomplished.

Establishing *objectives* is a critical first step and needs to be accomplished in light of the going-concern concept—most firms intend to do business with the same or similar customers over a period of time. All strategic decisions on marketing activities should be based on the needs and desires of the targeted group of customers. The activities facilitating exchange are the controllable marketing elements of the marketing mix—the product, price, distribution and promotion.

After studying the material in this chapter:
- You will know the definition and nature of marketing as a process.
- You will be able to explain the controllable marketing elements.
- You will understand the evolution of marketing and society.

MARKETING AND THE MARKETING PROCESS

Marketing is a central part of every society, influencing everyone in the society to some extent. Marketing has an increasing impact on the decisions being made not only by buyers and sellers but also by a diverse group including physicians, lawyers, politicians, and even the clergy. For example, a state politician may be trying to decide how he should allocate his promotional budget during the last two weeks of an election campaign. Should an expensive television advertisement be used? Should there be more radio spots? Or would additional advertisements in various newspapers across the state be a better use of the available money? Other decisions need to be made on where he should spend his time. Should precincts that are borderline be visited, or should emphasis be placed in those that are somewhat more favorable? These and many more basic marketing decisions are made throughout any local, state, or national political campaign.

Buyers of industrial goods are confronted with related yet different aspects of marketing. Should sources of supply be switched because of the superior quality and lower price of the new supplier? Will a new firm be consistently able to supply the quantity needed at this price? Will the new supplier deliver the product on time, in order to avoid any costly plant shutdowns that would result from an out-of-stock condition? An industrial buyer must carefully weigh many aspects of marketing in selecting the correct product and supplier.

Finally, consider the consumer—you and me—trying to decide on a hair stylist. Should the aspects of the number of awards, services offered, or number of employees be considered? Or, should the locational convenience of alternative hair stylists take priority? What about switching hair stylists: what are the factors in developing stylist loyalty?

Similar to what occurred in each of these examples, marketing impacts the lives of everyone in a society. This makes it important for everyone to understand the marketing process not only in order to have a better lifestyle but also to be able to work in an organization. Even managers not in direct marketing positions need to understand marketing principles, since marketing is the major force stimulating sales—which are, after all, the principal source of the firm's revenues.

MARKETING: AN INTEGRATED DEFINITION

But what exactly is this activity that has such an impact on our lives? The answer to this question depends on the perspective of the individual. Law, finance, economics, operations, and consumers all view marketing from a different vantage point.

The American Marketing Association developed its definition of marketing: "Marketing is the process of planning and executing the conception, pricing, promotion and distribution of ideas, goods, and services to create exchanges that satisfy individual and organizational goals."[1] In this strict definition, marketing begins with the production of goods or services and ends when the goods or services reach the consumer or user. A broader definition is more accurate in today's rapidly changing hypercompetitive environment. Marketing actually begins with an *idea* for a product or service and ends only after the consumer has had sufficient time to evaluate the product thoroughly, which might be months or years later.

In the changing hypercompetitive environment, the following definition of marketing is more applicable: *Marketing is the process by which decisions are made in a totally interrelated changing business environment on all the activities that facilitate exchange in order that the targeted group of customers is satisfied and the defined objectives accomplished.* This definition has four major aspects which need further amplification.

First, how does this decision-making process impact the accomplishment of defined objectives? While the specific objectives vary from firm to firm as well as from product to product within a single firm, it is impossible for good managerial decisions to be made without defined objectives. The basic objective of a profit organization is of course to make a profit. While this objective may not occur in the short run or for some of the firm's products, overall each firm must make a profit in the long run in order to continue to exist. Obtaining this objective under the going-concern concept—the organization plans to do business year after year—means that any profits realized cannot be at the sacrifice of customers or the environment.

Similarly, this going-concern concept is important in establishing and obtaining the objectives of a nonprofit organization. Nonprofit organizations' objectives do vary greatly: a church may have the objective to reach 1,000 people in the coming year with the biblical message; a doctor to establish a good practice by competently handling his patients' well-being; a university to attract the best students possible from a wide geographic area. Once established, the objectives should guide the strategic decision making of the firm, which sometimes does not occur. For example, one nonprofit organization with the established objective of helping orphans and disadvantaged youth by providing the best possible facilities and programs did not succeed because there were no image-building and fund-raising programs implemented to raise the necessary funds.

Satisfying Target Customers

The second part of the definition—the satisfaction of the target group of customers—requires that the customer be the orientation and focus of all the firm's activities. The customer's wants and needs must be constantly analyzed, enabling the firm's offering to be exactly what is desired—the essence of the *marketing concept*. Without this focus, a customer can just as easily choose an alternative offering from a competitive firm.

Activities Facilitating Exchange

All the activities that facilitate exchange, the third part of the definition, include all the controllable marketing elements of the firm available for use in customer satisfaction. These controllable marketing elements, which comprise the firm's offering, can be classified in four areas—product, price, distribution, and promotion. As is indicated in Figure 1-1, each element has its own mix where strategic decisions are needed in order to achieve customer satisfaction.

The product area includes all the aspects that make up the physical product or service being offered for sale. Decisions need to be made on quality, assortment, the breadth and depth of line, warranty, guarantee, service, and the package. All these aspects make the final product or service more (or less) appealing to the target market.

Closely related to the product and its mix is the price. While probably the least understood of the elements, the price of the product greatly influences the image of the product as well as whether or not it will be purchased. The price established needs to take into consideration the three Cs—cost, competition, and the consumer.

The third basic element of the marketing mix—distribution—covers two different areas. The first area—channels of distribution—deals with the institutions such as wholesalers and retailers that handle the product between the firm and the consumer. Physical distribution, the second area, deals with the aspects of physically moving the product from the firm to the consumer. This includes such things as warehousing, inventory, and transportation.

The final element—promotion—involves policies and procedures related to four areas:

    1. *Personal Selling.* Emphasis on personal selling and the methods to be employed in the manufacturer's organization and in the trade.

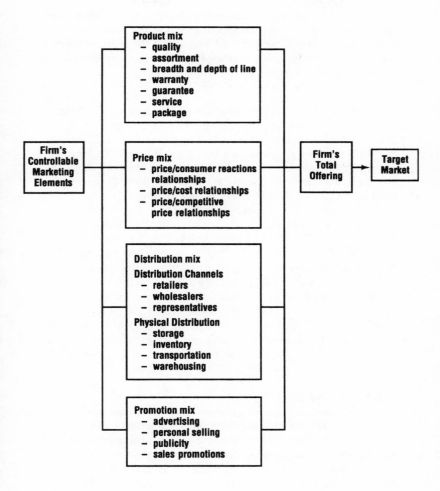

FIG. 1-1. *Marketing activities.*

2. *Advertising*. Policies and procedures relating to budget, message, and media.
3. *Sales Promotions*. Policies and procedures relating to budget and types of consumer and trade promotions and displays.
4. *Publicity*. Policies and procedures relating to a comprehensive program for good media coverage and a strong company image.

The final part of the definition indicates that marketing exists in a totally interrelated and changing external and internal environment. Decisions in the other functional areas of the firm as well as those made in competitive firms affect the rate of this change, as do the other variables in the external environment.

Two types of decisions are being made by marketing managers in this changing environment: strategic decisions and tactical decisions. *Strategic decisions* are broad-range decisions of a year or longer that establish an overall framework for the firm's marketing actions. For example, a strategic decision for many automobile manufacturers has been to increase their warranty from one year–12,000 miles to six years–60,000 miles.

Tactical decisions, on the other hand, are short-run, more frequently made decisions by which marketing activities are implemented and managed on a daily basis. In the case of the automakers' increase in the warranty time period, a tactical decision was the preparation and distribution of the new warranty cards to the respective dealers. One of the tactical decisions in the launching of Coast soap by Procter and Gamble was the distribution of free samples of the product in selected areas in New England.

THE MARKETING CONCEPT

More than any other functional business area, marketing helps develop the goals and direction of the organization. Overall, the basic philosophy operant within the firm's management should focus on the satisfaction of the target customer—the heart of the *marketing concept*. Under the marketing concept, the consumer becomes the dominant focal point of the firm, with all the resources and activities in the firm directed at generating customer satisfaction.

The adoption of a marketing concept by many firms in the United States as well as the rest of the world was precipitated by several factors. First, there has been an increase in the intensity of competition (hypercompetition) in both national and international markets, forcing organizations to place greater emphasis on consumers and their satisfaction. A second factor that has caused the adoption of the marketing concept is the high level of consumer knowledge and sophistication. Consumers are more aware of product alternatives and price than ever before. Just count the number of shoppers carrying calculators and coupons in your local supermarket.

As consumers become increasingly aware of the various options available, only those products and services that are recognized as "need satisfying" will be purchased.

A high level of consumer awareness has evolved in the United States and other developed countries due, in part, to the good communication systems. The communication system has informed consumers of faulty products (such as General Motors recalling specific models of cars and trucks), price increases (such as U.S. Steel announcing a forthcoming price increase on rolled steel), and fraudulent advertising (such as the Federal Trade Commission investigating the claims of American Express). The resulting increased awareness has enabled consumers to be much more discriminating in their purchase decisions.

An increase in production capabilities in conjunction with the development of worldwide markets has also led to the adoption of the marketing concept. Increased production capacity has led to economies in the scale of production—a decrease in per-unit production cost as the total number of units is increased. The increased units produced can only be sold through successfully selling to mass markets by focusing on customer satisfaction. This is the marketing concept.

Finally, the need for innovative products for survival has forced firms to place the customer first. Just a simple count of the number of times you have seen and heard the phrase "new and improved" indicates the size of the consumer appetite for new and supposedly better products. Yet, in spite of this hunger, somewhere between 80% and 90% of all new products introduced on the market fail. A key ingredient to successful new product introduction is knowing the needs and buying habits of the target group of consumers.

THE EVOLUTION OF MARKETING AND SOCIETY

Marketing has evolved historically through numerous stages. There are four distinct stages that occur during the development of an economy, beginning with the start of "exchange" between two parties. The four stages each have three specific areas: the level of industrialization; the values and attitudes of management toward marketing; and the degree of marketing knowledge. These three areas and their specific definition in each of the four stages are listed in Table 1-1.

Table 1-1
Principles Illustrated for a Primitive Society

Principle	Stage of Societal Development	Stage of Specialization of Labor or Resources Developed	Marketing Decision Needed
1. Product Planning	Tribe now using spears, arrows, and knives all made from stone. Demand for such known only in this tribe.	Gilligan had the best method of producing stone instruments demanding sharp edges.	Whether to make spears, toma-hawks, arrows, or knives—or per-haps a line of all these instruments.
2. Pricing	Game per capita was getting less plentiful and demand for bet-ter hunting instruments was increasing	Gilligan wanted to devote more time to stone instruments and less to hunting game for food.	How many or what part of an edible animal carcass should he demand for one instrument?
3. Branding Policies	Tribe now con-scious that cer-tain sharpened stone instru-ments were much better than others, but all qualities in the sharpened stone were not easily recognizable on sight. Further-more, there was now just begin-ning to be com-munication between tribes and a realization that this problem existed in other	Gilligan had now brought his entire family into the produc-tion process, further breaking down the job so that each mem-ber of his family was a specialist, such as: (1) the oldest child would search, find, and bring back the raw materials or the kind of stone needed; (2) one would shape a rough prototype	Gilligan real-ized the need for putting his family insignia in some form on his superior product so tribesmen could quickly recog-nize this. This was particularly needed for far-off tribes with whom he had no personal con-tact.

Table 1-1 (continued)

Principle	Stage of Societal Development	Stage of Specialization of Labor or Resources Developed	Marketing Decision Needed
	tribes. Tribes were also recognizing other forms of specialization useful to the group. For instance, some tribe members lacked the courage and stamina to stay days on the hunt, yet were found to be good at tanning and curing hides.	of the instrument needed; (3) one would finish-form the instrument; and (4) one would put sharp edges on the finished form.	
4. Fact Finding and Analysis	Tribes were now using more specialized sharp stone instruments for slicing meats, cutting wood, etc. Some difficulties had been experienced with some of Gilligan's stone instruments. In an effort to make these sharper he had started to use a harder but more brittle stone. Some of these instruments were breaking after 1–6 months of use.	Gilligan had found better stone for holding a sharper edge for all of his instruments. Gilligan was now sending one of his children out to visit each tribe to determine new needs and problems being encountered.	Whether to continue with present stone and find method of treating with heat and tempering to avoid brittleness or go to different stone. The new instrument to be made to satisfy user needs.

Stage 1

In the preindustrial (tribal, herdsman, or agrarian) stage, few if any individuals had accumulated capital, and life was devoted to meeting the basic needs of food, clothing, and shelter. This stage, usually reached within the family or tribal unit, has little specialization of labor or resources. In the marketing area all emphasis is on the production of useful, basic items. Most products are custom-made, fashioned by hand, and little attention is paid to anything like a "marketing mix." This is a state of unconscious ignorance. People "do not know that they do not know" that there are actually marketing principles and techniques in operation. Even though these techniques, values, and attitudes actually exist, there is no awareness of this.

Stage 2

In the beginning of industrialization, specialization of labor has become so developed that assembly-line production is occurring for standardized products. This is the selling concept stage, with production people feeling: "We make it. It's the sales department's job to sell it." Little emphasis is given to determining whether the product being made is the best one to satisfy the customers' needs. Emphasis is on selling the output of production. This stage is exemplified by Henry Ford's comment about the Model T at the time assembly-line production was just beginning in the United States: "You can have any color you want as long as it is black." The marketing people during this stage are aware of the existence of underlying principles and concepts. While the existence of such principles is acknowledged, they are not yet defined or clearly understood.

Stage 3

In stage 3, the society has evolved to an industrial base with the following characteristics. First, specialization of labor has become fully developed. Second, capital has been accumulated to permit large production units. Third, there is the capacity to overproduce. Management, at this point, has adopted the marketing concept, with emphasis on the customer. Consumers' needs are researched, and methods of informing them about products satisfying these needs are becoming increasingly more elaborate. The products are also readily and conveniently available. There is greater emphasis on marketing principles with the companies carrying out these marketing principles having greater success.

At this point, marketing people have developed conscious knowledge. Marketing concepts have been analyzed and defined, stages of development recognized, and theory and practice refined. There is also a conscious effort to understand and apply this knowledge.

Stage 4

The last developmental stage is the *postindustrialization* or *visionary stage*. Technology has solved most production inefficiencies, making the capacity to produce unlimited. Only shortages of raw materials and demand limit the actual production. Management has adopted more of a societal concept of marketing, with emphasis on the following: (1) how to dispose of the wastes from products without negatively affecting human health or lifestyles; (2) how to administer society to take into account any resulting shortages of raw material; and (3) how to promote nonprofit institutions that exist for the betterment of society. Acquisitions of products have diminished in importance compared to the freedom and time to develop a nice lifestyle. Quality of life is given more attention than quantity accumulated. Emphasis in marketing is on social needs rather than the need for more or better products. Marketing people have evolved to the point of unconscious application—subconsciously carrying out the proper principles without actually referring to them.

Two things are important in understanding this four-stage evolution concept. First, all societies do not move concurrently through these stages. Today there are tribes in Africa and in Brazil that are still in the preindustrial stages. A great part of the civilized world is in the industrialization stage, and the United States, Japan, and Germany are in the postindustrial stage.

Second, all enterprises within a particular country are not in the same stage at a given time. In the United States, there are corporations that are still in the product stage of marketing, while still others are in the consumer stage and selling concept stage. Some are in the societal concept stage.

SOCIETAL MARKETING CONCEPT

The significant growth in the influence and power of business and the simultaneous increase in environmental deterioration, world hunger and poverty, and knowledge and awareness of social issues by the populace that is occurring has brought about an increase in business scrutiny and a questioning of whether business is acting in the best long-run interests of consumers and society. This questioning and the finiteness of resources and damageable environment has led to a new stage (the fifth stage) emerging—the societal marketing stage. *Societal marketing* is when an organization, namely a business, understands the consumer's wants and needs and delivers the desired satisfaction effectively and efficiently in a way that preserves both the consumers' and society's well-being. Societal marketing means that social and ethical considerations are one aspect of every marketing decision and practice. This requires that the firm balance long-run consumer welfare with its long-term goal of profitability and include social, ethical, and ecological considerations in its product and market planning. Two companies have been identified as embracing the societal marketing concept—Ben & Jerry's (a producer of super-premium ice cream since 1978) and The Body Shop (a manufacturer and retailer of natural ingredient-based cosmetics in recyclable packaging since 1976).

Two concepts have taken the forefront in societal marketing—social responsibility and business ethics. *Social responsibility* means that the firm needs to consider and be concerned about its impact on society, particularly in its marketing activities. This social responsibility needs to be in the economic, legal, ethical, and discretionary areas. A prime example of social responsibility is the quick response of Johnson and Johnson to the Tylenol tragedy in 1982 when seven Chicago people died from cyanide-laced Extra-Strength Tylenol capsules. The company immediately withdrew all Tylenol capsules from retail shelves all over the United States and the packaging was changed to include a sealed cardboard box, a sealed plastic bottle top, and an inner seal covering the bottle. The cost to Johnson and Johnson was: product recall and lost profits, $50 million, and repackaging costs, $100 million.

The other concept—*business ethics*—is doing good or the right thing in a given human situation. Business practices are evaluated in light of human value, and profits should be achieved along with some human good. Business ethics refers to the individual marketing managers, whereas social responsibility refers to the entire marketing area or business concern. Together business ethics and social responsibility form the main basis for societal marketing, which redefines the bounds within which the marketing manager must satisfy customer wants and needs profitably while accomplishing the objectives of the firm.

CHAPTER PERSPECTIVE

Objectives, goals, and strategic and tactical decisions need to be made in a changing, interrelated, hypercompetitive business environment. Marketing must be synchronized with the production, finance, engineering, research and development, personnel, legal, and other functional departments within the organization in order to satisfy customer needs—the heart of the marketing concept under this concept. The consumer becomes the focal point of all decision making. This concept has been widely adopted because of several factors: increased competition, increased consumer awareness and sophistication, highly developed communication systems, increased production capabilities, the development of mass worldwide markets, and the need for innovative products in light of the high rate of new-product failure.

FOOTNOTE

1 Peter D. Bennett, editor, *Dictionary of Marketing Terms* (Chicago: The Association, 1995).

The Firm and the External Marketing Environment

INTRODUCTION AND MAIN POINTS

A firm functions in a complex, rapidly changing, hypercompetitive external marketing environment that must be continually monitored in order for the firm to survive and prosper in today's marketplace. Much of this external environment is beyond the control of the firm, but it still profoundly affects the firm's functioning. This external environment can be broken down into five distinct categories: economic, cultural and social, business, political and legal, and demographic.

After reading the material in this chapter:

■ You will understand the effect the external environment has on the firm's operations.

■ You will be able to discuss the impact of the economic environment, cultural and social environment, political and legal environment, business environment, and demographic environment on management decisions.

■ You will understand the value and source of information in making marketing decisions.

Marketing today, more than at any previous time, occurs in a rapidly changing, hypercompetitive external environment. While the firm or industry can have some degree of influence on this external marketing environment, these outside forces are not under the firm's control and are changing at an accelerated rate. Even though these forces cannot be controlled, failure to recognize their impact can be extremely damaging, such as occurred in many companies' slow response to the Internet and e-commerce.

One key to the success of an organization is the ability to predict change—one of the functions of marketing research—and to adapt the firm's offerings to that change. It is becoming increasingly important that a company constantly monitor the external marketing environment for new as well as changing needs.

This external marketing environment can be examined from various perspectives, as illustrated in Figure 2-1.

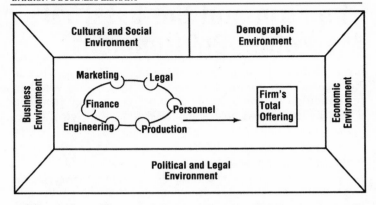

FIG. 2-1. *The uncontrollable environment of marketing and the business firm.*

ECONOMIC ENVIRONMENT

There is no more significant component in the external environment affecting marketing than the economic environment. The economic environment affects the operation of a company on both a micro (individual company) as well as a macro (a broader industry, state, national, and international) level.

Supply and Demand

When there is little or no government intervention and control, the basic underlying forces of the economic dimension are supply and demand. *Supply* is the amount of goods and services sellers are willing to offer at various prices in a given time period and market condition. *Demand* is the amount of goods and services buyers are willing to purchase at various prices in the same time period and market conditions. The intersection of these two forces determines the market price as well as the amount of the product that will be produced and sold. Often buyers and sellers do not agree, and the equilibrium price does not correctly reflect the value of the quantity of the goods and services in the market. When this occurs, there is either a shortage (excess demand vs. supply) or a surplus (excess supply vs. demand).

In a competitive market structure, when a surplus or a shortage occurs, changes occur until equilibrium is restored. In the case of a surplus, the price is usually lowered to meet the demand level in the short run. In the long run, either the supply will decrease, as the quantities offered are decreased by some firms making production cuts or by other firms going out of business, or the actual demand will change (increase) owing to buyers' willingness to purchase more of the product. When a shortage occurs, a company must carefully assess whether this condition is temporary or is actually a market need not being satisfied. For example, some felt that the shortage of home canning lids that arose during a canning season in the late 1970s indicated a long-run market need for an increase in the production of these lids. Since the cost of entering this market was very small (about $75,000), several companies were established to produce lids for this "shortage." These companies did not realize that the need was only temporary, caused by overpurchases and hoarding by traditional customers. The result was that most of the new companies went out of business within several years.

The Market and Exchange

In every market economy there is a way for the market equilibrium price and quantity to be achieved. The mechanism for doing this by bridging the gap between supply and demand is the marketplace itself. While there are several ways to think about the market, in the context of a changing environment, it is best to view the market as *the aggregate of buying and selling units, forming the relationship between demand and supply.* In the context of the economic dimension, the marketplace bridges the gap between what is produced (supply) and what is consumed (demand), making the right quantity available to meet the market need. In the case of a household, each unit builds up both homogeneous stocks of goods such as food products (accumulation) and heterogeneous stocks of goods such as a variety of hardware materials (assorting). Once the goods are accumulated, the stocks are broken down for use—that is, the box of cereal (homogeneous) is broken down (allocated) over several meals, on the one hand, and the nails, lumber, and hammer are broken down (sorted out) when building a home ice skating rink. Similar transactions occur on the retail, wholesale, and manufacturing levels as well as on the macro level of a nation or the world. These general dimensions of the market in a changing competitive environment are also reflected in the economic aspects of individual buying behavior, which includes the purchasing power of consumers, their actual willingness to purchase, and their spending patterns. (The latter is the focus of Chapter 4.)

General Economic Change
The economic conditions in a country and the state of a national economy change over time. Movements and fluctuations in the economy often follow patterns and have been described as "business cycles." These cycles historically have consisted of four stages: prosperity, recession, depression, recovery. Each of these general stages can be further complicated by various degrees of inflation, balance of trade, and balance of payments.

CULTURAL AND SOCIAL ENVIRONMENT
The cultural-social environment is reflected in the other four major environments external to the firm's marketing mix: (1) in the economic environment, in the types and amounts of goods and services purchased for consumption; (2) in the business environment, in the distribution structure developed for the delivery of goods and services and the strong interest in ecology; (3) in the laws and regulations, in the written law as well as the courts' interpretation of these; and (4) in all aspects of the demographic environment. For example, American consumers have gradually shifted from a savings and cash purchasing mentality to spending freely and purchasing on credit.

Lifestyle and Quality of Life
Lifestyle is simply the manner in which consumers and organizations behave in the marketplace. For consumers, lifestyles tend to focus on broad cultural trends and general needs, values, and activities closely associated with consumer behavior. These combine to develop an individual's overall behavior. Organizations have lifestyles, too, as reflected in such things as the prevailing dress standards, vacation policies, and willingness to innovate and change.

The lifestyle of consumers is further reflected in their standards of living. Business is expected to make available the products and services necessary to provide the desired standards of living and a satisfying quality of life. If the products and services that are desired are being produced and delivered, at the right price and quality, and with no associated negative impact in such areas as the environment, then no problems arise. When all these conditions do not occur, conflict occurs.

For example, consider the following alternatives: cleaner air occurring from stricter emission standards on automobiles—or better miles to the gallon; more dependence on fossil fuels (and foreign oil) to generate electricity—or solar power—or nuclear power; almost totally safe products at a much higher price—or products with a lesser margin of safety at a lower price; drugs more quickly available to cure illness with a possibility of side effects or completely safe drugs available only after many years of testing. There are no clear-cut answers to these and the other questions surrounding the production and distribution of goods and services. One thing is apparent: there are varying degrees of intervention by the federal, state, and local governments as well as special-interest groups in the final decisions on these and other important questions.

Consumers

The consumer (or customer) is the most important single force in the external environment of the firm. Without a consumer there is, of course, no market and no need for marketing. Although the management of a firm can influence consumer reaction to a product by tailoring the product to its target consumer, the consumers still decide which products they will buy and in what quantity.

Probably no single research study is more important in marketing than the clear, concise determination of buyer demand. This information identifies the deciding factors that will help mold the product most effectively. This process of molding the product to a defined market, called the *target market*, does not cease with the launching of the product. A progressive company is always interested in how it can further increase consumer satisfaction and acceptance of its product.

Consumerism

American consumers have in some instances become very disenchanted by various promotion messages, by faulty products, and by other aspects of the marketing process. In one instance, a leading manufacturer of liquor suggested that the consumer's dream man would be enchanted if she served the right (the manufacturer's) liquor. This type of promotional message as well as other activities such as unclear warranties and products not meeting expectations led to the resurgence of a movement called consumerism. What specifically is consumerism and some of its causes? *Consumerism* is a movement for promoting and protecting consumers' interests. The term has come to be associated with the rights of consumers to be informed and take action when necessary. The new consumerism movement began in the 1960s as a protest by consumers against unfair business practices, particularly in the marketing area.

The movement gained the support of various groups and individuals and has been involved in improving such business practices as the development of:
- higher quality, more dependable products
- less deceptive, more informative advertising
- more reasonable, accurate prices
- better-documented and supported warranties and guarantees.

In addition, the movement in the 1970s and 1980s spread to environmental hazards, air transportation regulations, credit and lending practices, and many other areas of daily life.

The federal government responded to this increasing consumer vocalism by putting more teeth into existing laws and by adding laws and regulations designed specifically to protect the consumer, such as the Consumer Product Safety Act and the Consumer Credit Protection Act (Truth-in-Lending Act).

Marketing and Social Responsibility

The rapidly changing values of society and the increased responsiveness in the social and cultural dimension have placed more pressure on marketing personnel to act responsibly, morally, and ethically. While previous deceptive advertising, fraudulent warranties, and defective products have eroded public confidence in business in general and marketing in particular, business is slowly regaining some of the lost trust and confidence. Marketing needs not only to provide the right quality of goods and services desired, but also to establish control procedures to inhibit unethical activities from damaging the company's image. As marketing views itself more and more as a social process concerned with the needs and wants of society in general, it will be better able to serve as the vehicle through which goods and services are effectively and efficiently delivered in the hypercompetitive changing environment.

BUSINESS ENVIRONMENT

The business environment consists of several factors: competition, raw materials, ecology, technology, labor, and the distribution structure.

Competition

The marketing system is predicated on competition, of which there are three basic types: intraindustry, interindustry, and international. Intraindustry competition is competition among firms in one industry. In the confectionery industry this would be between firms such as Hershey and Mars. If cough drops, chewing gum, acid indigestion drops are included in this industry, the competition would increase to include American Chickle with Certs or Chicklets. Interindustry competition, as the name implies, is competition among similar competing industries, such as ice cream, soft drinks, and confectionery.

For example, in some years, in the United States, an early drop in temperatures and a premature beginning of autumn has caused confectionery sales to increase more than usual in September and October, accompanied by a decline in ice cream and soft drink sales. Interindustry competition can also be between two entirely unrelated industries. For a particular target market family, competition exists between a firm making outdoor furniture and an airline promoting European trips. The family's limited discretionary income will be spent on only one of the items.

International competition is competition among companies in different countries. American auto manufacturers have encountered severe international competition from foreign car manufacturers; the same holds true for radio, steel, television, camera, and many other manufacturers.

Competition, regardless of its type, produces some beneficial results: (a) better products at lower prices; (b) an increase in the number of new or improved products; and (c) development of market efficiency in the distribution of products.

Raw Materials and Energy

The 1970s, 1980s, and 1990s have seen periodic shortages of certain raw materials; this situation is likely to continue in the next decade and beyond. Raw materials should be viewed in terms of their abundance and renewability. The supply and renewability of raw materials pose both problems and opportunities for companies. For companies whose products or entire operations rely on raw materials that are in limited supply, it may mean that the materials may become too costly even if they are available. For other companies, it may be an opportunity either to develop new sources of materials, use materials more efficiently, or provide substitutes for the materials themselves. Raw materials need to be protected and carefully used.

Probably nowhere else has the impact of overabundance and shortages of raw material and supplies been more severely felt than in the rise and fall of the cost of energy. The shortage of oil and its price fluctuations caused many obsolete factories to close as well as intensified the search for alternative energy sources. Coal became, for some, a substitute energy source, and numerous companies and inventors searched for ways to harness nuclear, solar, thermal, and wind sources of power. In addition, people began to make more efficient use of present energy through better insulation of commercial and residential structures and increased fuel efficiency in automobiles and other equipment. This was followed by a surplus that significantly reduced the price of oil.

Ecology

A closely related aspect to the business environment is the question of ecology. After years of little concern about damaging the quality of the natural environment, many consumers are now expressing discontent with the traditional methods of disposal of waste products, the littering of the environment, the level of ozone in the air, and the amount of pollution in the water. According to the Environmental Protection Agency, many U.S. rivers are so polluted that they are unswimmable for at least half the year. An even more critical issue is the handling of hazardous waste products.

It is becoming apparent that unless the U.S. starts cleaning up the environment, the health and life expectancy of its citizens will be adversely affected. But are Americans willing to pay the price, not only in terms of dollars but also in the loss of convenience and in adopting a different standard of living? Estimated costs of ending most air and water pollution range from $350 billion to over $500 billion.

Technology

One of the most dramatic forces in the business environment hat directly impacts individuals and corporate livelihood is technology. Technology provides a culture for developing new products and new methods for doing things, thereby developing new markets and opportunities. A company must carefully monitor all that is occurring in the technological environment or risk going out of business as its products become obsolete. In addition, the growth rate of an economy is directly related to the technological advances occurring in the form of major new products and services.

Labor

The work force is another uncontrollable factor in the business environment. This area has recently become less of a problem than when there were a large number of strikes and incidences of strikers defying court orders to go back to work. This absence has decreased the overall concern about the power of unions and their corruptness.

However, companies are confronted more and more by individuals wanting different things from their jobs, including more trust and respect from their employers, a guaranteed standard of living, and more control over the work environment, their personal lives, and vacation time.

Distribution Structure

The final aspect of the business environment that affects the firm's marketing is the developed distribution structure—*the methods and routes by which the product reaches the consumer.* Its importance can be seen by looking at the evolution of the home computer market. Many computer companies with good manufacturing technology were not familiar with, and did not have access to, the consumer market. The firm that had the initial advantage was Tandy Corporation, which sold its home computer products through one of its subsidiary companies, Radio Shack. Even though it did not have the name of IBM, Apple, or the other technical powerhouses, Tandy Corporation had a more important strength in the case of home computers—well-established channels of distribution. This advantage has been offset by direct sales by Gateway and retail store sales by IBM and Apple. The distribution system will become even more strategic for good marketing plans to be implemented in the changing environment of the future.

POLITICAL AND LEGAL ENVIRONMENT

The political and legal environment is another variable over which the firm has little or no control. Although a firm or industry can lobby Congress and state legislatures for or against certain laws and regulations, it is the lawmakers, not the business managers, who will enact the legislation. The automobile industry is a good example of this process. Even though the major car companies unsuccessfully lobbied vigorously against some of the antipollution measures and gas efficiency that Congress eventually passed, they were able to obtain a longer period of time for compliance than was specified in the original law—and they are still continuing to get extensions.

The influence of government on the business community is increasing each year, and now extends to all areas of business. Since detailed coverage of the laws and regulations affecting marketing would require an entire book, only a few specific aspects will be discussed here.

Consumer Protection Legislation

While there are many laws protecting the consumer, from a business perspective, two of the most important are the Federal Food, Drug, and Cosmetic Act and the Consumer Product Safety Act. *The Federal Food, Drug and Cosmetic Act*, passed in 1938, is a comprehensive law providing health safeguards for the consumer. These safeguards encompass a wide variety of items—foods, food additives, drugs, medical devices, and cosmetics. The food section of the act sets standards for foods, including raw agricultural products. These standards cover illegal foods, additions to foods, and their labeling.

The second part of the Act covers *drugs*—products used in the medical care of humans or animals. The law provides for the regulation of new prescription drugs, over-the-counter drugs, biological drugs (drugs made from human or animal substances), and medical devices. Violators of the Federal Food, Drug, and Cosmetic Act may be fined, imprisoned, or both. In addition, a manufacturer can be ordered to cease production and sale of a product.

The Consumer Product Safety Act of 1972 empowers a commission to establish and enforce mandatory product safety standards and ban the sale of unreasonably hazardous consumer products. The commission can inspect manufacturing operations, subpoena records, and require compliance tests. This Act, as well as a listing of other examples of consumer protection legislation, is presented in Table 2-1.

Regulation of Competition Legislation

In 1890 the *Sherman Antitrust Act* was passed. This act was the first federal legislation prohibiting monopolies that would cause restraint of trade. The legislation was strengthened by the *Clayton Act* in 1914, which restricted practices such as price discrimination, tying contracts (requiring a dealer to carry a manufacturer's full line of products), and exclusive dealings. Later the *Robinson-Patman Act* of 1936 was added to close loopholes in the Clayton Act. This Act prohibited price discrimination that was not based on a cost differential and also prohibited a company from discriminating in price between different purchasers of commodities of like grade and quality, where the effect of such discrimination may be a substantial lessening of competition or the creation of a monopoly.

Trademark and Packaging

Trademark law is another area of government legislation affecting firms. A *trademark* is an identifying word, phrase, symbol, or picture used to distinguish one company's products from another's. According to trademark law, the owner of a trademark has certain legal rights, including the right to prevent other companies from using the trademark in a confusing or deceptive manner. These rights are protected regardless of whether the trademark is registered with the United States. The *Lanham Act* of 1946 combined and replaced the old trademark act by simplifying and liberalizing registration of trademarks and providing prompt action for trademark violations.

Promotion

Any deceptive or misleading attempts to persuade people to purchase products or services have been prohibited for a significant period of time. Today, more stringent adherence to truthful, fair, and accurate promotional statements is required.

The Future

Upon examining Table 2-1, you will notice a decrease in the number and scope of consumer protection legislation after 1976 and then an increase, particularly in the area of promotion.

Table 2-1
Consumer Protection: Selected Legislation

Year	Law	Purpose
1906	Food and Drugs Act	Guards against unsafe and unadulterated food and drug products.
1906	Meat Inspection Act	Requires that meat shipped in interstate commerce be processed and packed under wholesome and sanitary conditions.
1938	Food, Drug, and Cosmetic Act	Amendment to the Food and Drugs Act, expanding the jurisdiction of the Food and Drug Administration to include cosmetics and therapeutic devices; also establishes standards of identity for food products.
1939	Wool Products Labeling Act	Makes fiber content labeling by percentages mandatory in products containing wool.
1951	Fur Products Labeling Act	Establishes mandatory labeling requirement for fur products.
1953	Flammable Fabrics Act	Outlaws the manufacture or sale of wearing apparel or fabric so highly flammable as to be dangerous.
1958	Textile Fiber Products Identification Act	Requires identification of the fiber content of clothing and textile fiber products.
1960	Hazardous Substances Labeling Act	Controls the labeling of packages of hazardous household substances.
1962	Kefauver-Harris Amendment	Amendment to the Food, Drug, and Cosmetic Act requiring that all drugs be tested for safety and efficacy.
1966	Fair Packaging and Labeling Act	Requires packaging and labeling of consumer foods. Provides for the voluntary adoption of uniform packaging standards.
1966	National Traffic and Motor Vehicle Safety Act	Authorizes the establishment of compulsory safety standards for automobiles and new and used tires.
1966	Child Protection Act of 1966	Amendment to the Hazardous Substances Labeling Act, which became the Hazardous Substances Act, prevented

Year	Law	Purpose
		marketing of potentially harmful toys and other articles used by children.
1966	Cigarette Labeling Act	Requires health warning labels on cigarette packaging.
1967	Flammable Fabrics Act Amendments	Broadens federal authority to set safety standards for flammable fabrics.
1968	Consumer Credit Protection Act (Truth-in-Lending)	Requires full disclosure of terms and conditions of finance changes in consumer credit transactions.
1969	Child Protection and Toy Safety Act of 1969	Amendment to the Hazardous Substances Act broadening its coverage to provide for ban on toys and other articles used by children that posed electrical, mechanical, or thermal hazards.
1970	Fair Credit Reporting Act of 1970	Amendment to the Consumer Credit Protection Act, stating conditions for the maintenance and dissemination of consumer credit records.
1970	Poison Prevention Packaging Act	Authorizes the establishment of standards for child-resistant packaging of hazardous substances.
1972	Consumer Product Safety Act	Establishes Consumer Product Safety Commission, which assumed many FDA product safety programs. Empowers the commission to set safety standards for a broad range of consumer products and to set penalties for failure to meet the standards.
1975	Fair Credit Billing Act	Provides consumers with an opportunity to dispute errors in billing statements. Requires creditors to make efforts to correct such errors.
1975	FTC Protocol on Deceptive Advertising	Used to enforce FTC policy against misrepresentation, omission, or practices misleading the consumer.
1976	Equal Credit Opportunity Act	Prohibits credit discrimination on the basis of age, race, color, religion, or national origin.
1976	Copyright Act	Gives a general grant of protection to original works of authorship fixed in any tangible medium of expression.

Year	Law	Purpose
1978	Fair Debt Collection Act	Makes it illegal to harass or abuse any person or make false statements or use unfair methods when collecting a debt.
1984	Toy Safety Act	Gives the power to recall dangerous toys quickly when they are found.
1987	Truth in Mileage Act of 1987	An act to amend Section 408 of the Motor Vehicle Informational and Cost Savings Act to strengthen, for the protection of consumers, the provisions respecting disclosure of motor vehicle mileage when motor vehicles are transferred.
1987	Home Equity Loan Consumer Protection Act	Makes home equity loans subject to the same disclosure requirements as other mortgage products and puts substantial limitations on the terms and conditions of home equity line of credit plans.
1990	The Consumer Protection Against Price-Fixing Act of 1990	Amends the Sherman Act in regard to competition. Provides that an agreement between a supplier and one of its customers to terminate a competitor of the latter because of its price discounting is per se unlawful.
1991	The Automated Telephone Consumer Protection Act	Covers five major areas of telephone solicitation regulation policy: (1) restrictions on the use of automated telephone equipment, (2) protection of subscriber privacy rights, (3) technical and procedural standards, (4) effect on state law, and (5) actions by states. The act's provisions became effective one year from the date of enactment.
1991	Telephone Consumer Protection Act of 1991	Regulates telemarketing activity and is intended to protect the home privacy interests of U.S. telephone consumers.
1996	Consumer Fraud Prevention Act	Ensures ethical practices and deals with protecting the rights of consumers.
1998	Consumer Bankruptcy Reform Act of 1998	Permits debtors that truly need bankruptcy to file in Chapter 7 liquidation and receive an appropriate discharge.

The government interest in consumer protection at both the federal and state levels should continue over the next decade. Concern about consumer protection is particularly impacting state legislatures and has resulted in a number of states such as New York, California, and Massachusetts passing consumer laws.

DEMOGRAPHIC ENVIRONMENT

Demography is the statistical study of certain characteristics of the population. Some of these population characteristics, or *demographics,* are: age, sex, education, income level, and geographical location. The demographic environment is a key variable of interest to marketing management, since people, channels, and businesses make up markets. By noting statistical shifts in the categories within these characteristics, marketing managers can both better meet the needs of present markets and identify future markets and the corresponding product and service opportunities. Demographics and business data can be used to forecast the growth and ultimate potential of present products and to provide a picture of future economic conditions. Such data can indicate any changes needed in present products as well as provide an evaluation structure for new product ideas. Similarly, as consumer markets shift, wholesalers and retailers can use this information to relocate merchandising units and channels of distribution.

Sources of Data

The single best source of demographic material for the marketing manager is the Bureau of the Census, U.S. Department of Commerce. The results of the census are readily available, along with many supplemental reports. The census covers population, housing, business, manufacturers, mineral industries, agriculture, transportation, and governments. Perhaps the best guide to census data is the quarterly *Catalog of the U.S. Census Publications*, published by the Bureau of the Census.

An excellent source of business data is the U.S. Department of Commerce. For source material to use in economic forecasting, there is probably no better publication than the *Business Conditions Digest*, published by its Bureau of Economic Analysis. The Department of Commerce gathers, analyzes, and distributes commercial statistics. Current studies cover: population, housing, business, retail trade, wholesale trade, selected service industries, manufacturers, government, transportation, construction, foreign trade, agriculture, and mineral industries.

Consumer Demographic Trends

Demographic trends are useful indicators for forecasting consumption patterns and buying behavior. These trends can assist marketing managers in identifying target markets and tailoring products and advertising programs to reach these markets. Conversely, they can also show marketing managers when to delete a product line or how to refocus product appeal in light of changing buying patterns. One excellent source of this information is the yearly "Survey of Buying Power" in *Sales and Marketing Management* magazine.

ACCELERATED PACE OF CHANGE

Many of today's common products, services, and institutions were not available just a decade ago. More new ideas are being worked on, and the time between the new idea and its market introduction is significantly decreasing. The use of personal computers, fax machines, the Internet, and the World Wide Web have radically changed the marketplace and the ways marketing managers can effectively respond to these changes. Many people now telecommute—that is, work at home instead of traveling to offices. This trend in itself should decrease auto pollution, develop closer family units, create more home-centered entertainment, and have an impact on shopping behavior. In the information age, success requires a totally new style of marketing management. No longer is it possible to maintain a hierachial pyramid organizational structure. A new flatter, more responsive, open structure is needed, allowing better customer response time. But this is not enough in itself, as marketing managers themselves must allow the individuals performing the various marketing tasks to take advantage of the fast pace of change in information technology and make responsive decisions that increase customer satisfaction and company profits. The role of the marketing manager often is to provide vision and direction to more educated and skilled individuals, providing these individuals the necessary resources and then allowing them to think and act independently. The successful marketing manager will guide employees toward achieving company goals, being unconcerned about his or her own status and giving more control to each individual.

CHAPTER PERSPECTIVE

In this chapter we discussed the external environment and its impact on the operation of a business. Understanding the economic environment in terms of how supply and demand will affect marketing decisions, particularly those about price and quantity. Even though the cultural and social environment is important in defining a target market, other key factors in the business environment include: competition, raw materials, ecology, technology, labor, and distribution. The influence of government on business through laws and regulations also affects the operations of a company. Demographic data are vital in forecasting trends for a particular product or industry. Although the business has little, if any, control over these external environments, managers must be aware of them and their impact in order to make effective decisions.

Planning and Controlling the Marketing Program

INTRODUCTION AND MAIN POINTS

In this chapter, we will expand your understanding of the importance of establishing a planning and control system by discussing how this will positively affect the marketing process. We will focus on the differences between planning, forecasting, and control for one versus multiple scenarios, and we will address the aspects of building a planning model and preparing the necessary forecasts and plans.

After studying the material in this chapter:

➤ You will understand the importance of implementing the planning process.

➤ You will be able to develop and implement a sales forecast.

➤ You will understand how the principles of control work in establishing a marketing control system.

THE PLANNING PROCESS

Every organization needs to establish strategic planning and control mechanisms to increase the effectiveness of its marketing activities. A strategic planning and control system takes into account the external and internal environments and provides important feedback for future marketing decisions.

Market planning, sales forecasting, and budgeting are closely interrelated aspects of a strategic system. Although market planning is the overall activity, sales forecasting provides the basic foundation for both budgeting and operations. Planning can be thought of as exercising foresight regarding the anticipated outputs of an organization in order to maximize the inputs available. If the required inputs in terms of advertising, promotion, production, and personnel are beyond the firm's capability, then the goal should be modified to reflect available resources. One way to develop an effective plan is to implement the following procedure:

1. Investigate the present situation
2. Consider alternative courses of action
3. Select one of the alternatives
4. Provide both human and material resources
5. Communicate with everyone involved so that each knows his or her particular role in the process
6. Evaluate progress periodically in order to ensure that action is taking place according to the plan.

The foundation of all market planning is the sales forecast, which is an estimate of sales in dollars or physical units for a specified future period under a proposed marketing plan or program and under an assumed set of economic and other forces outside the unit for which the forecast is made.

The development of a sales forecast usually starts with a forecast of general economic conditions followed by a forecast of the potential market for the particular industry. Then the sales for the product and the market share that can be attained by the product are estimated. Finally, the budget for the marketing mix elements needed for attaining the forecasted sales is established.

Planning and Forecasting

Most managers view administration as beginning with obtaining the facts and finishing with making a plan and a forecast for the planning period. Since each administrative phase is carefully evaluated and controlled throughout the period of the forecast, you need to analyze and forecast sales volume, profits, cash flow, and return on assets. Regardless of the level of sophistication, planning and forecasting are still a matter of studying the past and the present to predict the future.

As the need for making competitive business decisions in the future becomes even more pressing, the use of sophisticated planning techniques will increase. Even today, only the most backward manager would believe that a business can grow by making day-to-day decisions instead of having a strategic plan.

Multiple Scenarios

During a relatively stable economic and business era, the system of projecting a single set of conditions (a single scenario) into the future works relatively well. During times of rapidly changing technology, however, as we are presently experiencing, single scenario forecasting leaves much to be desired. A method for dealing with this problem is to develop more than one prediction—in other words, multiple predictions or scenarios for each situation. This usually involves three predictions: best case, worst case, and most probable case.

This system of forecasting is often called "multiple scenarios." Since the future is never an exact replica of the past, the use of multiple scenarios is a valuable tool in forecasting and planning. By treating the future in this manner, you do not deal with one particular sequence of trends and events but with ranges. This necessitates making future decisions for at least two other places on the range in the scenario. In determining the number of scenarios, their relative themes, and the techniques, you need to consider the number of issues as well as the width of the range.

Factors affecting corporate behavior in recent years, which in turn affects corporate plans, include government policy and economic growth. Relevant subordinate themes include social change, energy prices and availability, demographic patterns, land use, and environmental impact. The specified plan developed can cover any period of time, but long-term scenarios usually involve a period of three to ten years, while the short term is one or two years.

Techniques used by many companies in multiple scenario forecasting include the Delphi method, cross-impact analysis, and dynamic modeling. The Delphi technique involves interviewing a panel of experts on the types and timing of future events and product sales. Cross-impact analysis develops an array of events of varying probability and effect so that the consequence of altering any of the variables affecting these events can be assessed, thus generating a variety of scenarios from one set of events. Dynamic modeling provides useful insights into important processes.

Company Planning and Forecasting

The accuracy of and attention given to planning and forecasting vary greatly from one company to another. In some companies planning and forecasting are the foundation of the management system, and the achievement of objectives is required and compensated. In other companies, especially smaller ones, planning and forecasting are sometimes noted on the back of an envelope. Nevertheless, even this small amount of planning is better than no planning at all.

The data needed for making the marketing plan usually include: internal records of past sales and profits; a survey of salespeople to determine what they think they can sell; a survey of customers to determine what they think they will buy; and a discussion with other managers in the organization. In most cases sales forecasts are made on a basis of volume measured in either units or dollars. Forecasts are also made on volume, profit, and cash flow.

Internal records usually provide the best basis for marketing plans. Past sales results and performance can provide insight into any problems as well as into the effort needed to achieve various sales and profit objectives. You should pay particular attention to situations where the objectives were not obtained.

While the input of salespeople is helpful in formulating plans, it is difficult to accurately discount the level of optimism or pessimism in their forecasts. Surveys of salespeople can sometimes be used more effectively for motivational purposes in managing the sales force than for developing marketing plans.

The same problem occurs in data from reports of what customers think they will buy. Competitors' prices, economic conditions, and attitude changes can drastically alter actual customers' purchasing behavior from their stated intentions.

Plans can be well formulated by applying statistical and operational research techniques to internal company data and supplementing this with any relevant external information. Planning done in this manner, with upper-level management giving it a high priority and taking into account a multiple set of conditions rather than a single set, becomes a very important tool for both implementation and control.

Building a Planning Model

A procedure often used in the planning process by companies is building a planning model. A schematic overview of this model-building process indicates that building the model involves four factors:

1. Determining a time period
2. Categorizing the factors involved
3. Validating these factors
4. Implementing these factors into the base period.

The first step in building a planning model is to determine the time period of the plan. Should it be six months, one year, five years, or ten? While this depends on the needs and objectives of the company, since the longer the time period, the more inaccurate the plan, shorter time periods are usually better. The factors that can influence the plan can be placed into three general categories: controllable factors, uncontrollable factors, and factors associated with the stage in the product life cycle.

Some of the controllable factors to be considered include: the amount and nature of advertising effort; deals; sample distribution programs; development of new markets; introduction of new products; packaging and display; any price changes; any quality improvements; and sales force changes. Factors that influence sales and profits that are not controlled by management include: economic conditions; population changes; seasonal buying habits; competitive introductions; extent of competitive advertising, sales, and promotional activity; price and quality trends in competitive products; and sociological trends and cycles affecting product usage. Also, the stage in the product life cycle needs to be evaluated by looking at the following: whether distribution and penetration have plateaued; whether all markets and all territories have been opened; and whether sales levels have been achieved using trend line analysis.

The input factors can be validated by establishing a base for validation and then reviewing uniformity of base periods after index factors have been used. A factor's index number is the percent that factor is in relationship to one. For example, if the estimated sales for a four-week period without advertising are 4,000 units, the index number for the advertising factor is 1.25 $(5,000/4,000 = 1.25)$. In other words, sales due to advertising expenditures are expected to be 125 percent higher than normal for that period.

Sales can also be adjusted for a seasonal period in a month. For example, if the month of July is the low part of the seasonal curve of product sales, having sales of 3,000 units (computed over a five-year period), and if average monthly sales for the year computed over this five-year period are 5,000 units, the seasonal index for July would be .60 or 3,000/5,000. July sales for this company are therefore usually 60 percent of the average monthly sales for the year.

When the sales in a month in the base period are adjusted to take into account the effect of advertising or seasonal fluctuations, a more accurate figure for planning and control is achieved. When the monthly sales influenced by some advertising are divided by 1.25, a smaller figure is computed, which is the estimate of sales without the effect of advertising in the sales. Likewise, when July sales are adjusted by the seasonal index number .60, a higher sales figure is obtained, indicating sales with no seasonal influence present; in other words, sales given the seasonal index had been 1.0 for that period. This procedure should be implemented for each of the factors in the model for each of the eight base period months.

The base interval normally used consists of eight consecutive fiscal periods ending immediately prior to the twelve for which a forecast will be made. Each period of this interval is adjusted according to any known relationship between orders and the factors discussed, resulting in an estimate of the deseasonalized volume of orders for the final period of the base interval.

In practice, the actual orders are established by periods, and each period is adjusted by such things as the elimination of deals, deseasonalization, and application of changes in longer-range factors between each period and the final period. This process yields eight estimates of normal deseasonalized sales for the last period of the base interval. If a pattern of variation is evident, a new set of estimates results. When no assignable cause of variation occurs, then the plans proceed.

When a company first starts to use models for planning, usually much of the input data are lacking. When data are not available, three upper-level executives can give their estimates on a factor from which an overall estimate can then be determined. Even when a company has good data, some factors such as the lag effect on sales of an advertising dollar spent are relatively unknown.

Since there are usually significant differences between products, few generalizations from one product category to another are valid. For example, one company found that for one product 60 percent of the value of an advertising dollar spent was realized in higher sales attributable to the advertising in the first four-week period. After six months, there was no advertising effect left. On another product of the company, the effect of dollars spent in advertising continued for as long as three years, with the effect being slightly greater in the early period. During the first four-week period, the effect was small compared to the effect for the first product.

Developing the Plan

In developing a plan in a larger company with more than $10 million in sales, upper-level management prepared major expense and capital expenditure projects for the planning period with all capital expenditure projects being on a discounted cash flow basis; in addition, all monies invested in the project prior to the time profits were generated were charged the prevailing interest rate.

The plans of the company for the period and the probable effect on sales are also estimated on all the nine factors controlled by management. The effect on sales of any planned changes in advertising is estimated based on past experience which is reflected in the index terms.

Planning involves looking at the past of the entire organization. Marketing executives start with sales, past trend line, and the market share of the product and then use these as the basis to establish the sales goals for the planning period. If new products without previous sales history are to be introduced, estimates based on test market results are used in the sales forecast. If new territories are to be opened for the products, estimates should be made separately for these since these potential sales are not reflected in the past trend line of the product.

The final sales forecast developed should be communicated to all divisions of the company. The manufacturing division should plan for the necessary production facilities. The forecast should be translated into a staffing forecast for the personnel division. The sales division should plan for promotions needed for introducing any new products in order to obtain the needed distribution. Similar plans need to be made for opening new territories. The financial division should translate the forecast into financial needs for the future. If, for any reason, the demands made by the plan are beyond the material or personnel resources of the company, then the plan should be altered to match the available resources. Good managers use the overall plan to establish plans for interim projects.

After taking into account all the controllable factors, the seven uncontrollable factors should be added in. For example, the state of national economy during the planning period together with a forecast of any significant changes in consumer disposable income for the period, should be developed. The period data can then be interpolated and an index constructed using the same base used in the determination of base sales.

An index for the state in the life cycle also should be added to the plan by evaluating trend line characteristics. Any new markets in which the product will be sold should be reviewed and taken into account.

After the plan has been developed for the entire year, key periods should be checked to determine the reasonableness and accuracy of the plan. Period volume figures on a unit basis for each period should be reviewed by top management. If a satisfactory level of sales is not being achieved, plans should be revised accordingly along with the forecast. Such areas as the advertising budget, types and costs of deals, new territories being opened, and price should be modified and the overall plan revised. This stage is ordinarily called the first stage of simulation in a planning model.

While sales is the criterion in this stage against which changes are measured and evaluated, the ultimate criterion, return on assets, usually has not yet been computed. It is more important for line managers involved in the plan to review sales than return on assets.

Preparing Financial Plans and Statements

Based on the marketing plan, the forecasted income statement and balance sheet and the return on assets that will result can usually be determined by the accounting department. These estimates should be broken down by weeks for the first two periods and by periods for the remainder of the planning year, taking into account holidays and vacations. The period and weekly data, along with assumptions regarding planned deals, packaging changes, price and index weight changes for costing, are then used in constructing the production plan.

In developing the production plan, the present inventory condition, future inventory requirements, and desired product levels are also considered. The production schedule is closely monitored, especially at the times of deals, to avoid shortages in particular products, to make necessary adjustments in the forecast of shipments, and to determine whether adequate product capacity is available. After the schedule is reviewed with manufacturing personnel, the production forecast and plan, in appropriate units of volume for the next year, is used as a schedule for manufacturing and purchasing. A by-product of the production forecast and plan is the finished goods inventory forecast.

The profit forecast is then prepared for the next time period for each item appearing on the company's income statement. Monetary units of sales are developed from the shipments forecast. Costs are forecasted taking into consideration any future changes, such as new package weights, material changes, labor rate increases, advertising expenditures, and other promotional expenses.

A forecasted balance sheet is then prepared for the time period indicating any new funds required from sources outside the division or subsidiary during the period. Order, profit, cash flow, and balance sheet forecasts are tentative until approved by upper-level management. If the forecasts are not approved, then alternatives are developed, usually involving changes in the form of price changes, changes in the number and amount of deals, or changes in the advertising budget.

When both sales and return on assets are acceptable in the planning process, the company determines whether it has the necessary funds or will need to borrow money to finance projects. These figures are included in the final company plan.

When price adjustment cannot bring about the target return on assets desired, then all elements affecting the return on assets are examined. At this stage the president and key managers review all data affecting the return in the original plan. This allows upper management to exert considerable pressure on managers at various levels to make sure the forecast and plans are as accurate as possible. After a planning system has been in place for a period of two or three years, errors and problems significantly decrease.

Sliding Salary Scales for Managers

Many companies tie in the salaries of managers to the sales and return on assets achieved. If the target goal for return on assets is being achieved, then all managers would receive a salary which is sometimes 20 percent higher than the salary paid in the industry for a comparable position at a comparable sales volume. This increase is called a performance bonus. If the target return is not being achieved, salaries can be decreased depending on the degree to which the goal is not being achieved.

This type of salary control system makes the entire organization more aware of the return on assets as well as the sales growth goals while providing both growth and profit incentive. Although there is no incentive for taking huge profits over and above those needed for the target return on assets, most plans usually reflect a small safety margin above target. Anything above this level would slow growth. Another incentive for making managers responsible is the bonus method where the salary is stable and the bonus depends on sales volume and/or profit achieved.

METHODS FOR ESTIMATING DEMAND

Any demand estimation begins with defining the number of people in the primary market by focusing on the need that the product is going to satisfy and the number of people that have this need. In order to assess this need and the number of people possessing it, several methods are available. These can be generally classified as being either top down or build up in orientation. Top down methods use more of a deductive approach and start with an analysis of the total business system. Build up methods for estimating primary demand start with identifying each individual segment sharing a common need and cumulating these to determine the total demand for the product. Specific techniques often used to determine the primary demand for the product are the survey of buying power method, the SIC Code method, and the input-output method.

Survey of Buying Power Method

The primary demand for consumer products is often initially estimated by constructing an index of buying potential. Since there are so many final customers, there is a need to construct an estimating index from basic economic data.

Suppose a company is trying to determine whether or not it should market its new adult energy game in New York City. The company knows that the initial market success of the game is dependent on various market factors such as population and disposable income.

One approach that indicates the sales opportunity is the "Buying Power Index" published each year in the June issue of *Sales and Marketing Management* magazine. This index gives an indication of the ability to purchase in specific counties and cities in the United States. It is calculated by assigning a weight of 5 to the specific area's percent of the U.S. effective buying income, a weight of 3 to the area's percent of the U.S. retail sales, and a weight of 2 to its percent of U.S. population as indicated in the following equation:

$$BPI_i = \frac{5\ EBI_i + 3\ RS_i + 2P_i}{10}$$

Where:

BPI_i = Buying Power Index (percentage of total national buying power) in area i.

EBI_i = Percentage of national disposable income in area i.

RS_i = Percentage of national retail sales in area i.

P_i = Percentage of national population living in area i.

If New York City has 4.56 percent of the U.S. population, 4.14 percent of U.S. retail sales, and 5.485 percent of U.S. disposable personal income, the buying power index would be:

$$BPI_i = .5(5.48) + .3(4.14) + .2(4.56) = 4.89$$

This means that 4.89 percent of the sales of adult games in the United States would probably occur in New York City. This broadly based index gives an estimation of the potential for mass merchandised products sold at average prices. When the product needs to use more discriminating factors, graduated buying power indexes for the same city and county areas are also provided by the *Sales and Marketing Management* magazine.

SIC Code Method

Another market build up method which is very appropriate for industrial products is the Standard Industrial Classification (SIC) method, the way by which the federal government classifies manufacturing industries.

To determine the primary market demand using the SIC Code method, it is necessary to determine all the possible industry categories that have a need for the product or service being considered. Once the groups have been selected, the appropriate base for the demand determination should be established and the published material on the industry groups obtained from the *Census of Manufacturers.*

Consider the primary demand estimation problem facing a small manufacturer of a grill-cleaning compound that cleans hot working grills better than any commercial product available. While the cleaning compound could have home use, because of the limited resources of the firm located in the Chicago area, this market will be looked into at a later date. The more easily accessible market for the company is commercial restaurants, which have an SIC Code of 58—Eating and Drinking Places. This two-digit category is composed of 5812, Eating Places and 5813, Drinking Places. Information on this SIC Code obtained from the *Census of Business*, specifically from the *Census of Retail Trade*, is indicated in Table 3-1.

Since eating places appear to be the most likely prospects, the market is 377,760 eating places in the United States and 16,905 in the state of Illinois (see Table 3-1). Since approximately 1 gallon of grill cleaner is used by a restaurant every other week there is a potential primary demand of 9,821,760 gallons each year on a national basis and 439,530 gallons in Illinois—a viable primary market for the grill cleaner.

Input-Output Method

Another technique for determining the primary demand for a particular product or product category is the input-output method.

Table 3-1

Statistics on Eating and Drinking Places for the Total United States and the State of Illinois

SIC Code	Description	Number	Sales ($1,000)	Paid Employees for Week Including March 12 (Number)	Operated by Unincorporated Business Individual Proprietorships (Number)	Partnerships (Number)
United States						
58	Eating and Drinking Places	433,608	195,316,992	6,547,908	127,054	28,351
5812	Eating Places	377,760	184,203,215	6,243,862	106,768	25,576
5812 pt.	Restaurants	170,183	85,178,356	2,988,535	53,852	12,340
5812 pt.	Cafeterias	5,513	3,619,172	109,063	1,650	278
5812 pt.	Refreshment Places	164,341	77,685,530	2,651,779	42,728	11,395
5812 pt.	Other Eating Places	37,723	17,720,157	494,485	8,538	1,563
5812 pt.	Social Caterers	5,879	2,326,860	75,711		
5812 pt.	Contract Feeding	19,117	13,148,520	340,616		
5812 pt.	Ice Cream and Frozen Yogurt Shops	12,727	2,244,777	78,158		
5813	Drinking Places	55,848	11,113,777	304,046	20,286	2,775

Illinois				
58	Eating and Drinking Places	20,458	9,057,068	303,957
5812	Eating Places	16,905	8,402,286	287,167
5812 pt.	Restaurants	7,137	3,730,854	129,531
5812 pt.	Cafeterias	163	99,365	
5812 pt.	Refreshment Places	7,610	3,635,912	127,720
5812 pt.	Other Eating Places	1,995	936,255	26,650
5812 pt.	Social Caterers			
5812 pt.	Contract Feeding			
5812 pt.	Ice Cream and Frozen Yogurt Shops			
5813	Drinking Places	3,553	654,682	16,790

Source: U.S. Department of Commerce, Bureau of the Census. *1992 Census of Retail Trade.*

An input-output table is used to determine the number and size of the transactions occurring within specific sectors of the total economy. This table on a macro basis provides a summary of all exchanges between each industry grouping as well as between all industries and the final consumer. The total input-output structure of the U.S. economy is given on an 85-industry category basis with a sample being presented in Table 3-2. The table indicates that furniture and fixtures sold almost all of its output to final markets and would therefore be strongly affected by any changes occurring in these markets.

The relative primary demand among industries can be derived from input-output tables by allocating the proportion of total sales of an industry to each particular industry segment. Of the $86,865 million of lumber and wood products, 3.8 percent were sold to the furniture and fixtures industry and 7.5 percent to the paper allied products (excluding containers), suggesting that future new product efforts of the lumber and wood products group should be oriented toward the latter industry group as it provided the largest share of previous industry business.

SALES FORECASTING AND COMPANY MANAGEMENT

With the increase in competition and shortages of raw materials, increased emphasis has been placed on marketing planning and control, causing a need for accurate forecasts. These forecasts are used in all aspects of business planning as well as in formulating pricing strategies, planning research and development, product planning, advertising allocation, and assignment of the sales force.

A *company sales forecast* can be defined as the amount of sales a company expects to obtain during a given future time period in a specified area. While this sales level can be expressed in dollars or in physical units, it is usually better to forecast on a unit basis, therefore not reflecting price and price changes.

Forecasting Techniques

In order to handle the variety of various sales forecasting problems, it is necessary to be familiar with the available forecasting techniques. The better you understand the forecasting techniques, their applicability, and constraints, the more useful the resultant

Table 3-2

United States Input-Output Table (1992)

($ in millions)

Industry	Lumber and Wood Products	Furniture and Fixtures	Paper and Allied Products Except Containers	Paperboard Containers and Boxes	Personal Consumption Expenditures	Change in Business Inventories	Federal Government Consumption Expenditures and Gross Investment	State and Local Government Consumption Expenditures and Gross Investment	Total Industry Output
Lumber and Wood Products	26,156	3,314	6,508	37	5,155	945	31	210	86,865
Furniture and Fixtures	74	421	0	0	41,634	202	233	3,345	42,977
Paper and Allied Products, Except Containers	49	100	14,665	13,453	22,624	923	773	3,800	99,613
Paperboard Containers and Boxes	232	679	1,306	77	643	335	97	223	31,938

Source: This is an abbreviated table to give an indication of the complete tables found in *Survey of Current Business* published by the U.S. Department of Commerce.

forecasts will be for effective marketing decision making. Table 3-3 lists some of the most useful forecasting techniques by giving a brief description, the typical applications, data required, and a reference for more in-depth information.

Table 3-3
Some Marketing Forecasting Techniques

Technique	Jury of Executive Opinion	Sales Force Composite Method	Intention-To-Buy & Anticipations Surveys
Description	The views of the top executives regarding their beliefs about future sales are obtained. Although this method is easy to implement and can be used when there are no external or internal data available, its unscientific approach is often inaccurate.	The views of the salespeople and sales managers as to the future sales outlook are obtained. This information is from the people who can help ensure that the predictions are obtained. The forecasts are often understated as salespeople feel that the estimates will be the basis for the sales quotas.	These surveys of the general public (a) determine intentions to buy certain products or (b) derive an index that measures general feeling about the present and the future and estimates how this feeling will affect buying habits. These approaches to forecasting are more useful for tracking and warning than forecasting. The basic problem in using them is that a turning point may be signaled incorrectly (and hence never occur).
Typical Applications	Forecast of present and new product sales.	Forecasts of present and new product sales.	Forecasts of sales by product class.
Data Required	Each executive's response regarding	Each salesperson's estimates of probable	Several years' data are usually required to relate such

	future sales is recorded and then aggregated.	future sales by product/by customer in his or her territory are aggregated.	indices to company sales.
Reference	John E. Hanke and Arthur G. Reitsh, *Business Forecasting* (Upper Saddle River, NJ: Prentice-Hall, 1998).	William J. Stanton and Richard H. Buskirk, *Management of the Sales Force* (Homewood, IL: Richard D. Irwin, 1999).	Publications of Survey Research Center, Institute for Social Research, University of Michigan; and of Bureau of the Census.

Trend Projections	*Regression Model*	*Box-Jenkins*
This technique fits a trend line to a mathematical equation and then projects it into the future by means of this equation. There are several variations: the slope-characteristic method, polynomials, logarithms, and so on.	This functionally relates sales to other economic, competitive, or internal variables and estimates an equation using the least-squares technique. Relationships are primarily analyzed statistically, although any relationship should be selected for testing on a rational ground.	Exponential smoothing is a special case of the Box-Jenkins technique. The time series is fitted with a mathematical model that is optimal in the sense that it assigns smaller errors to history than any other model. The type of model must be identified and the parameters then estimated. This is apparently the most accurate statistical routine presently available but also one of the most costly and time-consuming ones.
Forecast of present products.	Forecast of sales by product classes, forecasts of margins.	Production and inventory control for large-volume items, forecasts of present product sales.

Varies with the technique used. However, a good rule of thumb is to use a minimum of five years' annual data to start. Thereafter, the complete history.	Several years' quarterly history to obtain good, meaningful relationships. Mathematically necessary to have two or more observations than there are independent variables.	The same as for a moving average. However, in this case, more history is very advantageous in model identification.
Ronald M. Weievs, *Introduction to Business Statistics* (Fort Worth, TX: Dryden Press, 1994).	Patricia B. Elmore, *Basic Statistics* (New York: Longman, 1997).	John E. Hanke and Arthur G. Reitsch, *Business Forecasting* (Upper Saddle River, NJ: Prentice-Hall, 1998).

Some of the descriptions of the techniques were adapted from: John C. Chambers, Satinder K. Mullick, and Donald D. Smith, "How to Choose the Right Forecasting Technique," *Harvard Business Review* (July–August, 1971), pp. 45–74.

Selecting the Best Technique

Any marketing manager who has used a sales forecast as the basis of a decision is aware of the importance of the forecast's accuracy and of selecting the best technique for the specific situation at hand. The selection of the best method depends on four basic factors—the decision-making situation, the attributes of the forecasting methods available, the amount of historical data available, and the stage of the product in the life cycle.

Each decision-making situation for which the forecast is prepared has characteristics that make one forecasting technique more appropriate than another. These characteristics include the time dimension, the number of products, the nature of the decision-control planning, the degree of stability, and the existing company procedures.

These characteristics of the decision-making situation need to be considered in light of the attributes of the various forecasting techniques. Each forecasting technique has specific cost, accuracy, time, and data patterns associated with its use. In implementing any forecasting technique, the cost must produce the needed accuracy.

Different forecasting techniques have various abilities to identify past sales patterns. For example, a product such as the newest Elan skis from Slovenia with seasonal sales requires a different technique than Cheer detergent with no seasonality. A particular problem occurs for a new product when no sales history is available. Here, analysis should be made of the sales of products that satisfy a similar need to provide a basis for the sales projection.

Finally, the selection of the best method depends on the stage of the product in its life cycle. Since each product has a pattern of sales, different forecasting techniques are more effective depending on the sales level and the competition in the particular stage of the product's life cycle.

QUALITATIVE FORECASTING METHODS

Various forecasting methods that use a less quantitative approach are available. These approaches are particularly applicable when no historical data are available, when no basic projectable pattern is evident from any available data, or when past conditions are changing. Four of the most widely used qualitative forecasting methods are the jury of executive opinion, sales force composite, buyers expectation, and the Delphi method.

Jury of Executive Opinion

One of the oldest and most frequently used techniques is the jury of executive opinion. The opinions of the top executives of the organization are elicited on a one-time or periodic basis depending on the forecasting need. For example, when a new product is being considered for commercialization, selected executives are usually queried at least once regarding their opinion on the probability of success.

The estimates of sales obtained from executives of such functional areas as marketing, finance, and production are often averaged in order to provide a broad-based forecast. The more information available to these executives, the more accurate their estimate of sales.

The jury of executive opinion has several advantages and disadvantages in producing reliable forecasts. The method can provide forecasts easily and quickly and brings together opinions from a diverse group of company managers who are thoroughly versed in the company's strengths and weaknesses as well as those of the competition's products. The greatest disadvantages of this method include: its reliance on opinion; its averaging of these opinions; and the difficulty in breaking the composite forecast of sales into product/market categories.

Sales Force Composite

Another method that can be used in the absence of internal and external data is compiling the views of salespersons. In the sales force composite method, salespersons project volume of usage by customers in their territory with or without consultation with the sales manager. Accuracy is increased through the use of the form indicated in Table 3-4. This form obtains sales estimates in units for a particular product on a customer-by-customer basis.

The major advantage of the sales force composite method is that the sales estimates are given by people closest to the cus-

Table 3-4

Form for Obtaining Salesperson's Estimates on Future Sales
Product ⸻

Customer	Sales Last Time Period (Week, Month, Year) in Units	Sales Next Time Period (Week, Month, Year) in Units	Reason for Change

tomers and then modified as needed by executives at various levels. In addition, the method lends itself to product, territory, or customer categorization. However, salespersons are often not aware of broad economic forces and future marketing activities of the firm. In addition, since the salesperson is evaluated on the basis of sales performance, not on the accuracy of sales forecasts, little time may be spent in making the projection. Probably the biggest drawback to using the technique is that the salesperson often understates the forecast in order to make the sales quota easier to achieve. This underestimating can be offset to some degree by establishing an "index of pessimism." A salesperson is a creature of habit and has a tendency to underestimate future sales by the same amount time after time. By tracking the difference between sales and estimates over time, an index can be established which can then be used to weight the salesperson's estimate. Forecasts obtained by the sales force composite method modified by the "index of pessimism" are very accurate, particularly for industrial products.

Buyer's Expectation Method

Since a forecast is a prediction of the amount a buyer will purchase in a future time period, one useful method is to ask the buyers themselves. Ultimately, the accuracy of this method depends on the extent to which buyers have clearly formulated purchasing intentions and the means to implement these plans.

The buyer's expectation method is best used in forecasting sales of industrial products. Since the firm buying is not concerned with the cost of inventory or overproduction, the buyer can overstate the demand. Industrial buyers, similar to salespeople, are creatures of habit and usually overestimate needs by the same amount each time. Therefore this inflated demand can be discounted by using an "index of optimism" established in a similar manner as the "index of pessimism." In the case of the small pallet company, forecasts became very accurate once this method was implemented (see pages 84–85).

Delphi Method

The Delphi method is a commonly used qualitative method for forecasting new product sales or new developments. In this approach, a panel of experts deals with a series of questions such as when a new production process will be fully available for implementation. Each expert is queried individually with the responses to the first set of questions summarized and used as a basis for establishing the next set of questions. This process is repeated until a reliable forecast is obtained. The Delphi method is particularly effective when new high-technology products or services are involved, but it requires a great deal of time to implement, depending of course on the number of repetitions needed, and the estimates of the experts may not be market based.

QUANTITATIVE METHODS

There are many different types of quantitative methods that can also be used to make the sales forecast. These can be classified into three overall groups: time series analysis, regression analysis, and the Box-Jenkins method.

Time Series Analysis

Time series analysis is a method of forecasting that involves the examination of past data to provide the basis for projections into the future. It involves attempting to relate variables with time. A time series is a set of ordered observations of a quantitative variable taken at successive points in time. In doing time series analysis, among the several techniques available the most useful is trend analysis. Trend analysis evaluates past sales to determine if any consistent pattern or trend is evident. The past sales history is then projected into the future. Three basic methods are used to determine the existence of a long-term trend: percentage-change, moving average, and curve fitting.

As the name implies, the percentage-change method evaluates the change on a percentage basis of past sales data on a unit basis between successive periods of time.

The moving-average method allows more recent time periods to influence the sales forecast, as each time a new sales figure occurs it is used in the computation while the oldest sales value is dropped.

A final method, curve fitting, is a method of analyzing any trends in sales data that express the relationship between the dependent variable of sales and time. The curves can vary from linear to more complex forms. The selection of the particular type to be used depends on which one best "fits" the past sales data, i.e., has the least errors occurring between the actual sales that occurred during the time period and the estimate of those sales that would have resulted upon use of the curve type. Once the best curve type has been selected, then the fitting formulas are employed to determine the forecast.

Regression Analysis

When sales can be related to something other than time, regression and correlation methods are useful forecasting techniques. These widely used statistical methods examine any possible mathematical relationships between sales and one or more variables. In this way, a functional relationship can be established indicating that a change in one variable accompanies specified changes in another in income. When a statistically significant relationship can be established, such as between income level and, say, car sales, then the variable can be used to predict future sales.

Box-Jenkins Method

One forecasting technique, the Box-Jenkins method, is becoming one of the more universally applicable and accurate methods available. The Box-Jenkins method produces information that allows for the particular model to be selected that best approximates the data. This approach differs from any forecasting technique discussed thus far as it does not pick a mathematical model on an a priori basis. Rather, a model is tentatively identified, checked for accuracy, and then used to generate forecasts. The problem with using the Box-Jenkins method centers around the availability of information and the costs involved. Oftentimes in a forecasting problem, the method cannot be used because too little sales data exist to provide a basis for model selection.

MARKETING CONTROL

Implemented marketing plans need to be carefully monitored and controlled. Marketing control provides management with feedback on how the plans are progressing. The feedback allows the manager to make any adjustments needed in the short-run marketing plan and guide the development of any long-run marketing strategy.

Short-run Control

Short-run control involves comparing the actual results with those projected in the marketing plan. This usually involves comparing market costs, sales in units and dollars, market share, and profit. These comparisons are made not only on a company-wide basis but on a geographic, product-line, and customer basis as well. The comparison and results should be done on a weekly basis but must be done on at least a monthly basis, with the results being disseminated to the appropriate marketing managers throughout the company. A good manager will look at the results and focus on those areas where major differences exist between forecasted levels and actual performance. This process is called management by exception.

Long-run Control

The long-run marketing plan and strategy must also be evaluated periodically. One of the best methods for doing this is the marketing audit—a systematic, unbiased, and comprehensive appraisal of the organization's marketing efforts and plans in light of the organization's capabilities and objectives and its external environment. The audit determines whether the current plans and strategies are appropriate and should be periodically done by individuals other than those closely involved in the development and implementation of the strategy to ensure that a fresh, unbiased appraisal occurs.

EFFECT OF QUALITY MOVEMENT

The quality movement and its associated concepts of total quality management and statistical quality controls have significantly affected marketing and marketing planning. The quality of the products and services as determined by the customers (not the producing company) is an important aspect of the initial as well as subsequent purchases. The quality of a product or service then becomes the customer's perception of the degree to which the offering meets his or her expectations. In order to achieve this needed level of quality for the customer from a marketing perspective, several things are needed. First, there needs to be quality of design derived by the company's determining what its customers want from its products or services. This determination from the customers allows the products or services to be designed to have the attributes needed to meet the customers' expectations. Second, there needs to be a quality capability in the production process itself. The production process needs to be capable of producing the attributes, design, and quality expectations of the product desired by the customer. Finally, there needs to be quality in every contact with the customer. Customers always need to be treated fairly and courteously with their needs and concerns attended to promptly. These quality contacts should occur throughout the marketing process from the initial contact to any installation and/or service to any complaint handling.

This emphasis on quality has led many firms to adopt total quality management (TQM), which is a set of management practices involved in an organization for improving and ensuring product and service quality to satisfy customer requirements. TQM builds long-term growth through improved customer satisfaction, which is an integral aspect of the marketing concept. TQM involves organization-wide focus from top to bottom to deliver customer satisfaction. It provides marketing with an organization-wide vehicle for cooperation and coordination with other functional areas to achieve a market orientation in the organization. With this emphasis on customer satisfaction and the associated quality tools, marketing managers can use TQM for effective implementation of the marketing concept. It allows the company, employees, customers, and suppliers to be together in one strong interconnected continuum.

CHAPTER PERSPECTIVE

In this chapter we have analyzed the components of corporate planning that are necessary in developing corporate and marketing plans using scenarios. Forecasts need to be made and continually revised. In building your planning model, you will need to identify and incorporate controllable and uncontrollable factors. A good sales forecast, which serves as the basis for other important forecasts, needs to be developed. Once the forecast has been established, managers' salaries should be established to maximize their performance and involvement in attaining the company's strategic goals.

Marketing Research

INTRODUCTION AND MAIN POINTS

In order to carry out effective planning and control, managers must have relevant and accurate information on a continual basis. This market information can be any verbal, visual, or written data that are relevant to the decision at hand. Many companies have gone beyond looking at data in a simple mode and have instead developed a formal dimension to their information management—a Marketing Information System (MKIS). Marketing research is a systematic and objective search for, and analysis of, information relevant to the identification and solution of any problem in the field of marketing. It must be systematic, objective, and able to be reproduced. And, the value of the information obtained must be worth the cost of the research activity used to obtain it.

After studying the material in this chapter:

- You will understand the aspects of marketing research.
- You will be able to implement a marketing research study.
- You will understand consumer and industrial research and how they differ.

Knowing and being able to respond quickly to a rapidly changing environment is becoming increasingly important in an era of hypercompetition and rapidly changing technology. Questions arise continuously in many areas of marketing activity. Who at the company actually makes the purchase decision regarding the new computer system? How much inventory do we have? Should we introduce this new product? What is our market share (our company's product sales divided by total product sales) in Chicago? Which of these package designs will customers prefer? How much of a profit margin should we have in our bid price on this government contract? Does our target market know the difference between our product and our competitor's? What do we need to do in order to achieve 10 percent market share? Which trade journals are most effective in reaching the target market? Is it worthwhile for us to exhibit at that trade show? All these questions require market research, and every area of company activity can benefit from the results of such research as well as from a good marketing information system.

MARKETING INFORMATION

Marketing information, an important resource that helps decision making, is any verbal, visual, or written data relevant to the decision at hand. This information can range from the results of a formal market research study on relative market share, to watching customers shop in a particular retail store, to a telephone conversation with a field sales representative regarding a key industrial account's hesitancy on issuing the purchase order. Similarly, the information can originate from sources both internal and external to the company and can be used in decision making in a variety of functional areas throughout the firm.

The types of marketing information needed and the corresponding types of activities undertaken have undergone extensive expansion in the past 20 years. While at first information was primarily collected on the market itself, marketing information now encompasses all aspects of marketing and is much more available through the Internet.

Marketing Information System

In order to make sure that there is enough marketing information of the right kind to aid in the decision-making process in today's competitive business setting, many companies have implemented a formal dimension to this information management—a *Marketing Information System (MKIS)*. This system provides for the determination, generation or gathering, processing, storage, and retrieval of data so that adequate information is available as the basis for sound managerial decisions. By anticipating potential problems, the MKIS is both future-oriented and preventive in nature. It operates on a continuing not an intermittent basis.

Marketing Research

Marketing research is an important aspect of any MKIS. The term marketing research ties two separate words together. The first term, *marketing*, has already been defined and involves a wide variety of activities used to satisfy customer wants and needs and thus to achieve the objectives of the organization.

The second word, *research*, indicates a systematic and objective process where a problem is investigated through the acquisition of relevant information. Research can be of two types—basic or applied. *Basic research* is research undertaken to extend the boundaries of knowledge in any field or area without attempting to give immediate application to an existing problem. *Applied research*, on the other hand, focuses on an existing problem by using existing information and knowledge. Regardless of whether it is basic or applied, good marketing research involves a systematic approach to a problem and frequently contains five aspects:

- Research objectives and budget
- Data availability
- Primary research
- Data analysis
- Conclusions and recommendations.

Research Objectives and Budget

One of the most difficult, yet important parts of the research process is establishing the objectives and scope of the marketing research effort. Clear objectives or goals must be delineated and agreed upon before the research project commences. These objectives can be as broad as the determination of the amount of effort needed to increase the company's market share by 5 percent in the New England states to as specific as the determination of the most preferred package of the five food package prototypes by women in the Chicago Standard Metropolitan Statistical Area (SMSA). The SMSA is the geographic area of a city as defined by the U.S. Census.

The difficult part in establishing objectives lies in part in the conflict between the value of information and the research budget. Since each piece of information has some cost associated with it, from a secretary making a copy of last week's sales figures to the results of a large research study carried out by an independent marketing research agency, it must be evaluated in terms of its value with respect to the decision at hand. This *value of information* should be the determining factor in the amount and type of marketing research effort employed in a given situation and its associated marketing research expenditure or budget.

Data Availability

Once the objective of the research project has been established, an assessment must be made of the amount and type of data presently available. These data are called secondary data—data already gathered and available, having previously been accumulated for a different purpose. Even though these data are assembled quickly and at a lower cost than primary data, sometimes they do not answer the research questions; after all, they were gathered for a different purpose and by someone else, whose reliability must be ascertained.

Secondary data can be classified in terms of internal (data originating within the firm) and external (published data originating outside the firm). Internal secondary data are all the data originating within the firm that were collected for some purpose other than the problem currently being addressed. Two of the most important types of internal data are sales and cost data. Also most companies have such internal data as records of daily sales reports, sales by product, customer, and territory, and customer complaints.

After the internal secondary data have been examined, in order to obtain additional information you can turn to published external secondary data. The principal sources of external data are (1) the government; (2) trade, businesses, and professional associations; (3) media; (4) trade journals; (5) universities and foundations; (6) corporate annual reports; and (7) commercial data services. Today, there is an overabundance of data available on various sites on the Internet.

The *government* is by far the biggest source of marketing data. While the data are available at a very low price, if any, once located, there is often a cost and time commitment in obtaining them. Some government publications are highly specialized, referring to specific studies of products or product classification. Other data are more general in nature. The prime source of general data is the Bureau of the Census. The principal publications are of course the *Census of Population* (market, sociological, and economic data by geographic area); the *Census of Business* (detailed information about retailing and wholesaling institutions and service businesses); and the *Census of Manufacturing* (detailed information on each manufacturing industry). In addition, the Department of Commerce publishes various statistical summaries, the most inclusive of which is the *Statistical Abstract of the United States*, published on an annual basis. For current information on business and economic activity, the Department of Commerce publishes a monthly, *The Survey of Current Business*.

State and local governments provide additional information. Data such as birth and death records and data on real estate sales and assessed values are public information that can be obtained from the specific state or local agency.

Trade, business, and professional associations also have general data on the various activities and sales of their constituency. For example, the American Dairy Association will have general information on producers and consumption patterns of milk and its related products. Although such data will of course not be company-specific, they are useful in gaining an overall perspective on the industry and its sales and other activities. Address and membership information for all associations can be found in the *Encyclopedia of Associations*, updated annually.

Most magazines, newspapers, and radio and television stations have marketing data available on their audience. In addition, media often do a periodic market survey of buying patterns and demographic information in their market area. For example, the *Chicago Tribune* does a study of consumers in its readership area in order to give advertisers a better understanding of the marketing potential of this area.

Trade journals also provide a wide variety of marketing and sales data and projections on the areas they cover. For example, if a market research effort was needed in the area of plastics, then trade journals such as *Plastic Design Forum, Plastics & Rubber Weekly*, and *Plastics Engineering* should be checked for any pertinent information. Probably one of the best sources of trade journal information is retail, wholesale, personal, and business data published on an annual basis in the "Survey of Buying Power" and "Survey of Industrial Buying Power" of *Sales and Marketing Management* magazine.

Universities and foundations undertake a variety of research projects. In addition to special studies supported by grants from the government, universities publish general research findings of interest to the business community through their research bureaus and institutes. Similarly, foundations such as The Conference Board publish reports on the findings of research efforts on special topics.

Corporate annual and 10-K reports are also useful sources of information on specific companies or general industry trends. Although the data are only as specific as is required by the Securities and Exchange Commission, you can gain at least a general picture of the nature and scope of the firms in an industry as well as their general direction from the information in these reports over a period of time.

Finally, there are many firms offering marketing research and commercial data services. Some, such as *National Family Opinion*, provide custom research; in other words, they design the research project specifically to meet the client's needs. Depending on the project, this can be costly. Others, such as *A. C. Nielsen*, offer standardized information, compiled regularly and made available to clients on a fee basis. Overall, outside research agencies can be divided into three groups: (1) those that collect data mainly in the home; (2) those that collect data mainly at the retail level; and (3) those that collect data mainly at the warehouse or industry level.

Primary Research

If all the secondary data sources have been checked and the needed data has not been found, then the third aspect of a research project is commenced—the collection of data through primary research. Primary research can be best viewed in terms of four areas: research design, sample design, questionnaire design, and data collection.

Research Design. The research design part of the primary research task involves deciding the methodology to be implemented to obtain the primary data needed to solve the problem. While there are many different ways to classify designs, one that gives a clear overview of the various procedures is based on three methods of generating primary data: experimentation, observation, and survey. Experimentation involves establishing a controlled experiment or a model that simulates the real-world marketing situation being investigated. Under the observation method, the primary data result from observing the respondents doing something.

The survey method involves collecting the primary data by interviewing a certain number of people. This is the most widely used method of obtaining primary data, with the data being usually collected by one of four techniques: personal interviews, telephone interviews, mail surveys, or focus groups.

Sample Design. Whenever a survey is undertaken, it is important to determine the group from whom information will be obtained—the population or universe; this is essentially all the units (consumers, stores, salespeople, manufacturers, representatives, buyers) possessing characteristics relevant to the problem. Although this may appear to be easy, it is often one of the most difficult tasks in a marketing research project because of the wide variety of factors affecting the determination. For example, it might be important that only recent purchasers of the product be queried. Or perhaps the users of the product and not the purchasers should be the primary focus of the research. Or perhaps the population should be composed of both users and nonusers so that a comparative picture can be obtained.

Once the population has been defined, you will have to decide the best procedure for representing this population within the time and cost constraints allocated in the research budget. Since there are many different methods used to draw this *sample—the group of units* composed of nonoverlapping elements that are representative of the population from which it is drawn— you must determine the best one to use for the specific research project.

Questionnaire Design. Regardless of the research and sample design employed, you must carefully develop the data gathering form to be used in the research study. The importance of this measuring instrument or questionnaire as well as the difficulty of designing it properly cannot be overstated. It is likely that you have seen poorly designed questionnaires. While the exact questions asked depend on the nature of the problem and the method of data collection to be employed, great care must be taken in choosing the types of questions and their wording so that there is minimal respondent bias. As is indicated in Table 4-1, there is a wide variety of questioning techniques— dichotomous, multiple-choice, preference, rating, ranking, and open-ended. Before the final questionnaire is developed, the advantages and disadvantages of each should be carefully evaluated in terms of the problem being investigated.

Data Collection. The most widely used methods of data collection are:
- Personal interviews
- Mail survey
- Telephone survey
- Focus group.

Primary research data are frequently obtained by *personal interviews*. For example, one might personally interview nonaffiliated doctors to determine their views on a particular hospital, or personally interview wholesalers to determine their movement of specialized oil and fat products, or personally interview a few

Table 4-1

Example Questioning Techniques

Questioning Techniques	Example	Advantages	Disadvantages
Dichotomous	Do you usually like to try a new store? —— Yes —— No	1. Easy to answer. 2. Can be used to screen before asking further questions. 3. Easy to tabulate. 4. Provides definite answer.	1. Forces a choice. 2. Provides no detailed information.
Multiple-Choice	Which of the following four stores do you like? —— Store A —— Store B —— Store C —— Store D	1. Usually avoids forcing an arbitrary choice. 2. Easy to answer. 3. Easy to tabulate.	1. Choices may not be all-encompassing. 2. Choices may not be clearly distinctive.
Preference	Which of these stores do you most prefer? —— Store A —— Store B —— Store C —— Store D	1. Gives information on preference. 2. Easy to answer.	1. Preferences may not reflect purchase choice. 2. Choices may present some confusion.
Rating	On a scale from 1 to 9 (with 1 being "did not like at all" and 9 being "liked it very	1. Gives important information on relative feelings about various product attributes.	1. Distinctions on scale may not be clear to respondent. 2. Provides scale gradations that may not

	much"), indicate your overall feelings about the overall store by circling the number that corresponds to your feeling. (did not like at all) (liked very much) 1 2 3 4 5 6 7 8 9	2. Does not force an arbitrary choice. 3. Provides a wide range of responses for comparative purposes.	be commensurate with knowledge of respondent.
Ranking	Rank in order from 1 to 5 (with 1 being the best and 5 the worst) your opinion of the following stores. ___ Store A ___ Store B ___ Store C ___ Store D ___ Store E	1. Provides valuable information on relative consumer opinions on products or attributes. 2. Provides a definite answer. 3. Yields information quickly.	1. Is probably the most confusing type of question for the consumer to answer. 2. Provides no information on how good the best product is. 3. Provides no information on relative differences between ranks of products.
Open-end Questions	Why do you shop at this particular store?	1. Does not bias respondent's response with established answers. 2. Provides a wide range of information. 3. Provides information of more depth.	1. Interpretation of answers requires skill and may vary between interpreters. 2. Difficult to tabulate.

This table is an adapted version of one in: Robert D. Hisrich and Michael P. Peters, *Marketing a New Product: Its Planning, Development, and Control.* Menlo Park, CA: The Benjamin/Cummings Publishing Co., 1978, pp. 99–100.

consumers to determine their views on a new line of merchandise for a small retail store. The primary advantages in personal interviews are:

1. The interviewer can adapt the question to the specific situation at hand.
2. Better response rates are obtained because individuals will usually respond when confronted in person.
3. Any misunderstandings regarding the questions can be eliminated on the spot.
4. Specific respondent reactions can be noted.
5. More in-depth and accurate information can be obtained.
6. The data received can be partially verified through observing the respondents and their surroundings.

There are some major limitations to this method of data collection, too. First, the interviewer can introduce bias into the process by asking leading questions or by giving some indication of the answer preferred. Any movement, facial expression, or voice intonation can affect the response obtained. Second, the interviewer can make errors in recording the responses. Finally, and probably most importantly, this is a very costly method of data collection: It takes a great deal of time, supervision, and interviewer training to successfully implement a survey involving extensive personal interviews.

Collection of primary data by *mail survey* involves preparing a carefully worded and ordered questionnaire, mailing it to respondents, and getting them to return the completed measuring instrument by mail. To encourage participation and ensure accuracy, the questionnaire has to be very carefully constructed and the introductory letter carefully worded. This method avoids any interviewer bias and has a much lower cost than personal interviews. Also, more spontaneous and accurate responses may be obtained if the respondents are assured of their anonymity. Finally, it is easier to reach some groups of individuals by mail, such as those in remote or inaccessible places, as well as to obtain combined reactions when a group such as an entire family is involved.

Perhaps the biggest drawback to the mail survey is the rate of return. The typical model response rate on a mail questionnaire is 20 percent; even this (or a better) result can be obtained only through the use of well-chosen techniques and incentives. There are many ingenious ways that can be employed to help increase this response rate. For example, one research firm obtained an amazing 78-percent response rate from a mail survey of purchasing agents by enclosing a quarter and indicating that this should be used by the respondent to enjoy a cup of coffee while filling out the questionnaire.

A second problem in a mail survey is that the responses actually returned often do not reflect the entire population. People who are more interested in the subject of the questionnaire and people whose training facilitates their ability to express themselves in writing are more likely to respond. A final limitation to a mail survey is that bias can result when a respondent does not answer the questions in order but rather reads the entire questionnaire before answering the first question.

Information can also be obtained by *telephone interviews*. With the cost-effective efficient telephone service available in the United States, this is probably the fastest and cheapest method for obtaining primary data, as any number of calls can be made to a specified area of the country for a fixed monthly rate. The interview process can be kept uniform by monitoring the calls on a regular or periodic basis.

Telephone interviews also have several drawbacks. The first one is that a telephone interview must be kept relatively short and interesting in order for the interview to be completed before the subject hangs up. Another problem is that certain types of questions (i.e., ratings and ranking questions) are very difficult to use. In spite of these limitations, given their timeliness and low cost, telephone surveys will continue to be the predominant method of collecting data. They can be of use to any size firm.

Another method for collecting primary data is the *focus group*. It consists of a meeting of 8 to 12 individuals with a moderator intent on encouraging in-depth and "free-wheeling" discussion of a topic. Rather than using a structured questionnaire, the focus group is led through the discussion by the moderator. Lasting about 1.5 to 2 hours, the focus group discussion allows for flexibility and provides in-depth broad knowledge that cannot be obtained through any other survey methodology. Through focus groups, new procedures, products, services, and techniques can be easily assessed prior to their implementation.

Data Analysis
Once the original data have been collected through primary research, they must be analyzed, along with any secondary data, to provide the findings to be used in the solution to the problem. This data analysis, whether it be simple numeric counting, per-

centage distributions, or more complex computer-assisted analytical techniques, should provide meaningful information appropriate for managerial decisions.

Conclusions and Recommendations

After establishing the objectives and budget, the availability of secondary sources, primary research, and data analysis, the final aspect of a research project can be generated—the development of the appropriate conclusions and recommendations. This is the most important part of the research project, but it does not always get adequate attention. The final measure of the value of the research project is whether or not the findings are successfully implemented in the company. This requires that the conclusions and recommendations be written in a clear, concise manner and be accompanied by the needed support material. This backup could include such things as original articles or tables from secondary sources, thorough description of the research methodology employed, the universe studied, sample description, original questionnaires, and the analyzed data.

CONSUMER AND INDUSTRIAL RESEARCH

Consumer research is a critical aspect of marketing. The likes and dislikes of consumers yield important information about a product's design, packaging, price, quality, utility, advertising, and distribution. With this information, management can solve present problems as well as anticipate and prevent future ones. There are many different types of consumer research: packaging, advertising, product, market distribution, and market share.

Many of these same types of research occur in industrial research with the major differences occurring in the research techniques used reflecting the nature of the products and the market. Also, most industrial research is more easily directed through the use of the *Standard Industrial Classification (SIC) Manual*, which is published periodically by the U.S. Government Printing Office and can be purchased for a nominal sum; the *SIC Manual* is also available in the business section of any good municipal library. The manual lists every single establishment where services of industrial operations are performed and assigns a SIC number to each. These establishments are classified into 11 divisions, plus one category for unclassified establishments. Within each division, major industry groups are classified by two-digit numbers. (See Table 4-2.)

Table 4-2
The Standard Industrial Classification System

Division	Industries Classified	First Two-Digit SIC Numbers Involved for Major Industry Groups
A	Agriculture, Forestry, and Fishing	01, 02, 07, 08, 09
B	Mining	10–14
C	Construction	15–17
D	Manufacturing	20–39
E	Transportation, Communications, Electric, Gas, and Sanitary Services	40–49
F	Wholesale Trade	50–51
G	Retail Trade	52–59
H	Finance, Insurance, and Real Estate	60–67
I	Services	70, 72–73, 75–76, 78–86, 88–89
J	Public Administration	91–97
K	Nonclassifiable Establishments	99

Source: Office of Management and Budget, *Standard Industrial Classification Manual* (Washington, D.C.: U.S. Government Printing Office).

CHAPTER PERSPECTIVE

In this chapter we have defined a marketing information system and marketing research. The marketing information system provides data from both internal and external sources to a company on a continuing basis in order to facilitate decision making. Marketing research is guided by specific objectives and is constrained by budget. Data used can be secondary (internally or externally generated) or primary. Primary research involves designing a method to gather information firsthand and to analyze it. Marketing managers need to utilize research to make sound decisions that result in effective marketing.

Analyzing Markets and Target Marketing

INTRODUCTION AND MAIN POINTS

The accurate determination of the market for a product is an important part in developing marketing strategy. Once these markets have been determined, a company must choose the markets that it can reach most effectively and profitably. Each market is unique in its makeup and demands. The most relevant characteristics of the market must be defined and the optimum marketing program designed in light of these characteristics.

Markets can be broken down into distinct categories, such as consumer product markets, industrial product markets, institutional product markets, military and government markets, and foreign markets. Within each of these, market segmentation can occur, based on a variety of criteria—demographic, geographic, product-related, brand loyalty, key element, just-noticeable difference, and psychological differences. Market segmentation is the process of identifying and classifying these parts of the market. The selection of a useful segmentation (classification) technique depends on the specific product category and the product/market situation.

After reading the material in this chapter:

■ You will be able to understand and successfully use various techniques for market segmentation.

■ You will know how to analyze consumer and industrial as well as other types of markets.

■ You will understand and see how to use market grids in defining your specific market segment.

A MARKET

There are probably no concepts in marketing more important than analyzing markets and target marketing. At the heart of these concepts is the *market* itself. But what exactly is a market? What criteria should be used in selecting one?

There are different types of markets: national and local markets, export and domestic markets, stock markets, furniture markets, wholesale and retail markets, and many more too numerous to mention. Each of these markets has several dimensions affecting the matching of the supply available with the demand (see Figure 5-1). These dimensions, sometimes called utilities, include time, form, possession, and place. The *time* dimension means that the product or service must be available at the correct time, not too early or too late, or else the match with demand may not occur and the goods will not be sold. The *form* of the product or service is also important. The correct quantity must be available for the final consumer as well as for the middlemen in the channels of consumption. A small retail store cannot take a shipment of 12 cases of Duncan Hines Yellow Supreme Cake Mix, nor is a home handyman interested in an entire case of nails. The possession or *ownership* dimension reflects who owns the product or service and is responsible for it. The final dimension, *place*, reflects the importance of transactional efficiency. Having diverse goods together and available in a market requires fewer transactions in order for exchange to take place than if the market mechanism were not in place.

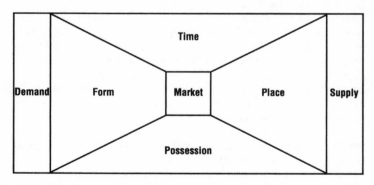

FIG. 5-1. *The dimensions of the market.*

Generally, a market is: (1) when buyers and sellers assemble, goods are offered for sale at prices and conditions that buyers accept, and a transfer of title occurs; or (2) a representation of the cumulative demand by buyers of specified products or services. The criteria used in defining a good market are (1) measurability, (2) accessibility, (3) profitability, and (4) stability.

The *measurability* criterion indicates the degree to which the size and other aspects of the market can be determined (measured). Certain markets are very difficult to measure. For example, it is very difficult to determine the number of people who wear sandals who would prefer a new rope sandal style. The *accessibility* criterion assesses the company's capability of effectively marketing and delivering the product to the defined segments. Even though the results of the segmentation process may look impressive, a market segment that cannot be profitably reached is not of any benefit to the company. The *profitability* criterion indicates whether the defined segment is large enough to be worthwhile. It is important that the size of the market segment justify the effort and expense of successfully reaching and serving it. For example, it is not worthwhile for a large manufacturer to develop clothes and shoes only for women who are very tall. Finally, the political *stability* of the market segment both now and in the future should be favorable. There is no payback in investing a large amount in a plant in a country only to have the plant shut down or nationalized at a later date.

By using these criteria to identify several market alternatives, the best market can then be selected for the particular product or service to achieve sales. This can result from: (1) a change in the marketing strategy or adopting a completely new one (the Arm & Hammer baking soda line increased sales using the new selling concept of deodorizing refrigerators); (2) a change in the size or type of packages (many canners of fruits and vegetables have added product sales by adding a very large can size previously only used in institutions such as restaurants and hotels); (3) a change in the communications system or an addition of another means of communication for reaching a market (Polymer Technology promoted its Boston Lens contact lens solutions in the Canadian market through flyers, price deals, trade advertising, and market representatives); and (4) the inclusion of a geographical area that was excluded as part of the original market (Puerto Rico, Trinidad, and many other Caribbean islands now sell Uncle Ben's Rice even though none of these markets were a part of the original market).

MARKET SEGMENTATION TECHNIQUES

The process of market segmentation is extremely important. Once the target market has been correctly defined, it is much easier to develop a marketing strategy and the appropriate combination of product, distribution, promotion, and price to reach that market effectively. Even though a market is rarely oversegmented, care should be taken to delineate a market only to the extent meaningful.

The overall segmentation techniques for all three types of markets (consumer, industrial, and government) are indicated in Table 5-1. The basic segmentation criteria—demographic, geographic, psychological, benefits, volume of use, and controllable marketing elements—can be effectively used to define a target market, whether the overall market be consumer, industrial, or government. It is particularly important to recognize and implement the capability of segmentation in the industrial and government markets. Firms in the consumer markets are generally much better at segmenting their markets.

Geographic Segmentation

One of the most widely used segmentation techniques is dividing the market into separate geographic clusters such as nations, regions, states or provinces, cities, or localities. Census information on both businesses and consumers as well as data from trade associations and publications is broken down on a similar geographic basis, allowing marketing efforts to be better directed. The market can also be evaluated in light of the distribution structure or market representatives either available or presently used in the market. In geographic segmentation, a firm can choose a market in which it enjoys a comparative advantage in terms of such marketing variables as distribution, advertising, and company image. For example, one producer of specialty oil and fat products for commercial bakeries and restaurants expanded its marketing in the New England, New York, and Pennsylvania area because of the cost advantages in transportation from a plant location close to this area.

Demographic Segmentation

When you determine that there are particular types of individuals who will be more likely to use a product, you are defining a market through demographic segmentation.

Even though demographics is not the only way or, in some cases, even the best way to define a market, it is the most widely used market segmentation method. This method is so frequently used because the demographic variables are closely associated with expenditure and preference patterns and the variables are easier to measure. In addition, the data are often already available in a published form from such sources as the U.S. Census. When

Table 5-1
Market Segmentation Techniques by Type of Market

Segmentation Criteria	Basis for Type of Market		
	Consumer	Industrial	Government
Demographic	age, family size, education level, family life cycle, income, nationality, occupation, race, religion, residence, sex, social class	number of employees, size of sales, size of profit, type of product line	type of agency, size of budget, amount of autonomy
Geographic	region of country, city size, market density, climate	region of country	federal, state, local
Psychological	personality traits, motives, lifestyle	degree of industrial leadership	degree of forward thinking
Benefits	durability, dependability, economy, esteem enhancement, status from ownership, handiness	dependability, reliability of seller and support service, efficiency in operation or use, enhancement of firm's earnings, durability	dependability, reliability of seller and support services
Volume of Use	heavy, medium, light	heavy, medium, light	heavy, medium, light
Controllable Marketing Elements	sales promotion, price, advertising, guarantee, warranty, retail store purchased service, product attributes, reputation of seller	price, service, warranty, reputation of seller	price, reputation of seller

Source: Robert D. Hisrich and Michael P. Peters, *Marketing a New Product: Its Planning, Development, and Control.* Menlo Park, CA: The Benjamin/Cummings Publishing Co., 1978, p. 168.

original published data are not available, then primary research first involves using questions to determine whether an individual is appropriate or qualified for the target market the manufacturer is interested in reaching. If you are doing a study of consumer preferences for cold cereals, for instance, the first survey question could be, "Did you eat any cold cereal yesterday?"

Once the person qualifies for the market, the interviewer would continue to obtain the necessary demographic data (such as age, sex, and income). Many marketing managers believe that the demographic method should be used only on products with low brand loyalty and that a survey of all brands in the product category should be used to determine the potential of a single brand.

Using demographic segmentation is much easier because of the availability of data from the *U.S. Department of Commerce, Bureau of Census*, and trade publications, which provide data in each of the demographic categories, not only for the entire United States, but also for regions and geographic divisions within the country.

Brand Loyalty Segmentation

Brand loyalty, the strength of preference a consumer has for one brand over another, indicates the tendency of a consumer to purchase a particular brand on a regular basis. In using brand loyalty as a segmentation technique, the amount of brand loyalty is indicated by its location on the continuum of brand loyalty. Brand loyalty also varies greatly by product category. For example, canned vegetables have generally low brand loyalty. Cigarettes, on the other hand, are a product category where there is high brand loyalty. In the case of cigarettes, a consumer does not switch brands very often, perhaps only once in a lifetime. A similar wide variation in brand loyalty also occurs in service industries. While a bank generally has a high brand loyalty, a laundromat has low brand loyalty.

Just-Noticeable-Difference Segmentation

Another useful segmentation technique involves a just-noticeable difference. This technique enables a company in a category like long filter cigarettes or colas to determine quickly and inexpensively whether or not the consumer can discern any difference between its product and others in the category. This technique will not indicate whether or not the product is preferred over others in the category, but only whether or not the consumer can detect a difference when the products are consumed under normal conditions (the conditions under which this type of product is typically consumed).

Key-Element Segmentation

Another excellent segmentation technique is key-element segmentation, where key market elements for product success are developed. For example, there are three levels of value for wristwatches: (1) some people want to pay the lowest price for a watch that works reasonably well; (2) some people buy to obtain a dependable watch for price paid; and (3) some people buy for prestigious reasons, for example, as a graduation gift that symbolizes prestige and success.

Since the low-price fields had not been seriously entered by other manufacturers, it was the market chosen by Timex. The timely tactics of Timex proved very profitable in a market with relatively high brand loyalty.

Typical key elements used are value, usage of the product, degree of susceptibility to change, attitudes, individualized needs, and self-confidence. Once the proper key element of segmentation is found, then the numbers or percentages of users in the entire market can be determined for each of the categories on the continuum reflecting the key element. From this, a category with sufficient potential that has not yet been developed by some other company can be selected.

Product Segmentation

Product segmentation can be used to uncover new market opportunities. Usually, consumer preference for a product along some key dimension of the product is distributed along a normal curve. This leaves the smaller, most unexploited markets at the extremes of this normal curve, since most manufacturers aim at the big markets found at the median or center of this normal curve. For example, most manufacturers want to include just the proper amount of chocolate in their chocolate cakes so as to satisfy the majority of the population. Consumers who desire a strong chocolate flavor and consumers who like a light chocolate flavor are at opposite ends of the curve and are often ignored, even though they represent a viable unexploited market.

New product opportunities are also found by asking consumers to calculate how close each brand is to every other brand. Whenever a proposed new product is found that has preference over existing brands, this proposed product can be developed to conform to the consumers' perception of what it should be.

Psychographic Segmentation

Psychographic segmentation measures attitudes and lifestyles in large surveys with more than 100 items on a questionnaire and with consumer sample sizes as large as 1,000 to 10,000 or more. In one sense, psychographics is similar to the motivation research studies previously discussed. After the large amount of data is obtained from the large sample in the field, it is analyzed, usually using a computerized factor-analysis-clustering technique, which separates all respondents with similar answers on a question into groups or clusters. These clusters often are given names such as the self-made businessperson, the successful professional, the contented housewife, the chic suburbanite, the retiring homebody, the devoted family man, the militant mother, the old-fashioned traditionalist, the elegant socialite, and the frustrated factory worker.

Even though the named clusters are easily recognized, the real question is whether a manufacturer and an advertising agency can develop a marketing package for any of these clusters and obtain more sales than they can by marketing to all clusters. This can be illustrated through the experience of a large eastern candy manufacturer that manufactured products with low brand loyalty and therefore experienced considerable shifting of consumer purchases to and from its brands. Their research indicated that there might be two or three main clusters of candy eaters as well as many small clusters of candy eaters who prefer chocolate nut or chocolate coconut. Using a questionnaire and colored pictures of the product, a sample of respondents was personally interviewed. Based on conclusions reached through computer analysis of the data gathered, different product packages were designed and each brand was assigned its own advertising message. In some instances, brand name and the package were changed to identify more with the cluster. Each of the three products, the same but with a different package and advertising message directed to a different cluster, were put into a test market. In addition, a fourth test market was used in which the product, package, and advertisements were directed at the entire candy-eating market regardless of clusters. This latter product sold so much better than the others that the idea of clusters was dropped.

Multivariable Segmentation

Another method of finding a niche in a market, particularly in an area where a given product differs little from competing products, is by applying a technique that incorporates a wide variety of marketing variables. Multivariable segmentation is probably most useful in product categories where it has already been determined that "no just-noticeable difference" exists between the firm's product and each of the others in the product category. Unable to find or make the product unique, the company must turn to a form of being "firstest with the mostest" with its marketing campaign. This analysis often results in such advertising campaigns as "you only go around once in life—you deserve the best" or "now it's Miller Time" and all the connotations these messages bring forth.

In other words, the company seeks a niche in a psychological benefit market and wants to convey the idea of a *unique* benefit. The concept involves combining all the consumer conceptions of the products in the class with the particular desires or needs of these consumers. This can be portrayed effectively on a graph, as in Figure 5-2 (see page 82). As is indicated, this figure portrays the results of an analysis of 500 malt beer drinkers drawn from Chicago households belonging to a consumer mail panel. Actual beers on the market were used as well as the person's ideal beer.

The two dimensions accounted for 90 percent of the discrimination among the eight products. The horizontal direction was best suited to describe quality, price, and prestige, while the vertical dimension described "heavy vs. light" users. The circles of the lower figure indicate clusters or market segments, the size of each circle being proportionate to the importance or size of the particular segment. These clusters represent individual consumers who have distinct demographic, psychological, and preference characteristics.

Many other methods, such as *social structure, family life cycle*, and *personality traits* exist for segmenting markets. Each method can only predict potential product areas if the product sale correlates highly with the factor used for segmentation. For example, when family life cycle is used to classify individuals as a single person, married without children, married with children in the home, or married with no children in the home, purchasing susceptibility of certain segmentation categories would be highly correlated with the sale of certain products such as baby carriages. Obviously, the category "married with children in the home" identifies the most likely market for a baby carriage manufacturer. Research has indicated that social class structure is useful for predicting type of store outlets chosen, family lifestyle, or skill in communication.

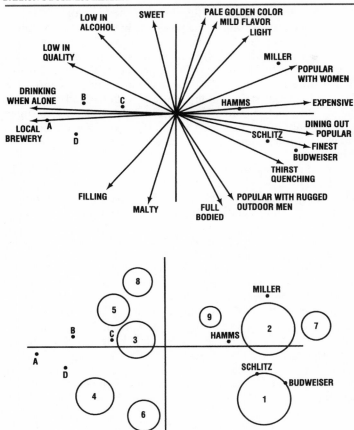

FIG. 5-2. *Location and magnitude of different psychological beer markets.*

Source: Richard M. Johnson, "Political Segmentation," *Proceedings,* American Marketing Association (April, 1969).

DETERMINING A CONSUMER MARKET

Each of the previously discussed methods has been used for market segmentation to various extents. The selection of the particular technique depends primarily on the specific product category and the product/market situation. When research has failed, when everything possible has been done to find a product difference or an advertising campaign that will differentiate the product from its competitors—all to no avail—it may be necessary to find a unique market niche with high potential through the use of a variety of psychological attitudes and beliefs.

In deciding how a market should be segmented, once a product differential has been found, you should first determine the degree of brand loyalty. Where is the product on the brand loyalty continuum? If the product category is one of low brand loyalty, then the market probably should be delineated through demographic segmentation. The demographic method is useful for determining (from the whole population) the types of users as well as the extent or degree of usage of products in the product category. For instance, if you are introducing a new type of canned peas, you would not fashion the new can of peas (through product tests) to appeal only to the canned pea eaters; instead you would attempt to appeal to consumers who eat other canned vegetables as well. Similarly, advertising would not be aimed at just those who eat canned peas. The demographic data in the market collected from the market segmentation analysis would help formulate the entire marketing plan.

If the product falls into the category of high brand loyalty, then product segmentation and/or key elements of segmentation can be used by implementing the following procedure. First, assemble 10 to 25 typical consumers of a product at a long table containing every product in the category being studied. Second, using a focus group interviewer to stimulate group discussion, have respondents group the products into clusters in such a way that they believe the ones within a cluster are more or less alike. Third, have each person tell the entire group the major differences between the clusters of products. Fourth, since participants are now expecting a new and improved product concept, have each one take a sheet of paper and record ideas for new products. Fifth, determine where these new product ideas fit into the present product structure of the company by having the group rank all products and new product concepts from best to the worst. Finally, determine the key elements the group is using for segmentation (i.e., value, aesthetic qualities, durability, heavy concentration of an important ingredient or material). The approximate market size of the new product concept can then be determined through a more quantitative study.

This technique was used once to help a milk company find a new product in the milk market. At various times in a two-hour discussion with a group of 20 housewives, the key element of segmentation varied among these three elements: quality of milk, price, and types of containers. When the product concepts were written and analyzed, the majority favored milk in a different type of container. The presently used cardboard containers were disliked for several reasons: the jagged cardboard edge affected the flavor, children spilled too much milk, and the milk took on flavors from other foods when stored in the refrigerator because of the poor seal on an open carton. The majority of the group preferred to go back to the old glass bottles even though it would be necessary to return the bottles. Another good idea that emerged was putting an inexpensive plastic pour spout, similar to that on Morton salt, on the cardboard package.

ANALYZING INDUSTRIAL AND INSTITUTIONAL MARKETS

The problem of identifying distinct markets or market segments also exists for industrial, institutional, and government products. For instance, a manufacturer of farm machinery may find that there is a demand among earth-moving contractors for a particular piece of equipment. This demand, in all likelihood, would take separate approaches for media and direct sales. Likewise, within a single market—such as farm machinery sold to farmers—there will usually be a need to do some type of segmentation within the market. Farmers with different crops—for example, a Southerner raising peanuts and a Midwesterner raising wheat—use different equipment. Because the number of users is much more limited than with consumer products, most of this analysis of separate markets as well as segmentation within the same market can be performed through the use of published market data.

MARKET GRIDDING FOR TARGET MARKETING

In determining a target market, you may need to employ a variety of techniques. One technique that has proven helpful in both industrial and consumer markets in both analyzing and displaying results is the market grid. A market grid graphically delineates the total market for a product on two or three or more dimensions. The breakdown is based on the appropriate market segmentation characteristics. A grid's usefulness is dependent on the segmentation characteristics used as well as the amount of information available on each of the segments identified.

As is indicated in Figure 5-3, the market grid can determine the best marketing plan for reaching the target market. In this example, a multivariable three-dimensional segmentation of potential customers for a pallet firm located in Indiana indicates that medium-size food firms in Indiana and Ohio interested in all

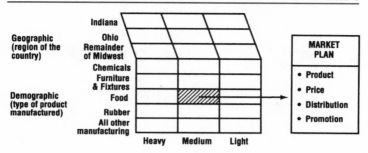

FIG. 5-3. *Market gridding for the market plan.*

the elements of marketing—product, price, distribution, and promotion—would be the best target market. The marketing plan for this group was then developed and used to reach this target market successfully.

CHAPTER PERSPECTIVE

We have discussed the importance of defining the target market in order to determine the overall marketing strategy. Marketing segmentation criteria include the following: demographic, geographic, psychological, benefits, and volume of use. In determining consumer market segmentation, you should first determine the degree of brand loyalty. In industrial markets, which usually have a more limited number of users, analysis and segmentation can be performed more easily with published data in secondary publications. The market grid is a useful technique for visually identifying the best market for the development of the marketing plan.

The Marketing Organization

INTRODUCTION AND MAIN POINTS

In this chapter we will expand your understanding of marketing organizations and structures. We will focus on the fact that each marketing organizational structure has three elements: a chief executive responsible for ensuring that the marketing activities are performed in such a way that they result in consumer satisfaction and in organizational objectives being accomplished; a marketing function for the effective development, delivery, and promotion of goods and services to the customer; and marketing support services such as marketing research and advertising.

After studying the material in this chapter:

■ You will understand the relationship between marketing and the other functional areas.

■ You will understand various marketing organizational structure alternatives.

■ You will know the characteristics of a product management system.

MARKETING AND OTHER FUNCTIONAL AREAS

The relationship between marketing and the other functional areas of the business is important for everyone to understand in order to facilitate the coordination of all the firm's activities. For nonmarketing people the understanding is important to ensure that interactions flow smoothly and effectively. These individuals may in fact have direct line or staff responsibility for some aspect of the marketing activity. For example, the comptroller needs to understand marketing in order to better manage the sources and uses of funds, since a large percentage of the firm's expenditures is in the marketing area.

It is similarly important for marketing personnel to understand the relationship between marketing and the other functional areas, as they frequently interact with other managers in the firm.

For example, a product manager who wants to penetrate new markets may have to work closely with the accounts receivable area in order to establish the criteria for credit ratings as well as the amount of credit to be extended.

The relationship between marketing and the firm's other functional areas such as finance, engineering, production, personnel, and legal is indicated in Figure 6-1. In the financial area, decisions made on credit, accounts receivable, and accounts payable have an effect on the scope of marketing. For instance, credit terms established affect not only the cash flow position of the firm but also the nature and number of distributors that will handle the firm's offering. The size and extent of accounts receivable also affect these two areas. For example, if a firm is not willing to live with a 90-day payment period, some retailers may not be

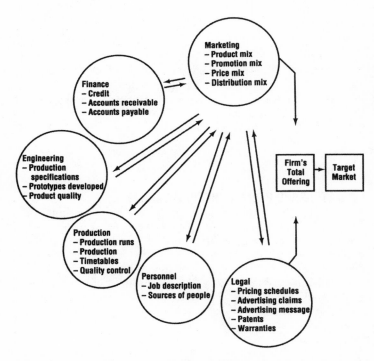

FIG. 6-1. *The interrelationship between marketing and the other functional areas in a firm.*

willing to handle the product. Many discount and department stores allow 90 days to lapse between the receipt of goods and issuing payment. The length of the accounts payable period established could affect the firm's suppliers of raw materials and component parts and equipment as well. One small firm was able to secure a supply of excellent component parts for their end product—a large industrial machine—because the company was willing to pay the supplier promptly upon receipt of goods instead of taking the usual 30 to 45 days.

The engineering area similarly makes strategic decisions affecting marketing. For example, the product specifications established affect not only the sources of supply but also product performance and price. Similarly, the nature and availability of prototypes can help or hinder a potential customer's purchasing decision. One small firm was having difficulty obtaining new accounts for its motors because prototypes could not be developed on a timely basis. The quality of the final product is, of course, directly related to some engineering decisions. Quality can be too high or too low for a specific target market. One small firm developing and marketing fader units (devices that control multiple projectors that show films simultaneously on multiple screen areas) developed a product line that would dissolve or fade the image on the screen at high rates that the market could not detect. A reduction in these rates with the accompanying cost savings and price reduction made the product more appealing, thereby significantly increasing sales.

Marketing must also work closely with the personnel department, particularly in such areas as establishing appropriate job descriptions and communicating the firm's needs to the people most qualified to fill these positions. This is particularly important since various levels of qualification as well as skill levels are frequently needed. For example, in the area of marketing research, it is important to determine not only the level of research skills but also the degree of quantitative and computer programming ability needed. In addition, the best source of supply for individuals with the appropriate qualifications should be ascertained, generally based on an analysis of the backgrounds of good employees presently in the positions. One company attempting to establish an appropriate recruitment procedure for salespeople grouped its sales force into three categories: high volume, medium volume, and low volume. Then the backgrounds and employment documents of each of the salespeople in each category were carefully analyzed to determine their underlying traits and work patterns. From this analysis, a recruitment procedure was established to hire more high-volume salespeople.

Finally, the marketing and legal departments must interact on such issues as the price of the product, terms of sale, content of the advertising messages, and wording of patents and warranties. All the offerings of the firm must be within established legal guidelines. For example, the Robinson-Patman Act must be followed in establishing the price, quantity discounts, and discounts for prompt payment for each customer. Also, the legal department in conjunction with marketing must ascertain whether or not patent protection should be sought for a new product as well as monitoring to make sure no patent infringements have occurred. Patent protection can provide a very important competitive edge for the small firm, particularly if a technological breakthrough has occurred. While there are some commonalities in the way patents are handled in every organizational structure, there are some differences, mostly depending on the nature of the product being marketed. For example, the procedures followed by consumer product companies are often different from those of industrial product companies.

Organizational Structure of the Small Company

When companies are small and have a limited number of products, one person, usually the president, often does most of the work of the marketing department. In a small company, the president often performs the following tasks: innovates new products, improves old products, helps create advertising for new products, changes old product advertising, creates promotional specials, creates new package designs, decides on the sales personnel, and determines the advertising budget.

When there are more than a few major products, it becomes difficult for even the best CEO to handle all the marketing activity. The problem is compounded even further when, in an effort to cover all bases, the president allows others in the organization to help in recommending new products, advertising, and price changes. For example, when the sales manager fills this role, the innovations and suggestions are often trade-channel-oriented, not consumer-oriented.

Brand management is an organization system in which responsibility for one product or group of products is delegated to a person or a group of persons if the sales volume warrants. This organizational structure is delineated in Figure 6-2.

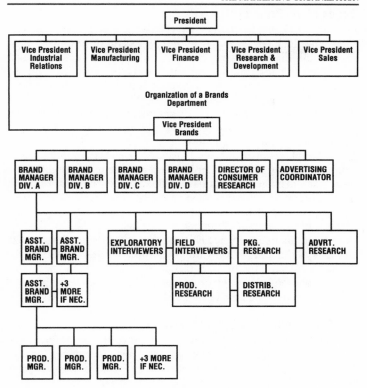

FIG. 6-2. *A consumer product organization.*

Quaker Oats uses this form of organization and assigns categories of products to division (brand) managers. For example, one brand manager has pet foods, another has breakfast cereals. In some organizational structures one brand manager has high-consumption consumer products, another has low-consumption consumer products, another has commodities, and another has industrial products. Any structure that divides the brands so that sufficient attention can be given to each one is generally beneficial. Under each brand manager there can be as many as six assistant brand managers. Each of these, in turn, could have as many as six product managers in an organization managing up to 400 to 430 products. If more products than this existed, another vice president of brands could be added. The brand management form of organization is a method of focusing proper attention on products regardless of the number of products in the organization.

Duties of the Product Manager

Product managers are the key executives in a brand organization. They should have as much authority as possible and be held responsible for the success of their products. A product manager is responsible for: innovating new products; working with the advertising agency or company advertising department to create copy and media plans; developing any promotion deals needed; determining the quality standards and price; and making forecasts of sales, profit, cash flow, and return on assets for each product. These are not the only job responsibilities of product managers. Even though product managers usually make wide-ranging decisions on many functions, similar to a president in a small company, such managers do not have authority over the sales division, the manufacturing division, or the finance area or division. Since a significant part of the job must be accomplished through these areas or divisions, a combination of two factors is needed for success. First, the company needs to recognize that no other organizational system places this much emphasis on marketing the products. Second, the product manager should have the necessary training and ability to obtain cooperation from others. A product manager needs to be able to successfully sell ideas to others.

The Functional Marketing Organization

Another type of consumer product organizational structure has either a marketing manager or a product manager under the vice president of marketing. As is indicated in Figure 6-3, sales, products, and advertising are under the same person, making it easier to coordinate product management and sales.

In this structure there can be as many echelons below the product manager or marketing manager as there are in the brand organization. While the product managers are usually responsible for product innovation and improvement as well as promotion, the advertising manager is responsible for all advertising. In this structure the product managers can be organized in a way similar to the brand type of organization but without the responsibility for advertising. Since it is usually more difficult to learn the peculiarities of each product, product managers may work under the marketing manager when the products vary greatly.

These are just a few of the many different types of organizational structures for consumer products. The important thing for the small firm is to establish an organizational structure that is flexible and responsive to consumer needs and to the firm's maintaining its profitability.

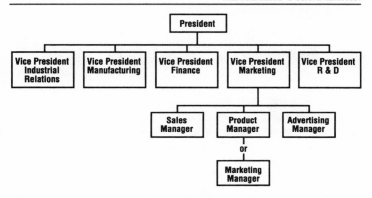

FIG. 6-3. *The marketing manager organizational structure.*

VENTURE TEAM

One organizational structure that is well suited to the design and development of products and services that either do not fit the ongoing business of the organization or else require special attention is the venture team. This structure is also sometimes called a venture group. A venture team is separate from the remainder of the organization and contains members recruited from various functional areas such as engineering, production, finance, and marketing for the period of time needed to accomplish the task at hand. The lines of authority and responsibility are usually different from those of the actual organization; the team operates with a manager who usually reports directly to the chief executive officer. Unless the manager of the venture team is given the authority to make the final decision, the authority to make any decisions is often a problem.

The use of a venture team allows the firm to develop and market new products and services, which would be very difficult within the existing organizational structure particularly when revolutionary technologies are involved. Since members of the team are not bothered by the day-to-day decisions of their previous jobs, they can focus their efforts on the task at hand, which provides a strong motivation for success. Apple Computer used the venture team approach to create and market the Macintosh. Several companies have also successfully used venture teams to develop and implement their e-commerce activities.

STRATEGIC BUSINESS UNITS

A structure with even more responsibility and independence from the organization than the venture team is the strategic business unit (SBU). Strategic business units are used to establish a mini organizational structure that is responsible for a particular group of customers or a particular group of products. Members of the SBU are usually from all areas except legal, systems, and human resources; they are part of the strategic business unit for a longer period of time than occurs in the venture team. SBU members are rewarded based on the sales and profits of the strategic business unit and often never return to their original position in the firm. IBM has successfully used strategic business units in a variety of situations. Each unit is a separate organization with its own mini board of directors, autonomous decision-making authority, and bottom-line responsibility for sales and profits. The strategic business units in IBM have developed and marketed such products as the IBM personal computer, automated teller machines for banks, and industrial robots.

INDUSTRIAL VS. CONSUMER PRODUCT ORGANIZATION

There are some differences between industrial and consumer organizational structures. In most consumer product companies few if any members of the company are in contact with the final consumer. On the other hand, industrial, institutional, and government product companies usually have more people calling on the buyers of their product.

Although the basic principles in selling are the same for both industrial and consumer goods, industrial salespeople frequently need more technical training. Some knowledge of the technology, composition, and engineering involved is usually needed to sell a technical product or service to a technical person. Consumer product salespeople, on the other hand, need to know more about the operations of the wholesale and retail channels as well as the sales promotion deals and cooperative advertising allowances than about the technology involved. Generally, this training is much shorter than technical training.

There is also a difference in the length of time needed to make a sale of consumer and industrial products. While an industrial salesperson often needs anywhere from one month to two years to make a sale, a consumer product salesperson usually makes a sale within 45 minutes. In addition, an industrial product salesperson often calls on committees composed of representatives from product manufacturing, quality control, engineering, and purchasing rather than one individual buying a consumer product.

In advertising and promotion, the industrial product company needs a more technically trained copywriter who is able to clearly express the technical advantages of the product. The media used for industrial products are often professional trade journals, not radio or TV, since most buyers are interested in written descriptions of the technical aspects or qualities of the product.

On the other hand, the consumer product company needs copywriters who can develop the product benefits for the consumer, knowing that the consumer is usually not as interested in the technical aspects of the product.

The industrial market researcher's qualifications are also somewhat different from those of a consumer product researcher. Because of the small number of customers, industrial marketing research often involves a survey of all members in the segment. Sampling is frequently not needed. Although customers are few, the amount of sales to each customer is usually large, with the sales resulting from derived or joint demand.

Buyers in the industrial market are more technically trained and somewhat more rational than consumer buyers, who may be more influenced by emotional appeals. It is often standard procedure for an industrial buyer to obtain at least two bids. Buying by specifications that often call for specific aspects and quality of goods or services is also common, with the lowest priced product not always the one purchased. The salesperson is usually dealing with a committee whose membership can change as the evaluation proceeds. For example, there could be representatives from the production department on the committee at the start of the decision. Later, engineering and purchasing departments may be involved. If the commitment is large enough, the vice president of manufacturing or the president may make the final decision. Marketing research personnel need knowledge of product characteristics and must be able to relate their research findings to technically oriented executives in their organization.

INDUSTRIAL PRODUCT ORGANIZATIONS

Channels of distribution for industrial products are usually short and direct, with a manufacturer-to-customer direct link being quite common. When indirect channels are used, industrial marketing representatives and/or distributors are typically used, particularly in the case of small firms.

While information for pricing and other decisions and the effect on sales is often obtained through research studies, quality, performance, technical assistance, and reliability in delivery are often more important than price. Negotiated prices frequently occur, sometimes involving penalty clauses for failure to deliver as well as discounts for various quantities ordered. Bid pricing is common.

The Industrial Product Manager

Just as is the case for consumer companies, when too many demands are placed on the president of a small industrial company, proper attention to improvements in old products and the development of new products frequently does not occur. The more difficult the technical aspects of the products and the more diverse the Standard Industrial Classification (SIC) Code of the customers, the faster this impasse is reached. One solution to these problems is the product manager or brand manager structure.

There are many possible forms of organization. Figure 6-4 indicates one that uses managers and product managers for each product or product line In this organization all product managers for product line. A report to the area manager for product line A. The area manager is more a strategist than technician, becoming involved in problems of market share, distribution, advertising, and promotion.

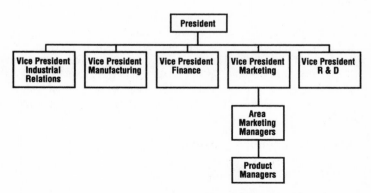

FIG. 6-4. *Organization in which regional markets are given priority over products.*

Another type of product manager structure might prevail in a company that has 70 product managers or more in such areas as large-scale and medium-scale computers, peripheral services, guest services, and product description. The product managers in this organization work closely with the salespeople in the field, putting together the promotional materials, sales and operational manuals, and advertising. They frequently go on sales calls and occasionally hold meetings with customers. In the new product development area, they work with engineers on ideas, particularly contributing on marketing aspects of the new product or service being designed.

Another unique organizational structure consists of salespeople and product managers paralleling each other, with both reporting to the product or commodity area supervisor in the department. One company with this structure has four product areas (flexible containers, aircraft components, building products, missile and undersea) and one area specifically responsible for the development of all new products. The new product is turned over to its respective area when ready to be launched. Each of the commodity areas has its own sales force of five to nine engineers who are capable of designing products on the spot to solve problems.

As these examples indicate, depending on the industry, the products, the customers, and the problems, different types of industrial organizational structures are best.

CHAPTER PERSPECTIVE

In this chapter we have expanded the discussion of the duties of a product manager. Besides delineating the aspects of a brand management structure where one person or a group of persons is responsible for the marketing of one or more products, we have also explored the differences in marketing between consumer goods companies and industrial goods companies. Primarily reflecting the small number of customers in industrial product companies, these firms generally have different organizational structures than consumer product companies.

Consumer, Industrial, and Government Markets

INTRODUCTION AND MAIN POINTS

In this chapter we will expand the concept of a market by developing the notion that a market means different things to different people and takes on a variety of meanings for an individual. The product classifications, attributes, and buying characteristics of each of three major markets—consumer, industrial, and government—will be presented.

After studying the material in this chapter:

■ You will be able to make better marketing decisions by understanding the nature and dimensions of a market.

■ You will know how to develop a successful marketing program by developing a knowledge of the consumer, industrial, and government markets.

■ You will understand the similarities and differences between and among these three markets.

MARKET

In terms of its economic aspect a market is a mechanism that bridges the gap between supply and demand in the marketplace. In this sense a market is the aggregate of all buying and selling units relating the aspects of supply and demand by building up and breaking down goods and services in order that exchange occurs. For example, the market for home computers consists of major sellers such as Apple, Dell, Compaq, Gateway, and IBM on one side and the people (consumers) interested in a home computer. In bridging the gap between supply and demand, the market creates the four basic utilities—time, form, place, and possession of a product or service (see Figure 7-1) The presence or absence of any one of these utilities can affect the nature of any transaction or exchange that may (or may not) occur.

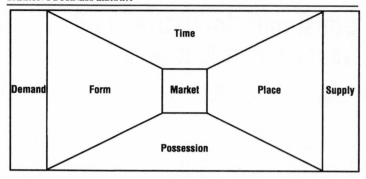

FIG. 7-1. *The dimensions of the market.*

Transactions in the market take place in a variety of ways, depending in part on whether the goods to be exchanged are physically present. There are three basic methods of transactions: inspection, sampling, and description. In transaction by *inspection* the goods are physically inspected by the consuming unit. This usually occurs when there is a high degree of perishability, a lack of standardization, a significant amount of self-service, or a newness or mistrust in the exchange relationship involved. For example, close inspection occurs in both the wholesale and retail sale of fruits, vegetables, and flowers. A lack of standardization occurs not only in large machinery and component parts and equipment in industrial products but also in such consumer goods and services as oriental rugs, paintings, and hairstyling.

When a solid business relationship has been established between buyer and seller, when a total inspection is too time-consuming, or when the inspection consumes or alters the product, the buyer or inspector can test a sample that is representative of all the products in the transaction. Transactions by *sampling* occur most often in the commodity and materials markets as well as when a new product is added to a line in the store. For example, in order to tell the quality of a commodity such as coffee, General Foods makes some coffee from the raw commodity beans, therefore consuming them in the process. When commodity sampling such as this occurs, an elaborate sampling plan is developed so that the product (in this case the coffee beans) is selected from various parts of various bags. This ensures that the quality of the final product (i.e., the brewed coffee) is controlled at least in terms of its raw materials. Similarly, sometimes it is important to have a sample of the new product for the buyer to evaluate in order for the transaction to occur, resulting in the new product being added to the wholesaler's or retailer's line.

The final method of transaction is by *description*. For this type of transaction there needs to be some confidence and trust between the buyer and seller. This relationship can be established over time; however, standardization, good quality controls, accurate product description, and selling techniques such as lease/buy, guaranteed sale, or consignment selling have facilitated this type of transaction by increasing the seller's credibility and reducing the buyer's risk.

The type of transaction that will occur has implications for the marketing program developed, as each method requires varying emphasis on the channel of distribution, the physical distribution system, the promotional program, the selling system, and support services—all aspects of the marketing mix.

CONSUMER MARKET

The consumer market is the market where products and services are purchased and consumed for personal satisfaction or use. Indeed, the American consumer should be "king" not only because of the direction of legislation but also because the consumer has more money to spend and more time to spend it than ever before. Given this increase in amount of time and money, it should be no surprise that the largest number of different products are available in this market. Since most of these products are not unique, the ones selected depend on the consumer's evaluation of the product and its benefits in terms of its ability to satisfy a need compared to other products available. In the food industry alone, the consumer can choose from over 20,000 items. And, new products are constantly being added to the large number of items already available.

Consumer Market Segments

While each product is at the center of an individual purchase transaction, the final success or failure of a product depends on the evaluation and resulting purchase decisions of all the consumers in the particular market. The composition of each of these markets is constantly changing. For example, one way in which the total U.S. market is changing is that the number of people 65 or older is larger than ever before and still increasing. With the majority of the elderly having good disposable incomes, this market segment has been identified as an attractive one enticing a wide variety of new products and services as well as special pricing arrangements.

For instance, many airlines have special fares, banks offer special accounts and personal planning packages, colleges offer continuing education classes and courses, and there are special clubs such as the senior citizen clubs at McDonald's restaurants around the country.

Buying Roles

In addition to its wide diversity and large size, the consumer market is distinctive in that three buying roles are involved in each transaction. These roles—consumer buyers, purchase deciders, and ultimate users—can be fulfilled by the same person or by two or three different people. The consumer-buyers are the members of the family who do the actual buying. In this group are the child who buys her favorite Barbie doll, the housewife who buys Ivory soap for the laundry, the housekeeper who purchases the can of Libby pears for dinner, or the husband who buys the Toro lawn-mower. The purchase decider is the member of the family who actually makes the decision regarding which product or service is to be purchased. Examples are the housekeeper who specifies that Drano be purchased for the clogged drain; the youngster who wants Cinnamon Life as a breakfast cereal; the father who decides that Atra razor blades should be bought; or the mother who feels that Crest toothpaste should be purchased to minimize cavities. Finally, the ultimate users are the members of the family or someone else who actually consume or use the product. Products have various usage lives from a single use (Duncan Hines Deluxe II cake mix), an extended use (the Cougar automobile), or even unlimited life (a Sarouk oriental rug purchased three generations earlier).

Market Characteristics

The capability to successfully market to the consumer market depends a great deal on the company's understanding of the general market characteristics. These characteristics also distinguish the consumer market from the other two markets and have caused specific distribution and selling systems to evolve. The characteristics common to the consumer market are:

- Largest number of buyers and sellers
- Wide variety of heterogeneous products
- Small size of each individual purchase
- Wide geographic dispersion

These characteristics require extensive, economically viable channels of distribution systems that link sellers and buyers, who can obtain a small amount of a wide variety of heterogeneous products. In addition, a sophisticated communication system has evolved for information purposes as well as to help eliminate price discrepancies resulting from geographic dispersion. These characteristics have caused a wide variety of products to be developed.

Product Classifications

Although there are many methodologies for classifying consumer products, one of the most effective classification schemes is based on the buyer behavior activities associated with the product purchase. This behavioral classification system delineates five types of consumer goods—convenience goods, shopping goods, specialty goods, unsought goods, and services.

Convenience goods are those products that consumers purchase with the minimal amount of time, money, and effort possible. These are products that the consumer purchases immediately and frequently with little ongoing comparison of alternatives—tobacco products, candy, gasoline, soap, and newspapers. Convenience goods can be further subclassified into three groups: staples, impulse goods, and emergency goods. Staples are goods purchased regularly and frequently, with brand loyalty playing an important role as it allows the purchase to be made quickly and easily with no alternative comparisons. Examples here include aspirin, bread, milk, soft drinks, and beer. Individuals choose Bayer aspirin, Wonder Bread, Hoods milk, Pepsi Cola, and Miller Lite on a regular basis. Impulse goods are those products purchased without previous planning or expenditure of any search effort. These goods not only have to be available in many retail outlets but also have to be strategically located in each outlet so that they receive maximum exposure to the consumer. Candy bars, gum, and magazines are placed next to the cash register to attract the attention of customers who have not planned on purchasing them. Emergency goods are purchased immediately and only when the need is urgent; snow tires, boots, and shovels in a snowstorm and an umbrella when one is caught in the rain are examples of emergency goods. One key to successful marketing of an emergency good (or service, such as automobile towing) is its availability.

Shopping goods, products that consumers will expend time and effort in comparing and purchasing, are the next general category of consumer goods. The expected value of receiving better products at lower prices is high for these products with respect to the effort, money, and time involved in the buying process. Shopping goods can be further subclassified into homogeneous and heterogeneous goods. Homogeneous shopping goods are perceived by consumers as being fundamentally alike in quality but varying in price. This price variance warrants the expenditure of time, effort, and money in comparison shopping. Examples are branded appliances such as toasters or dishwashers, grade A extra large eggs, or branded drug items. When price and quality vary, making the products dissimilar, the shopping good is a heterogeneous one. Examples of heterogeneous shopping goods are clothing, furniture, carpeting, and records. For these products a consumer is likely to overlook minor price differences in order to obtain such product attributes as different options, color, style, or quality. It is important for there to be a wide enough assortment of merchandise to satisfy the tastes of different consumers, along with good sales personnel to disseminate information on the various alternatives available.

Goods that consumers will expend a considerable amount of time and effort to obtain are called *specialty goods*. These goods have such unique product characteristics and/or are so important to the consumer that the search and purchasing process is very elaborate. In most cases, except when the process becomes too drawn out, the consumer enjoys comparing and evaluating alternatives and finally making the purchasing decision. Automobiles, books, cosmetics, stereo components, photographic equipment, oriental rugs, and paintings are examples of specialty goods. For these goods the product itself is the most important element in the purchasing decision.

Unsought goods are those goods that the consumer either does not know anything about or has no interest in purchasing. In the case of unsought goods, the consumer must not only be informed about their availability but he or she must also be presented with the attributes and value of the goods through unique advertising and personal selling efforts. Examples of unsought goods are cemetery plots, encyclopedias, gravestones, and life insurance as well as each distinctively new product in the marketplace.

In addition to the preceding four product classifications of goods, there is also the *service* sector. This is an important classification of goods in the consumer market—in fact, an ever increasing percent of total consumer expenditures are for services. There are two primary categories of services: services from goods and performed services. Services from goods involve the rental of the wide variety of products available. Products that fit this category are those that are used infrequently, that require a great deal of storage space or maintenance, that are very expensive, or that have a great deal of risk or uncertainty attached to their purchase. Glasses, paintings, tables, tents, trailers, crutches, mowers, wheelchairs, chainsaws, and videos are just a few examples of the myriad of products available for rent. The concepts of investment, maintenance, and infrequent use can easily be seen in the renting of a chainsaw to cut four cords of wood for the winter. The performed services category includes those services performed for an entire audience such as spectator sports events, lectures, concerts, theater, as well as more personal services such as dental care, physical therapy, drawing up a will, hairstyling, or automobile repair. This market will continue to draw an ever-increasing share of expenditures by consumers.

INDUSTRIAL MARKET

The industrial market is composed of a wide variety of different entities involved in the purchase and/or resale of products. The primary difference between the industrial and consumer markets is that the industrial market does not purchase for final consumption. The industrial market purchases products for further processing, use in operations, and/or resale. There are four basic types of purchasers in this market: retailers, wholesalers, institutional users, and manufacturers. *Retailers* are those members of the channel system purchasing for resale to the ultimate consumer; they provide the final link in the chain between the manufacturer and the ultimate consumers. Retailers play a vital role in breaking down the bulk into the appropriate size as well as in displaying various products in an appealing manner. There are over a million retail establishments in North America, ranging in size from a small "Mom and Pop" store to a large Wal-Mart store, from a very narrow line of merchandise such as a men's accessory store carrying belts, ties, and shirts to a large department store carrying selected products in a wide variety of categories such as clothes, stationery, tools, and dishes.

The retailer can eliminate good access to the consumer market either by improperly displaying the merchandise or by not even carrying it. For example, the Fantasia lamp, a fiber optic display lamp, only sold in stores where the overall light was dim enough so that the impact of the lamp and its tentaclelike features could be seen. The lamp did not sell well in traditional furniture stores and furniture departments in department stores with higher levels of light. Only in small, unconventional, more dimly lit stores did the lamp sell. Many of the new consumer product ideas developed never actually have the chance of competing for consumers' attention because they are not accepted by the retailer. Thus, small businesses, especially, must at times spend as much effort selling to channel members as to the final consumer.

Wholesalers are those institutions that obtain goods from manufacturers and distributors for resale to retail and other establishments. The wholesale system allows the manufacturer to access the retail and the ultimate consumer markets in a very cost-effective way.

Institutional customers are a mixture of government and private enterprise such as nursing homes, hospitals, hotels, restaurants, colleges, schools, churches, rest homes, ships' stores, and military canteens. These markets can be addressed similarly to the ways industrial products companies reach their customers.

Manufacturers are those entities that acquire products for the use in or production of final products. The Standard Industrial Classification (SIC) Code divides this market into nine major categories: Agriculture, Forestry and Fisheries; Mining; Manufacturing; Construction; Transportation; Communication; Public Utilities; Banking, Finance and Insurance; and Services. This market accounts for more transactions and business activity than the consumer market.

Market Characteristics

The industrial market has certain characteristics that need to be considered when designing a marketing strategy: derived demand, volatile demand, concentrated demand, fewer buyers, larger purchases, more involved global market, and different transaction terms. By far the most important characteristic distinguishing the industrial market is *derived demand*—the demand for the industrial product is ultimately derived from the demand for the consumer good involved. A semiconductor chip is purchased because of the demand for the computer in which the chip is a key component. When one firm dominates a significant percent of the supplier's output, the supplier may need to help that firm market its final product in order to increase sales.

The demand for industrial products tends to have much greater fluctuation than the consumer market, particularly for purchases requiring significant expenditures and/or long lead time. This *volatile demand* is often referred to by economists as the *accelerator principle*. A rise of 20 percent in consumer demand can increase industrial demand by as much as 200 percent in the next time period. A decrease can cause an equally significant decrease.

Demand for industrial products tends to be much more *concentrated*. Even though this geographic concentration does vary by industry, a significant number of manufacturing firms can be found in a few states. Geographically concentrated industries include citrus fruit, computers, petroleum, rubber, steel, textiles, and tobacco. This geographic concentration of course reduces the costs of marketing and allows for a more concentrated effort to be undertaken. Also, there are *fewer buyers* in the industrial market compared to the millions in the consumer market.

Purchases of industrial products also tend to be larger, in that a few firms tend to account for the majority of purchasing. This version of the 80/20 rule, or Pareto's curve, indicates that 80 percent of a supplier's sales are accounted for by 20 percent of the supplier's customers.

Not only are the purchases of a larger size, but the individuals doing the purchasing are more *knowledgeable*. The buyers are professionally educated and trained to make the best products available to the company at the lowest possible cost. This level of knowledge is compounded when buying committees are involved in the purchasing decision. The more knowledgeable and sophisticated the buyer, the more knowledgeable and sophisticated the salesperson must be in order to secure an order.

The final differentiating characteristic is in the *transaction terms*. These terms include direct purchasing, leasing, and reciprocity. In direct purchasing, most of the products are purchased and received directly from manufacturers; only rarely is an intermediary involved. Leasing is frequently used by manufacturers to obtain equipment, particularly when there is a lease/buy agreement where a percent of the lease can go toward the purchase of the product.

Industrial Product Classifications

A good classification system for industrial products based on their use and cost has three major groups: capital items, noncapital items entering directly into the manufacturing process, and supplies and services.

Capital items are products that are not used up in one accounting period. Most of these items are major purchases and are usually depreciated over a period of years (the life of the product), rather than their full expense being allocated in the period of the purchase. Examples of major purchases include buildings and such equipment as machine tools, blast furnaces, drill presses, and computers. Major capital equipment purchases are sold directly by one company to another, with the transaction process spanning a long period of time, sometimes as long as five years. During this long period representatives of the selling company usually meet frequently with members of the buying team, which is generally composed of higher level management from different areas such as production, marketing, finance, research and development, and sales.

Minor capital equipment is used in the production process, but of course does not become a part of the final product. This category is composed of factory tools and office equipment. Trucks, fork lifts, portable drills, typewriters, adding machines, and filing cabinets are just a few of the myriad of products in this category. These products can be sold either directly through a salesperson or indirectly through a wholesaler, the latter particularly in cases of wide geographic dispersion and small volume of purchases. The purchase is usually made on the basis of quality/price in a short period of time by a buyer, not a buying committee. Depending on the cost of the item and the policies of the company, the decision may need upper-level management approval.

Noncapital items are all those industrial products entering directly into manufacturing, and thus are expensed and used up in one accounting period. Noncapital items can be further delineated into three categories: raw materials, semimanufactured products, and component parts. Raw materials can be either farm products or natural products such as vegetables, livestock, cotton, iron ore, diamonds, coal, and copper. The marketing practices depend a great deal on the degree of perishability of the product, the fluctuation of demand, and the number of suppliers in the field.

Raw materials that have undergone some processing but are still further changed in the manufacturing process are called semimanufactured goods. Sheet steel, lumber, leather, and textiles are all semimanufactured goods that will go through further processing as they become a part of the final product. Since these products are often very homogeneous in nature, little product differentiation is available. Price and guaranteed supply are probably the most important determinants in the purchasing process. Usually no single supplier has 100 percent of a company's business.

The final category of noncapital items is component parts. While becoming part of the final product, component parts enter the finished product without further change in form. Small motors, automobile batteries and tires, and hinges are just a few examples. Most component parts are bought on a yearly contract with scheduled periodic deliveries and cancelation clauses. When the supplier deals directly with the buyer, price, quality, and service are important factors in buyer selection.

Supplies and services represent the final major group of industrial products. These items do not enter directly into the final product and as such are the most vulnerable to downgrading or a purchasing freeze when the purchasing company's sales are off. These groups of products are composed of maintenance and repair items (brooms, paint), operating supplies (stationery, lubricating oil), and services (consulting contracts). Due to the low unit volume, wide geographic dispersion, and small order quantities, intermediaries are often used, though not for services or when large, very important accounts are involved. Often a company deals directly with its most important customers. In the purchase decision for maintenance and repair items and operating supplies, price and service become very important because there is little product differentiation. Business services vary from engineering and management consulting, legal and advertising, to repair and maintenance. Since these services are generally provided by only a few alternative suppliers in a particular geographic area, price becomes a secondary factor in the buying decision, below the supplier's reputation and quality of personnel. Maintenance services are often provided by a contract with the original equipment manufacturer.

Industrial Product Customers

Industrial product customers can be subdivided into:
- Original equipment manufacturers
- User customers
- Industrial distributors

The *original equipment manufacturer* (OEM) buys the product or service to incorporate into another product, which is sold either to other industrial product companies or to consumer product manufacturers. An example would be an electronic insert molded part that might be sold to a manufacturer of television sets or to a company producing a lathe-starting mechanism. In the latter case, the final product would be sold to another industrial manufacturer rather than to a consumer product manufacturer. The *user customer* is one who uses a given product to make other products for either consumer or industrial product companies. An example of a product that could be sold to a user customer is a milling machine or an industrial drill press. The *industrial distributor* is a wholesaler who takes title to goods purchased and in turn sells products or services to other smaller industrial distributors or to OEMs or producer user manufacturers. Each of these product customers is usually called on by a salesperson representing the company.

GOVERNMENT MARKET

The government market is composed of customers in four broad categories:
- Municipalities
- County government
- State government
- Federal government

Expenditures for all governmental units generally revolve around education, public safety, public health and welfare, highways and streets, parks, and other miscellaneous administrative functions. Not only do governments have a large economic influence because of the sheer volume of goods and services purchased, they also provide outlets for a wide variety of products. There is hardly a product that is not purchased by the U.S. government.

There are many federal agencies, each with somewhat different purchasing practices, but there are three major government sources of help to firms seeking to break into this market: the *Commerce Business Daily*, the Small Business Administration, and Small Business Development Centers. The *Commerce Business Daily* lists not only proposed defense and civilian agency procurements but also recent contract awards. The latter, of course, provides leads for possible subcontracting opportunities. The Small Business Administration (SBA) provides help to small businesses in a variety of ways, such as through individual counseling on how to bid more effectively on government contracts and how to become certified on the appropriate bidding list. Also, counseling and seminars are provided to companies by Small Business Development Centers throughout the United States.

Since the federal government buys almost every product imaginable, you should understand the two major types of buying procedures employed: competitive bidding and negotiation. While competition is involved in both forms of government procurement, it is probably at its highest form in *competitive bidding*, where requests for proposals (RFPs) are sent to each qualified supplier on the competitive bidding list for the particular product. The RFP includes the description and specification of the product, the government product identification number, the quantity, the terms and conditions of delivery, the terms of the contract, and the due date of the bid. On that date the contract is awarded to the lowest bidder, unless the government deems that the company supplying the lowest bid cannot fulfill the contract. In these instances numerous forms must be filed justifying this determination before the contract is awarded to the next lowest bidder. In *negotiation*, the government agency works with one or only a few companies. This form of procurement usually takes place when state-of-the-art technology is involved or where the contract is very large and risky with few, if any, competitors available.

CHAPTER PERSPECTIVE

In this chapter we have expanded your knowledge on the aspects of supply and demand by building up and breaking down goods and services, resulting in exchange or transaction. These transactions can take place in three ways: by inspection, by sample, and by description.

The consumer market is a unique segment of the total market with three buying roles fulfilled in each transaction: a consumer-buyer, the purchase decider, and the ultimate user. The industrial market is differentiated from the consumer market in that the industrial buyer does not purchase for final consumption, but rather for further processing, use in operations, and/or resale. There are the four basic classifications in this market: retailers, wholesalers, institutions, and manufacturers. The unique industrial characteristics include derived demand, volatile demand, concentrated demand, fewer buyers, larger purchases, and different transaction terms.

We have also explored doing business with the government, which usually involves competitive bidding or negotiation. Despite being time-consuming and complex, the government market is attractive due to the volume of goods and services that are purchased at the federal, state, and local levels.

Consumer Behavior

INTRODUCTION AND MAIN POINTS

In this chapter we will expand your understanding of marketing by focusing on one of its major ingredients—the behavior of the consumer. We will focus on the general models of buying behavior, the psychological and social influences, the factors affecting the buying decision, and the stages in the buying process.

After studying the material in this chapter:

■ You will understand some of the aspects of consumer buying through the various models introduced.

■ You will know how to determine the psychological and social influences impacting a particular buying decision.

■ You will be able to identify some important factors affecting the purchase decision.

The consumer behavior process is reflected in the following two purchase scenarios. On Friday afternoon at 3:00 P.M., a 32-year-old woman, mother of two children, walks into a grocery store and buys her family's groceries for the week. She stops at the candy rack, selects two Mars bars for her husband, a Twix candy bar for herself, and continues on her way to the checkout counter.

A 27-year-old bachelor enters the same store at 7:30 P.M. on the following Tuesday evening. He walks over to the cake mix area, selects a box of Duncan Hines chocolate cake mix and a can of Pillsbury Ready-to-Spread frosting, and walks to the checkout counter.

Why did the woman buy Mars and Twix rather than Hershey, Clark bar, or Heath bar? Why did the bachelor buy Duncan Hines rather than Betty Crocker or Pillsbury? Or, why did he buy chocolate rather than vanilla or lemon? Millions of dollars have been and continue to be spent on research trying to answer these and other questions. Although explanations vary considerably, there is one underlying notion: It is important to understand the forces that lead consumers to behave as they do.

THEORETICAL MODELS FOR BUYER BEHAVIOR

For years many physiologists, psychologists, sociologists, economists, and marketers have attempted to answer the question, "Why does a particular consumer buy a particular brand in a particular size, color, and package at a particular price on a particular day in a particular store?" In the attempt to answer this question, several models have been developed, focusing on some important buyer motives and the buying process. Although no one model provides a complete explanation, you can use the elements and structure identified in developing your marketing plan.

Stimulus–Response Model–Learning Model

The stimulus–response model is based on the work of classical psychologists such as Pavlov and Watson, who found that all organisms have physiological drives directly related to their need for survival. There are two basic drives: primary and secondary. The primary drives include the need to avoid pain and the need for belonging. Secondary drives such as guilt, pride, and acquisitiveness are learned drives that are acquired in the attempt to satisfy primary drives. An example of an advertisement attempting to apply this general model through stimulus generalization is indicated in Figure 8-1. In this advertisement the goal is to have the reader generalize from the various stimuli—"Your server is your showroom. Are the doors always open?"—to the response desired: Buy Compaq.

Advocates of the stimulus–response model contend that the sequence of steps—drive, motive, stimulus, cue, response—fulfills human needs and eventually results in brand loyalty (the allegiance to one product over another). A drive is a strong inner force or need that can cause an individual to act; motive is a directed drive; stimuli are things that activate a drive or need and may elicit a response; cues are minor stimuli; response is a reaction to a given set of stimuli and cues. In addition, reinforcement is a satisfying response or action that results in reinforcement of the stimuli and cues, thus increasing the likelihood that a person will respond in the same way again, leading to the degree of satisfaction achieved and the level of brand loyalty established.

Psychoanalytic Model

Since human needs occur at different levels of consciousness, it is only through probing with special techniques that the various levels of needs can be identified. These needs begin to operate on the instinctual level during early childhood. As children grow

FIG. 8-1. *Advertisement attempting to develop stimulus generalization.*

Source: *Newsweek*, October 4, 1999, p. 51.

older, they realize that blatant behavior such as crying is not an acceptable way to satisfy needs and gradually develop better, more subtle ways of satisfying needs. According to Freud, as an individual grows older and has more experiences, the psyche (the repository of human drives) becomes more complex, developing a three-part structure: the id, the superego, and the ego. The id is the unconscious part of the mind, where strong desires and instinctive urges reside. The superego is the conscience; it internalizes societal rules and attitudes, and is the part of the mind that must find socially acceptable ways of satisfying the id's needs and desires, thereby avoiding shame and guilt. The superego is only partly conscious. The ego is the "control center" of the mind. As an individual grows, ways of satisfying needs and expressing desires that are acceptable are learned. The ego must balance the uninhibited actions of the id against the repressiveness of the superego. The ego is frequently appealed to in a wide variety of advertisements, such as the one appearing in Figure 8-2.

According to psychoanalytic theory, a buyer's motives are very complex. One group of buyers may be motivated by functional concerns while still being driven by symbolic concerns. For example, a man who says he is buying a certain make of automobile because of its maneuverability may actually be buying a sense of masculinity or a feeling of security or belongingness.

The rapid success and subsequent decline of the first cake mixes illustrates the use of psychology in the marketplace. In these first cake mixes, all that had to be done was add water. At first the cake mixes were a great success, but then sales dropped sharply due to several factors. First, many homemakers didn't lead the "active life" referred to in the advertisements and did not lack time to bake a cake. Second, homemakers did not like merely adding water to the mix, feeling they should put forth more effort in making cakes. In response, cake mix manufacturers redesigned their products so that consumers would "Add a cup of milk and one egg." Sales then increased.

Unfortunately, the task is not always this simple, as indicated in the failure of the Ford Edsel. While designed with the best available psychological research to appeal to the automobile buyers' need for security, it was rejected by consumers. Sales for the Edsel's first year on the market were poor, then fell even lower during the next two years. This failure illustrates one problem with the psychoanalytic model: A person's motivations are frequently buried so deep in the subconscious that it is difficult to determine the proper motive at a given point in time. Various projective techniques such as word association, sentence completion, picture interpretation, and role-playing have been developed that can sometimes bypass the individual's ego control and give a view of the individual's hidden dreams, hopes, and aspirations. However, even these research techniques may fail, and even when successful in identifying motives, an individual's attitudes may change before the actual purchase decision is made.

PUSHING THE ARTFORM

Wynton Marsalis, the most acclaimed jazz musician and composer of his generation, as well as distinguished classical performer. Recipient of the Grand Prix du Disque of France, Edison Award–Netherlands, 23 Honorary Doctorates, and 1997 Pulitzer Prize for Music: The first ever for jazz.

Movado, maker of some of the most acclaimed timepieces in history, holds 99 patents, over 200 international awards for design, and has watches in museums on five continents: A leader in innovation.

Museum Safiro™.
18K gold micron finish.
Sapphire crystal. $795.

MANN JEWELERS
Beachwood, OH 800-272-6266

MOVADO WATCHES ARE EXHIBITED IN THE PERMANENT COLLECTIONS OF MUSEUMS WORLDWIDE

MOVADO
The Museum.Watch.
S W I S S
www.movado.com

FIG. 8-2. *Advertisement featuring an ego appeal.*

Source: *Newsweek*, October 11, 1999, p. 38b.

Hierarchy-of-Needs Model

In general, these previously discussed two models have been criticized for their limited usefulness in explaining motivation and behavior. An alternative model is the hierarchy-of-needs model formulated by Maslow (see Figure 8-3). Human beings have five basic needs, which can be grouped into three categories: physical, sociological, and self. The *physical* needs comprise physiological and safety needs and are concerned with survival—food, shelter, and clothing. An individual's first needs are obviously to satisfy hunger and thirst. After these are satisfied, then he or she is concerned with *safety needs*—the need for security, protection from harm, and stability.

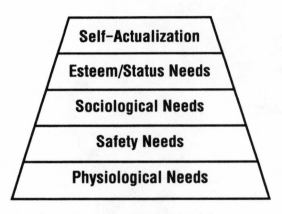

FIG. 8-3. *Maslow's Hierarchy-of-Needs Model.*

The *sociological* needs include belongingness and love as well as esteem and status. Everyone has a need for affection and acceptance by others, to feel close to family and friends. This need is reflected in our joining clubs, conforming to dress codes, and behaving in expected ways. The desire for belongingness and love has a strong effect on an individual's behavior. The needs for *esteem* and *status* are reflected in our desire to succeed and to feel important in relation to others. The desire to master our environment, to have a good reputation, and to enjoy prestige are included in this category.

The self needs center around *self-actualization*—the need to know and understand ourselves and build systems of values that express this. Self-actualization is the need to realize our full potential. Since the need system is a hierarchy, the "higher" social and self needs become important only after one's basic needs have been fulfilled. For example, only after one is fed and clothed and has a feeling of security, belonging, and esteem can one focus on self-actualization, which is the need appealed to in the AXA Advisors advertisement in Figure 8-4.

FIG. 8-4. *Advertisement featuring a self-actualization appeal.*

Source: *U.S. News and World Report*, October 4, 1999, p. 48a.

Even though Maslow's model is not universally accepted, it can be used as a marketing tool to identify consumer motivations in different segments of society for your product. For example, a toothpaste may be sold on the basis of its sex appeal, not its hygienic value, and a well-prepared dinner can be sold as a sign of love, not eating the right food. To a certain extent Maslow's hierarchy-of-needs model describes the growth of the individual in a way that parallels the growth of society.

Sociological Model

The sociological model represents another attempt to explain consumer behavior. While psychoanalysts emphasize the development of the individual self, sociologists emphasize the role of groups in society, as in the advertisement for the family van in Figure 8-5.

The central premise of the sociological model is that the behavior of the individual is primarily the consequence of forces exerted by the external environment. People form ideas of what they want from four basic social configurations: culture, subculture, social class, and reference groups. *Culture* is the total knowledge, beliefs, values, and customs that people use and pass down to succeeding generations. *Subculture* is a group within the dominant culture of an area that shares common values and belief patterns that differ to some degree from those in the mainstream culture. *Social class* is the grouping of a society in which individuals and families share similar values, lifestyles, and/or income. *Reference groups* are groups that positively or negatively influence an individual's attitude or behavior. While the importance of these influences varies from individual to individual, all of them play a role in shaping behavior. The individual will tend to behave (i.e., buy a particular product) according to which forces predominate.

Economic Model

Economists approach the issue of consumer behavior from a different perspective than do social scientists. According to economists, the consumer lives in a rational world that functions by means of rational economic principles. The consumer makes buying decisions on the basis of rationally perceived self-interest, given a limited amount of money for gaining satisfaction by satisfying a number of wants and needs from a range of products available. The effort to maximize self-interest in light of these demands is called *utility maximization*.

FIG. 8-5. *Advertisement featuring family and fun.*

Even the most addicted chain-smoker would not spend *all* of his or her money on cigarettes. The proudest homeowner will spend no more than a certain amount on furnishings or lawn and garden spray. The most fashion-conscious individual will draw the line somewhere and stop purchasing clothes. The reason is simple: Everyone, sooner or later, reaches a limit beyond which they will not go. This phenomenon is the basis of the principle of *diminishing marginal utility*.

While indeed there is frequently some degree of rational economic thinking behind most purchases, there is an emotional side involved in the purchase as well. And sometimes the emotional, nonrational side predominates or is the sole force behind the purchase. It is doubtful, for example, that the majority of the people who buy gag gifts such as pet rocks have a rational basis for doing so.

PSYCHOLOGICAL AND SOCIAL INFLUENCES

As the previous discussion has indicated, an individual's behavior is influenced and shaped by many forces. Some of these forces are psychological—the instinctive need to feel safe and secure—and others are sociological—the pressure exerted by a peer group to conform. To provide a better understanding of why people behave as they do, we will discuss some of the more important influences of behavior. These influences are aspects of the models of buyer motivation previously discussed.

Self-Concept

To a great extent our behavior is influenced by our self-concept; we act in accordance with our view of ourselves. Much research has been done on the relationship between behavior and self-concept and its main components: the ideal self, the real self, and the looking-glass self.

Marketing managers tend to think in terms of groups or masses of people, since a company doesn't make a profit by selling *one* pencil or *one* blouse to *one* customer. Profit comes from selling to many people. When planning a mass-market strategy, however, you must consider the consumer on an individual basis. People's needs, aspirations, and self-concept affect their buying behavior. A person is likely to choose products that either are compatible with his or her self-concept or will help that person move closer to his or her ideal self. A product that does not appeal to the consumer's real or ideal self-concept is less likely to be purchased.

Culture

Culture is the totality of beliefs, values, and customs of a group of people that are passed on to succeeding generations. How we view the world, what we see and feel, what we value, and how we respond to our environment are all culturally based to some extent. Through culture we adapt to our environment and express our relationship to it. Cultural values, of course, are not instinctual; they are acquired through societal institutions that take us through the process of *socialization.*

Even though cultures and the values they express can change with time, the institutions that reflect cultural values are much slower to change. "Generation gap" and "future shock" are just two terms used to describe the problems that both individuals and institutions struggle with when they are confronted with rapid change. When institutions respond reasonably well to changes in culture, the society is relatively stable. However, when change is too rapid and/or institutions are unable to assimilate changes quickly enough, society can become unstable.

A marketing manager must be sensitive to changes in cultural values. A sociologist, for example, might attribute the failure of the Edsel to bad timing. The Edsel, which appeared in late 1957, was a family car in the medium-price range, designed to appeal to a consumer's basic need for stability and security. The Edsel was marketed near the end of a period of relative social stability when people still had little need for security; their need for a sense of adventure, self-expression, and fulfillment was greater. If the Edsel had been on the market during the 1930s, a period of uncertainty and unrest, it might have sold better.

Up to this point the word "culture" has been used in the singular sense. However, there are many cultures, just as there are many societies. A firm that becomes involved in international marketing needs to be aware of cultural and societal differences. For example, the concept of personal space—the distance that people keep between themselves and others—varies from region to region or country to country. Northern Europeans keep a greater distance between themselves and others in formal situations than do southern Europeans. If you positioned yourself while speaking to a northerner in terms of southern European "space," you might be considered too familiar. If you conducted yourself with a southerner as though he or she were a northern European, you might be considered cold and unfriendly, possibly even hostile. You need to be careful in dealing with any customers or potential customers by understanding their overall culture, including their "space" requirements.

Subcultures

Just as culture can differ from country to country, it can also vary within countries. In the United States, sociologists distinguish five to six distinct regions. If you are Bjorn Peterson, an outspoken Lutheran who lives in South Boston, or if you are J. Whitney Waspworth IV, an active Republican who lives in the Lawndale area of Chicago, you and your views are in a distinct minority. South Boston is almost exclusively Irish and Catholic, whereas Lawndale is predominantly black.

These examples illustrate several of the main subcultural divisions in a society: nationality, religion, race, and geographic region. Many groups are more or less distinct from the general population. For example, the Amish and the Hutterites, two religious sects, live in more physical isolation in the Plains states. Also, people in the same geographic region share many distinctive lifestyles and values.

While these subcultures are often separated physically, their emotional separation is much more important. The different values, attitudes, and feelings of subcultures represent potential markets for specialty-oriented companies and possible problems for the unwary marketing organization. Not only do subcultures represent potential markets, they may also force the company to market the same product differently.

Social Class

While subcultures represent one major division of a culture, social class represents another. A social class is a reasonably stable and long-lasting social grouping. Members of a class place importance on similar things, live similar kinds of lives, are interested in similar pursuits, and value certain kinds of behavior. Classes can be very rigid. In some countries they are called castes and are a permanent form of status. In countries like the United States, classes are considerably more flexible and fluid, though they are definable. Social classes are ranked according to the values of the particular society and represent distinct market segments that can be appealed to.

Sociologists usually identify six social classes in U.S. society: upper-upper, lower-upper, upper-middle, lower-middle, upper-lower, and lower-lower. The upper-upper class is the closest parallel in the United States to an aristocracy. The members' wealth is inherited, their children attend private schools, and they usually maintain more than one home. Striving to get ahead in the traditional American sense is not part of their class ethic—they have already arrived. Low visibility is more important. The upper-upper class comprises less than 1 percent of the population.

Many people who consider themselves to be in the upper class are usually classified as lower-upper by sociologists. The distinction between the upper-upper and lower-upper is based on the source of money—earned income (lower-upper) versus income from investments and previous generations (upper-upper). Because one ambition of the lower-uppers is to attain upper-upper class status for their children, members of this class tend to be prominent in social, political, and cultural affairs. Capitalizing on the prominence they have earned through success and ability in business or the professions, they like to hold symbols of upper-class status such as political office and other highly visible positions in society. While this class comprises about 2 percent of the population, some of its members personify the term *nouveaux riches*. Others are members of the jet set. This class is often a reference group for lower social classes.

The upper-middle class makes up about 12 percent of the population, with its members usually being in the professions, such as law, medicine, engineering, science, and education. While they tend to be strong supporters of education, high culture, and the development of the mind, they value a comfortable, well-furnished house and the ability to entertain guests. They seek continued mobility within their class and are a market for quality items, especially those related to the home and education.

The lower-middle class is primarily composed of white collar workers and higher-ranking blue collar workers such as firefighters, plumbers, and electricians. This class comprises about 30 percent of the population, with its members being industrious and supportive of traditional values (home, church, and country). Like the upper-middle class, the lower-middle class places a high value on a good home. But unlike the upper-middle class, this group is a market for conventional, mass-produced furnishings since it does not have a large amount of discretionary income.

The upper-lower class, or working class, comprising about 35 percent of the population, generally has little education and mainly work in unskilled manual jobs. Upper-lower class shoppers have a high degree of brand loyalty and frequently buy impulse goods.

The lower-lower class, about 20 percent of the population, includes the urban slum dwellers, the rural poor, welfare recipients, and the chronically unemployed. People in this class tend to overpay, to buy on credit, are not quality-conscious in their buying decisions, and buy impulsively.

Reference Group

While culture, subculture, and social class influence a person's buying decisions, any individual or group who changes a person's behavior or attitudes may be considered a *reference group*. An individual reference group may be a baseball player, movie star, or a teacher. Examples of group references are parents, fellow employees, trade unions, or private clubs. Whether individual or group, if day-to-day contact is possible, the members are considered a *primary reference group*. Less influential are *secondary reference groups*, those with which day-to-day contact is not maintained. Besides frequency of contact, another way to classify reference groups is based on the individual's view of the group. For example, an *aspirational group* is a group that the individual wishes to belong to sometime in the future. For a high school girl who plays on the intramural basketball team, an aspirational group might be the varsity basketball team. A *disassociate group* is one to which the individual never wishes to belong or even be associated with. This could be a church group not of the individual's faith or people who frequent health food stores. Also, reference groups may be *normative*, where behavior standards for members are set—a street gang, for instance. These groups may also be *evaluative*, in which case the individual evaluates his or her performance by comparing it to the standards of the group. An example might be a member of a particular faith.

Because most people desire to belong to some group, reference groups affect the individual's attitudes, behavior, and feelings—and purchasing behavior. Reference groups can create pressure for conformity as well as nonconformity. Since this pressure can greatly influence purchasing decisions, the implications of reference groups are important for advertising. If a company can show a potential buyer that its product is used or highly valued by one of that person's positive reference groups, it has a good chance of positively influencing the individual and obtaining a sale.

The importance of reference groups varies. Some are very strong; others are not. A strong reference group can be a virtual closed society with the ability to communicate information, attitudes, and beliefs almost instantaneously. A tightly knit reference group can exert a strong influence over its members and, thus, their buying decisions. This influence is especially strong in areas where the product is highly visible, such as an automobile.

STAGES IN THE BUYING PROCESS

There are five stages in the buying process—need arousal, information search, evaluation, purchase, and postpurchase. Of course, not every purchase involves all the stages (see Figure 8-6). For example, when the purchase is a routine one in which the consumer buys the same brand as before, there is no need for an information search or an evaluation of alternative products.

FIG. 8-6. *Five-stage model of the consumer buying process.*

Need Arousal

The first step in a buying decision is the recognition of a need. People buy things because they feel they need them. Stimulus of the need recognition can come from within (we become hungry or thirsty or hot or cold) or from outside forces (we see a poster advertising Coke and become thirsty, or we admire a friend's new computer and decide to buy one too). Sometimes recognition of these needs comes instantly, and we satisfy our needs very quickly. Other times these needs are more subliminal or simply not pressing, and we act on them only after a long period of deliberation.

Information Search

In some situations all the elements needed to make a sale are present. There is an intense need, a well-defined object that will gratify the need, and the object is readily available. The sale is practically assured. The purchase of fast-service foods is an example of this type of situation. You are hungry, a cheeseburger and fries will satisfy your hunger, a fast-food restaurant is located nearby, so you stop and purchase the food.

In most situations, however, the sale is not this easy. The consumer cannot immediately gratify the need because something is missing. For example, the consumer may not be sure which brand of product will best satisfy the need, or the consumer does not know where to buy the product. In these situations the consumer will simply take note of whatever information is already available and will remember it for a future purchasing activity.

An ongoing sense of need can lead to one of two situations. In one, now that you are aware of a need, you are more conscious of product-related information on its satisfaction. You have probably experienced this state of mind. The refrigerator doesn't seem to be working as well as it did in the past. It still runs, but eventually you are going to need a new one. With this in mind, you pay more attention to advertisements on television and appliance store displays that feature refrigerators. Although you don't make the purchase immediately, you accumulate information that will be beneficial when you have to buy a new one. You are in what is called a *heightened state of awareness*.

A second, more intense condition is called an *active search for information*. While you haven't noticed that the refrigerator is getting worse, suddenly there is a problem—and the technician tells you that the refrigerator will last only a few more weeks. You begin conscientiously looking for as much information as possible. In this instance you will go after much more specific information than if you were simply in a heightened state of awareness.

Consumers usually get their information from one of four places: personal sources, commercial sources, public information, and personal experience. Personal sources such as friends, family, and close associates are frequently asked about buying alternatives. Commercial sources include advertisements, displays, and information from salespeople. Government publications, reports by consumer organizations, and mass media reports comprise public information. Finally, information is gained from personal experience—examining the product and, if possible, trying it for a test period.

Evaluation

While all stages of the buying process are important, the evaluation stage is often the most critical point. Several factors play an important role here.

Consumers evaluate the quality and characteristics of various products based on certain characteristics such as speed, strength, safety, or long product life that vary by product category and with particular consumers. For example, consumers will evaluate a convenience good differently than they would evaluate a specialty good. People purchasing an item for professional use will evaluate it differently than would a person purchasing it for a hobby.

Utility of the product is also evaluated. Simply stated, this concept concerns the nature of the benefit that a consumer expects to get from a product of a particular quality. The consumer's goal is to obtain the best quality and most utility within a certain cost.

Purchase

Even after the consumer has made this evaluation, he or she may not buy the product selected. Social factors and anticipated conditions can influence this purchase intention. *Social factors* reflect the reactions others may have to the purchase. The importance of social factors depends on the degree to which the other person likes or dislikes the choice and the importance of the person's opinion. Primary reference groups have a strong influence here. *Anticipated conditions* are the consumer's expectations of what external conditions will be like. Changes in these conditions, such as an economic recession, may cause the consumer to postpone the purchase.

Postpurchase

During the actual buying process, most consumers ask themselves several questions: Will I be satisfied with this product later on? Will I get my money's worth? These same questions can also recur after the purchase has been made. It is therefore important to pay attention to the consumer's feelings after the purchase has been made. Feelings of dissatisfaction or uncertainty about a purchase can be attributed to *cognitive dissonance*, which is an uncomfortable state that occurs in a person when he or she receives information in discord with his or her own feelings. This state of mind can be changed by discrediting the credibility of the source or by changing one's own position. Cognitive dissonance is especially prevalent among purchasers of major items such as houses and automobiles. For example, the owner of a new car may find that the car gets 17 miles per gallon, not the 20 he or she expected. When this occurs, the consumer needs positive reinforcement. Many loyal consumers such as those who will buy only General Electric appliances or Chevrolet cars were positively reinforced in some way during their postpurchase phase by advertisements and direct-mail pieces affirming their purchase decision and the product value they received.

CHAPTER PERSPECTIVE

In this chapter we have examined the various aspects of consumer behavior. The primary differences among the theoretical models of buyer behavior were explored, as were the various aspects of the psychological and social influences. By understanding these influences and the various stages in the buying process discussed, you will be in a better position to market your particular product or service effectively.

Government, Industrial, Nonprofit, and Service Marketing

9

INTRODUCTION AND MAIN POINTS

In this chapter we will broaden your understanding of marketing of consumer goods to include marketing to the government, industrial, and nonprofit markets as well as service marketing. We will focus on the characteristics and buying processes of each of these markets in developing the best marketing strategies for each.

After studying the material in this chapter:

▬ You will understand and be able to develop an effective organizational structure to service the three major markets.

▬ You will know the important aspects of government and service marketing and be able to use these in effectively marketing to each.

▬ You will be able to plan and implement a marketing effort in the nonprofit sector.

Government, industrial, and nonprofit marketing are becoming more and more important as marketing is being used, to some extent, in almost every organizational setting. In approaching these markets, several factors should be kept in mind. First, as in the consumer market, there are many markets, not just one or two. Second, unlike consumers, the various industries, institutions, and government agencies tend to base their buying decisions on more "rational" motivations. Also, the buying decision in these markets usually goes through a lengthier review process, often involving several levels of individuals, than that used in the consumer market.

GOVERNMENT MARKETING

The government consumes a significant amount of products and services in performing its duties and responsibilities. Even though the government is sometimes a very difficult and expensive market to access, the size and the amount of purchasing is so large that you need to carefully consider it as a potential customer.

Government as Customer

The government consists of customers at the federal, state, and local levels. As a group, these governmental units account for the largest expenditures of any group in the United States. The federal government spent $990 billion in 1986, $1,454.6 billion in 1997, and $1,487.1 billion in 1998 for a variety of goods and services needed to support operations in such areas as highways, mass transportation, national defense, police and fire protection, protection against faulty products and services, and education. Specifically, the federal government spent $340.4 billion on national defense, $18.2 billion on education, $22.6 billion on transportation, and $317.9 billion on health in 1998.

For marketing purposes, government units can be grouped into three major categories: departments of federal, state, and local governments; administrative units such as school or sanitary districts; and government-created autonomous agencies such as the Port Authority of New York and the Tennessee Valley Authority. These latter two categories have a substantial amount of autonomy and independence in making purchase decisions. The expenditure patterns of state and local government units tend to follow the distribution of population in terms of size and expenditures.

Government Marketing

Marketing to the government is somewhat more complicated than either consumer or industrial marketing, owing to the uniqueness of the government buying process. The basic steps involved in large government purchases are:

1. A department discovers it needs a particular item.
2. If the purchase is covered by the current budget, the department head draws up a requisition describing the item and giving all the necessary specifications.
3. The requisition is sent to the purchasing office where it is reviewed by a government buyer; when necessary, it is rewritten to ensure competition.
4. The purchase is approved by the appropriate governing body.
5. A public advertisement announcing a call for bids is placed, and companies on the agency's bid list receive invitations by mail.
6. Interested companies submit sealed bids, which are opened publicly at the time specified in the announcement and entered in the public record; the winning bid is then announced. The bid selected will be the lowest bid, unless the bidder is deemed unable to fulfill the contract.

Most government units operate under statutory regulations that allow informal bids to be accepted when purchasing items below a specified dollar level. When purchasing items below this amount, two or three possible suppliers are contacted to obtain comparative pricing, and the items are purchased without any formal bidding procedure.

To be notified of upcoming bids, other than through the advertisements, a company must be on the approved bid list. You can do this by submitting the list of the products for which your company is qualified to bid to the government agency or agencies who may require the item. Your company and its products will be approved for the bid list or otherwise notified. When a product has so many suppliers on the bid list that it is not economically feasible to notify all companies on the list for each bid, suppliers are notified on a rotation basis.

In addition to purchasing through bids, some major purchases by government units and agencies are negotiated. When buying by negotiation, the process usually begins with a bid or quotation that is modified to reflect the conditions and factors relevant to the particular procurement situation. Negotiations are usually carried on by the government unit simultaneously with a number of competitive suppliers. This usually results in proper procurement in terms of price, quality, and service; the strength and experience of the suppliers is also taken into account. Negotiations often occur when the government unit is purchasing a product or service at the cutting edge of the technology. For example, purchases of highly technical products by the National Aeronautics and Space Administration (NASA) are almost always accomplished through negotiation.

In order to market to the government successfully, particularly when the purchase is being made by bid or negotiation, you must be particularly conscious of the costs involved—not only the costs of your company but the costs of competitors as well. These costs can establish realistic price limits and guidelines for use in the bidding procedure, and thus will eventually secure or lose the sale and result in a profit or a loss.

INDUSTRIAL MARKETING
Owing to the nature of the buying decision and the size of the purchase, industrial marketing is different from both government and consumer marketing. The unique characteristics of this market are particularly evident in distribution, the buyer organizational structure, and the industrial sales environment.

Channels of Distribution

There are two major differences between the channels of distribution used in industrial marketing and those used in consumer marketing. First, the channels are much shorter for industrial marketing, reflecting the larger purchases and geographic concentration of this market. Second, in industrial marketing, the intermediaries are less numerous, consisting primarily of manufacturers' representatives or agents and distributors.

The most common channel in industrial marketing is the manufacturer's own salespeople selling direct to customers. This arrangement has two distinct advantages over using intermediaries. First, the manufacturer's interests will always be given top priority and attention. Second, direct selling provides a better means of communication between manufacturer and buyer, with better rapport being established and market information being obtained.

One disadvantage of direct selling is its high cost, as an industrial sales call costs more than any other sales call. Also, an industrial sale has the highest cost to close. For a startup or a company short on capital, it is better to pay the variable cost of a representative's commission than the cost of a salesperson's salary. After all, a manufacturer's representative is only paid when a sale is made.

Systems contracting is being used more and more in industrial distribution because it increases system productivity and customer service and decreases such costs as purchasing and inventory. In a systems contracting arrangement, a buyer arranges with a particular distributor to procure a variety of products at competitive prices. In turn, the supplier guarantees 48-hour delivery for about 95 percent of the items once the order is received.

Personal Selling

Usually industrial marketing has more job specifications and requires a more technically trained salesperson. While the principles for sales training and administration of the sales force are the same for industrial consumer marketing, training in industrial marketing is usually lengthier because of the more technical nature of the product and the more knowledgeable buyers.

Pricing

While price is not the only variable in the marketing mix influencing the demand for industrial goods and services, it certainly is a very important one. A price that is too high cannot only bring about buyer resistance but also invite competition, while a price that is too low can negatively impact profits and can even deter a sale by connoting a low-value product.

Buyer Organizational Structure

The buyer organizational structure should be determined for each potential customer in order to eliminate time wasted in calling on the wrong person. Although buyer organizations differ even in the same product category, there are some important distinctions.

The buying structures of industrial companies differ based on the size of the company and the contribution purchasing makes to profits. For example, in a very large chocolate-manufacturing firm, the cost of cocoa beans accounts for half of the net sales dollar. In addition, the price of cocoa beans can vary from as low as five cents up to two dollars a pound. Whether the company makes a profit and continues in business depends to a great extent on the expertise of the cocoa bean buyer. This buyer, as well as buyers in other industrial companies who significantly impact sales and profits, will generally have important positions in the organization, perhaps vice president.

The Industrial Sale

There are three major differences between an industrial sale and a consumer sale. First, the industrial sale is usually made by multiple buyers, such as committees of two to five people. The membership of the committee can change as the sale progresses. Second, the industrial sale goes through many stages before the actual sale occurs. Third, the industrial sale takes much more time to consummate, often three months to two years.

The stages of an industrial product sale are indicated in Figure 9-1 (see page 136). An industrial sale can go through seven different stages, which can be classified into three categories: (1) organizing the idea, (2) justifying the possible purchase, and (3) receiving bids and making the final purchase decision. Throughout this time-consuming process, the members of the purchasing committee involved can be different in the several industrial organizational structures used by companies to facilitate the buying process (see Figure 9-2, page 137).

Key Decision Maker

In industrial as well as government marketing, it is often very difficult to determine the Key Decision Maker (KDM) or Key Buying Influencer (KBI). While orders are often initiated by

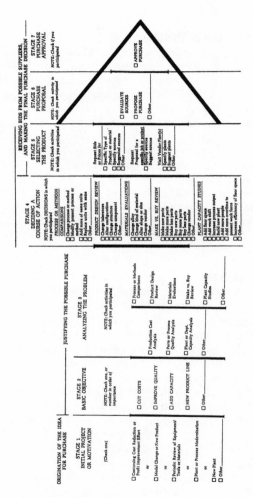

FIG. 9-1. *Stages in an industrial sale.*

Source: Richard M. Stanfield. *The Dartnell Advertising Managers' Handbook* (Chicago: The Dartnell Corporation), 1970, pp. 94–95.

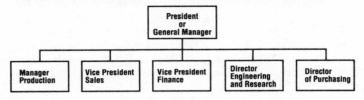

COMPANY ORGANIZATION WITH PURCHASING DEPARTMENT IN FIRST ECHELON

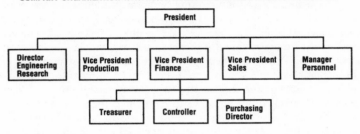

COMPANY ORGANIZATION WITH PURCHASING DEPARTMENT IN SECOND ECHELON

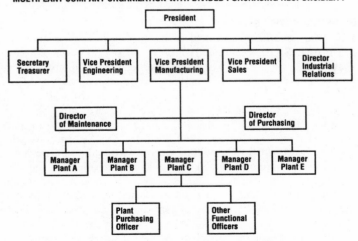

MULTIPLANT COMPANY ORGANIZATION WITH DIVIDED PURCHASING RESPONSIBILITY

FIG. 9-2. *Various industrial purchasing organizational structures.*

Source: Richard M. Hill, Ralph S. Alexander, and James S. Cross. *Industrial Marketing* (Homewood: Richard D. Irwin. Inc.), 1975, pp. 69–72.

top management, most of the purchases are actually carried out by middle management and even lower echelons. In other words, the purchaser does not actually initiate the order and start the buying process. Also, some company policies that indicate the desirability of soliciting three bids are not always followed. In many instances, only one or two suppliers are contacted, and in the final sale it may be only middle management who makes the purchasing decision in conjunction with the purchasing department.

Given this buying decision process, you can understand the importance of identifying the Key Buying Influencer. This can be accomplished by following some general guidelines. First, you should observe individuals in the purchasing department. Who has the most clout? Second, be careful not to make presentations too many times or spend unnecessary time with assistants and secretaries. Third, you need to respect the customer company's bureaucracy. Don't step on sensitive toes! Rarely does the purchasing department choose the supplier by itself. Fourth, you should do everything possible to determine the customer company's problems, buying procedures, politics, and attitudes. Finally, when you have identified the KBI, do not let anything deter you from making a presentation.

Industrial Advertising

Industrial advertising is a cost-effective way to support the selling effort. Since a sales call is very costly, any wasted time should be minimized as much as possible. The company's name, products, customers, record, and reputation, as well as any differential advantages of the company and its offering, should be communicated to customers and prospects through advertising in advance of a sales call. This will provide the necessary groundwork. Also, advertising can often reach the Key Decision Makers when they are either unknown or inaccessible to the salesperson.

Since the time required for making the sale may be one month to two years, it is often too costly to have a salesperson continually visit a potential customer. When this occurs, advertising can be used to keep the company name and product in front of prospects.

Institutional advertising that is not for direct sales purposes can lay the groundwork for a later sale by improving the company's image. *Institutional advertising* is advertising aimed at developing the company or brand image of a firm in certain segments of the market. Of course, image improvement alone cannot perform the entire selling function. Any institutional advertising should be evaluated with a before-and-after attitudinal survey of each segment of the market at which the advertising is directed—consumers, stockholders, financial institutions, employees, nonemployees, or residents of the area surrounding a plant. While the "before" survey should determine the level of company or brand image, the "after" survey should determine the degree to which the specified objectives were accomplished and the image increased.

Direct mail can be a particularly useful medium in industrial advertising. This method of approaching potential customers can develop and categorize sales leads in order of importance so that the salesperson can call on the most important leads first. It can also announce improved or new products to current customers, thus decreasing some of the time needed by the salesperson. Usually direct mail uses the company's own mailing lists, or else an appropriate list is purchased from one of the many list brokers.

One of the greatest problems in industrial advertising is the same problem that occurs in personal selling—identifying the Key Buying Influencer. Until the KBI has been identified for each Standard Industrial Classification (SIC) Code customer using the procedure previously discussed, the most effective copy cannot be developed, nor can the best media be selected.

Industrial Promotion

Most industrial companies do not differentiate between advertising and promotion, so that the same personnel administers both. Promotions such as catalogs, trade shows, dealer and distribution materials, directories, and specialty advertising such as calendars, pens, and note pads effectively support the salesperson. Of these, business publications, catalogs, and trade shows are the most frequently used sales promotional devices.

A catalog is a comprehensive printed compilation of information about a product or products and is designed for demonstration and referral. Buyers constantly refer to catalogs when purchasing in order to compare vendors' specifications and prices. If a manufacturer's catalog is not available in the purchasing department, the company may not get the sale.

The importance of trade shows in industrial sales cannot be overstated. These shows give salespeople an opportunity to talk to prospective as well as current customers at a very low cost per contact, especially in comparison with an industrial sales call. Many sales are actually made at the show. Trade shows also give the company good sales leads and provide an excellent opportunity to introduce new products and to show nonportable products.

Another important promotional device is dealer and distributor material, such as dealers' show kits, posters for dealer sales offices, price lists, and direct-mail material for dealer use. Publicity and public relations are used in industrial sales to obtain favorable publicity for products or for the company itself. While the company does not directly pay for this exposure, there may be indirect payment, perhaps in the form of entertainment expenses. While certain promotions such as catalogs and trade shows are a must for most industrial product manufacturers, tight control on the costs of these promotions, especially trade shows, is needed to avoid any excessive expenditures.

NONPROFIT MARKETING

Traditionally marketing has not been considered applicable to nonprofit situations, but this has reversed itself significantly in the past few years. The increased nonprofit marketing has focused on people, places, ideas, products, and services. Instead of focusing on products, nonprofit marketing tends to focus much more on ideas such as nonviolence, drugs, child safety, gun control, ecology, clean cities, not smoking, and energy conservation. This marketing, used to increase the acceptability of social ideas, is often called social marketing.

Objectives of Nonprofit Marketing

Why should a nonprofit organization be interested in marketing? There are basically two reasons. First, by using marketing, a nonprofit organization can better satisfy the wants and needs of its target market, thereby accomplishing its objectives. If an organization does not participate in marketing, its constituency is apt to be poorly served.

Second, nonprofit organizations need marketing in order to generate revenue. For example, the image of the organization is a significant factor in the results of any fund-raising effort. Through marketing, the primary constituencies of a nonprofit organization—clients and donors—can both be satisfied in an efficient, timely manner and the needed funds raised.

The lack of the profit motive and bottom-line responsibility makes goals, objectives, and controls sometimes very difficult to establish in a nonprofit organization. Since charitable organizations, hospitals, museums, welfare agencies, and universities have complex, interrelated reasons for existence, it is often more difficult to establish clear objectives to serve as the basis for developing the plan.

For example, until the entering college class in the Fall of 1997, colleges and universities went through a period when there were fewer children of college age and therefore faced a significant change from the prior years of rapid growth in enrollment. During this time when there were decreasing numbers of college students, only a few highly selective sought-after colleges experienced overall full enrollment or any growth. Some schools did experience some growth in selective areas such as law and business. These enrollment problems, which started to improve in the Fall of 1997, reflected the lower number of high school graduates in the decreasing population. During this period, in order to help offset this decline, many schools became actively involved in continuing adult education. Others offered courses and degrees in such disciplines as business at both the graduate and undergraduate levels. Still others effectively segmented their markets and marketed to the selected segments. These colleges successfully identified new market opportunities and created new products (such as adult course offerings) for these markets.

The Nonprofit Marketing Mix

Developing the marketing mix for a nonprofit organization is similar to developing one for a profit organization. In both cases the marketing mix must be designed to accomplish the objectives of the organization while satisfying the needs of its constituencies.

One of the biggest differences occurs in the product area. After all, the marketing of ideas and concepts is much more abstract than the marketing of more tangible products and services. This problem is made more difficult when the nonprofit organization provides a wide range of benefits. For example, imagine the difficulty in delineating for a potential volunteer the benefits of the Peace Corps, which has a broad range of services including nutritional assistance and training, construction, education and vocational training, health services, and community development.

Similarly, price is also a somewhat different element in the marketing mix of a nonprofit organization. Price for these organizations must be looked at in terms of its broadest economic definition—value or opportunity cost—the value forgone by choosing one alternative over another. Some nonprofit organizations must decide whether at least a token price should be charged for the services received. The amount to charge is a very difficult decision when you consider that price is an indication of quality and value. For example, churches have realized greater attendance at a concert when at least a token admission fee is charged than when the concert is free. The charging of a price sometimes is necessary to attract a target audience even when the objective is not to obtain revenue.

For other nonprofit organizations, the price, determined by a board or commission, is usually established to recover most of the costs of providing benefits. For example, the YMCA is chartered to provide educational and physical benefits to its constituency. The prices charged for program participation and membership do not cover all the operating costs in most YMCAs, requiring that yearly sustaining fund drives be undertaken to make up the deficit.

The other two components of the marketing mix—distribution and promotion—are not as unique, as decisions in these areas are similar to those made in the profit sector. A nonprofit organization needs to make sure that its clients and donors are aware of its existence and that its offerings are available through appropriate distribution.

SERVICE MARKETING
Service marketing is also a very important area of marketing. While services are just as real as physical products, the consumer cannot physically touch them in the purchasing process. Services such as hairstyling, legal assistance, hospital and medical care, dental work, dry cleaning, air travel, professional sports, and consulting have the largest amount of marketing expenditures.

Characteristics and Scope
The types of services available cover a wide range, from the performed services of a professional football team to those of a real estate rental agency. Two main characteristics distinguish services from products: intangibility and variability.

Services are usually intangible, not able to be physically touched during the purchasing process. One exception to this is of course the large rental goods service market. This characteristic makes it difficult for service marketing to make sure the potential customer clearly understands the benefits of the service, as these benefits can only be described. In addition to making sure that the benefits derived from the service are as explicit and understandable as possible, service marketing must try to make sure demand is smooth and is not concentrated in a short time period. For example, a beauty salon needs to attempt to get customers on Tuesday and Wednesday as well as the usually busy Thursday, Friday, and Saturday.

The second characteristic, variability, must also be taken into account in developing the marketing mix for services. Variability occurs not only from one service provider to another but over time from a single service provider. Standardizing a service is difficult because of its labor intensity. This is particularly the case for personal services such as beauty care, hospital care, or consulting, where the service received is directly related to the skill of the individual.

Extent of Service

There is a wide variety of services available, particularly in the United States, which is the leading service economy in the world. Today, the largest percent of the labor force in private enterprise is employed in the service sector, and the largest percentage of the typical family's budget is spent on services. Increasing expenditure patterns on services is equally prevalent in the industrial and government markets.

More and more firms are planning their future growth in terms of increased sales of present or new services. Sears, for example, already operating one of the largest retail chains, also has Allstate Insurance, a car rental company, an income tax preparation firm, car repair services, home improvement centers, and a financial services operation that is competing in an area traditionally dominated by banks.

Service Marketing Mix

The use of marketing in service firms has lagged compared to its use in companies manufacturing products, particularly those in the consumer nondurable goods area. Many service firms are so small that marketing personnel are not even a part of their operations. Some service organizations were at one time prohibited from doing marketing by their association or peer pressure. This was the case in the medical and legal professions until 1978 when the Supreme Court ruling permitted advertising by professionals.

Of course, effective promotion has been and continues to be an important part of the service marketing mix. Three effective ways to promote a service are indicated in Table 9-1 (see page 144). Different methods are more (or less) effective in different areas of the service business. In virtually all cases, the promotion needs to stress both tangible and performance attributes, as exemplified in the good service promotion indicated in Figure 9-3 (see page 145).

TABLE 9-1
Methods for Promoting a Service

1. Develop as tangible a representation of the service as possible. For example, a credit card, although not a financial service itself, still serves as a physical product with its own image and benefits.

2. Associate the intangible service with a tangible object that is more easily perceived by the customer. The insurance industry has done this very successfully as demonstrated in the following examples:

   "You're in good *hands* with Allstate."
   "I've got a piece of the *rock*."

3. Focus on the relationship between the seller of the service and the user of the service and avoid the intangible aspects of the service itself. Promote the competence, skill, and concern of the tangible agent or service employee to facilitate the sale and to start developing a client relationship.

In developing the marketing mix for a service, three areas need concentration: eliminating wide fluctuations in demand, ensuring quality with minimal variation, and developing a unique pricing and promotional strategy. One of the most important objectives in service marketing is eliminating the wide variations in demand by either altering the nature and timing of demand or controlling supply. For example, a movie theater needs to increase attendance at its weekday matinee shows while it is filled to capacity on Friday or Saturday evenings.

Another objective is to decrease variability in the quality of service. One carpet cleaning service had to adjust its operation because the quality of the service significantly decreased when the owner of the business was not on location performing at least some of the cleaning. The quality of the car repair service received can vary greatly in the same service station or car dealership, depending on the day and the nature of the problem.

A unique pricing and promotional strategy needs to be developed to help solve these problems. The price can be used to affect demand and even to indicate a differentiation in quality. For example, a service station can charge different prices for services performed, depending on the day or the mechanic. Movie theaters can have different price structure during matinees versus weekend performances.

FIG. 9-3. *Service advertisement.*

Source: *U.S. News and World Report,* October 11, 1999, p. 46a.

CHAPTER PERSPECTIVE
In this chapter we have covered the special applications of marketing to government, industrial, service, and nonprofit sales. You have learned about the procedures involved in submitting bids or negotiating to secure a government order. Industrial marketing involves a specialized salesperson and identification of the

Key Decision Maker (KDM) or Key Buying Influencer (KBI). In addition to personal selling, good advertising and promotion are also important. If you are developing a marketing plan for a nonprofit organization, you need to take special care with the unique problems of product and pricing in the marketing mix. Finally, in services, you should focus on dealing with variability in demand and the quality of service being offered as well as effective promotion. In these special cases you will be adapting the fundamentals of the marketing mix to create a successful marketing plan and selling effort.

International Marketing

INTRODUCTION AND MAIN POINTS

In this chapter we will introduce you to the important aspects of international marketing. We will look at the economic, political, legal, and cultural characteristics of a foreign market that need to be evaluated in determining whether to do business in that country. Then we will discuss how to assess which target markets are viable and the risks and returns involved. We will then introduce the various organizational structures appropriate for entering selected markets. Finally, we will discuss how to decide on the appropriate marketing mix—product, price, distribution, and promotion—for foreign entrance.

After studying the material in this chapter:

■ You will understand and be able to employ the alternative methods of engaging in international marketing.

■ You will know the characteristics of multinational companies.

■ You will know the aspects of an international marketing program.

NATURE AND SCOPE

International business and marketing is taking on an ever-increasing role in the global economic context. Firms from most developed countries effectively sell their products in a variety of market areas. From Rome to St. Petersburg to Rio de Janeiro, the familiar sign of Coca-Cola can be found. L'Oreal has a significant share of the world's cosmetics market. And, the U.S. markets have been successfully penetrated by international firms, particularly those from Japan. For example, it is obvious to anyone who drives that Toyota, Nissan, and Honda have captured a significant share of the United States automobile market.

Indeed, as formerly agricultural countries become more and more developed industrially, the distinction between foreign and domestic goods becomes somewhat blurred. What was once only produced domestically is now produced internationally. Yamaha pianos are now produced in the United States. Digital Equipment Company has plants in Puerto Rico. Many U.S. companies have domestic and foreign joint ventures, some of which are in such state-controlled economies as the People's Republic of China. This blurring of national identities is likely to continue as more and more products are introduced outside domestic boundaries through successful international marketing.

What is international marketing? Simply put, it is conducting marketing activities (product, price, distribution, and promotion) outside the home country of a company. It can be as simple as a British firm placing a help-wanted advertisement in a Rome newspaper or as complex as a South Korean contractor building a factory in Brazil.

There is always a certain degree of apprehension about expanding abroad. Until recently, most American companies preferred domestic to international marketing since domestic marketing is easier to understand and involves less risk. When international marketing takes place, if often means that managers must learn another language, a different currency, and the culture and customs of another country. The problem is further compounded by political and legal uncertainties. As a general observation, companies are usually drawn into international marketing by either a weakening of their domestic economy or market conditions, or by growing market opportunities for their product in foreign countries, or both.

INTERNATIONAL MARKETING TERMINOLOGY

In order to understand the nature and scope of international marketing, it is important to understand some of the key terms and concepts.

An *export market* is any country or alliance of countries in which a foreign company agrees to sell its products that are manufactured outside the borders of the countries in which the products are being sold.

While there are many different definitions of a *multinational firm,* in general, such a firm is one that engages in business in many countries. The term is also used to indicate a company with physical facilities in different countries.

Host countries are countries within which a multinational company operates, excluding the country of origin of the multinational.

Tariffs are a schedule of duties (defined in terms of the country's currency) levied by a government on either imports or exports. Tariffs may be computed on a dollar basis in terms of the value of the shipment or on a physical basis such as tons or cubic feet.

An *embargo* on certain goods exists when a nation prohibits the import or export of these goods. For example, the U.S. government, in the interest of national defense, has an embargo on the sale of certain computers to some countries.

A *quota* is often set on foreign commodities, meaning that only a stipulated quantity of these commodities may enter the country each year. As an example, the United States has a quota on sugar imports to protect the growers of sugarcane and beet sugar that results in the price of U.S. sugar being about two or three times higher than the price of sugar on the world market.

Licenses in international business are of two types: (1) a permit by the government of a country that allows a company to transact business there, or (2) the granting of permission by a company to another company in a different country to use its technology or name in conducting business in that country. Technology is often licensed to a company in a less-developed country. Also, an exporter should help the agent or buyer secure the needed licenses. Finally, licenses or franchises are often the preferred method of doing business in a country that has significant political risk.

A *turnkey project* is often used in external marketing instead of a license in an underdeveloped or less-developed country. In a turnkey project, a company builds a factory or other facility, trains the workers and management to run the operation, and then turns the operation over to local owners. This allows the foreign company to become involved with trade in a country where it could not have been involved via another mechanism. This is essentially the arrangement Union Carbide had for its plant in Bhopal, India, where an industrial accident cost thousands of lives and threw the parent company into protracted turmoil.

A *management contract* is another way for a company to become involved in international marketing. In this case a company contracts its personnel to run non-company-owned facilities in foreign countries. This has been done by American oil and construction companies in the Middle East.

A *value-added tax* occasionally occurs when raw materials from one country are sent to another country to be processed or semiprocessed and then exported back to the raw-material exporting country when processing is complete. In a value-added tax, only the materials and labor supplied by the processing country are taxed on export. Occasionally, this tax is levied on imports and rebated on exports. When this occurs, the tax is a *border tax adjustment.* (This is not to be confused with the value-added tax, or VAT, added to domestic purchases in what is essentially a broad-based tax on consumption.)

There are several *alliances* in the world today. The European Union (EU) (formerly known as the European Community and European Economic Community) is the best known. In the EU, tariffs between member countries have been eliminated and a single market has formed for goods and services. Goods move easily across borders of countries in the alliance because of the lowering of the tariffs between member countries. Present members of the European Union include: Belgium, Denmark, France, United Kingdom, Ireland, Italy, Luxembourg, the Netherlands, Germany, Spain, Portugal, Greece, Austria, Finland, and Sweden. In the coming years, new countries will be added.

There are several other alliances or common markets. The Latin American Free Trade Association (LAFTA) is composed of Mexico, Colombia, Venezuela, Ecuador, Peru, Bolivia, Chile, Brazil, Paraguay, Uruguay, and Argentina. The Central American Common Market (CACM), composed of Costa Rica, Guatemala, Nicaragua, Honduras, and El Salvador is another. A third is the European Free Trade Association (EFTA), composed of Austria, Iceland, Finland, Norway, Switzerland, Liechtenstein and Sweden.

These trade communities operate similarly, though they are not as far along the road to economic unity as the European Union. Tariffs have been lowered between countries in the communities, and usually a significant part of each country's international trade is with other countries in the alliance. This can be as much as 50 to 60 percent of the total trade of the country. Most of these trading communities also encourage the movement of both capital and labor between member countries.

A *foreign purchaser in a local market* is a foreign buyer who is located in a country for the purpose of actively purchasing various domestic products for export. This is perhaps the easiest way a domestic company can export products since the sale is just like a domestic sale. The only difference is that the product is then shipped out of the country by the foreign buyer.

An *export management firm or trading company* is a firm representing many companies in a foreign market for a fee. Located in the same country as the manufacturing company, this firm handles all the activities involved in the export process.

A *joint venture* is a method by which companies from different countries become involved in international marketing by forming either a local distribution or manufacturing facility. The more traditional form of a joint venture is when two firms (such as a Canadian and a Japanese firm) form a third company in which they share the equity. Another joint venture arrangement is when a firm purchases 50 percent of the equity of a foreign firm.

THE IMPORT-EXPORT ARENA

There has been significant growth in both imports and exports as a percentage of the overall U.S. business activity (see Table10-1). The difference between a nation's imports and exports is called its balance of payments. The balance may be either positive or negative, depending on the extent of exports versus imports. The United States has been in an increasingly negative trade position since 1980. U.S. exports and imports represent a wide variety of goods, with the largest export item being capital goods. Industrial supplies and materials, and food products follow in size. Leading

Table 10-1

Exports and Imports of Goods and Services ($billions)

Year	Exports	Imports
1980	271.8	291.2
1981	294.4	310.6
1982	275.2	299.4
1983	266.1	323.9
1984	291.1	400.2
1985	289.1	410.9
1986	308.8	448.6
1987	347.8	500.6
1988	430.3	545.7
1989	488.3	579.8
1990	536.1	616.0
1991	580.0	609.4
1992	615.9	652.9
1993	641.8	711.7
1994	702.1	800.5
1995	793.5	891.0
1996	849.8	954.1
1997	938.5	1,043.3
1998	933.9	1,098.2

Source: *Survey of Current Business* (July 1999).

import categories include industrial supplies and materials, capital goods, and automotive vehicles and parts.

MULTINATIONAL COMPANIES

Direct investment by a parent company in a host country is frequently used in international marketing. The parent company makes the investment and has a certain amount of control over the operations of its subsidiaries. Sometimes the investment is in the form of majority ownership belonging to the parent company. Usually a business in the host country shares in the investment and has at least a minority position in the new enterprise. Some countries have established laws requiring that a certain percentage (sometimes more than 50 percent) be owned in the host country.

A foreign subsidiary in which the parent company owns a minority of the stock is another form of ownership. Usually the parent company furnishes the technology for production and marketing in this situation regardless of the ownership situation.

As the domestic market has become increasingly competitive, franchisers have expanded into international markets. For instance, fast-food companies such as Kentucky Fried Chicken and McDonald's have outlets in Japan, England, Germany, and other countries. A McDonald's in Budapest, Hungary, is one of the company's busiest outlets in the world. The number of countries and franchisers is continually increasing. Another form of international business activity is licensing, through which a firm grants a foreign company the use of a trademark or patent.

Occasionally a company will contract with a foreign firm to market or manufacture its product. For example, the Uncle Ben's Rice patent was first developed and owned by a German scientist named Huzenlaub, who licensed the use of his patent to firms in each of five countries around the world.

Economic integration requires the establishment of transnational rules on economic activity and exchange. A group of countries can establish (usually with great effort) a set of rules on trade and other economic relations among members that can result in increased commercial activity across borders. Generally these efforts involve smaller groups of countries (five to ten) in close proximity to one another. One notable exception was the General Agreement on Tariffs and Trade (GATT), which involved 90 nations throughout the world. GATT, an institutional structure established by industrialized countries after World War II, maintained a permanent staff of about 300 people in Geneva, Switzerland. The main function of the staff was to collect information and carry out studies on trade issues relevant to the governmental negotiations that occur under GATT auspices. One fundamental concept in these negotiations was the most favored nation (MFN) principle, which requires that any tariff reduction negotiated between any two members be extended to all members of GATT.

In 1995, the World Trade Organization (WTO) formed as the successor to GATT. The WTO, with more than 100 members, is now the main body overseeing international trade. It resolves trade disputes between its member countries, administers treaties and trade agreements, and maintains statistics.

In addition to the WTO, world trade conferences are held to correct any maladjustments or problems. Also, debates over inequalities in international trade often occur in the United States.

U.S. Tax Advantage for Multinationals

U.S. multinationals have two tax advantages. First is the deferral principle, whereby the multinational does not have to pay taxes on the income made from a foreign subsidiary until the profit actually enters the United States. Therefore, a profit made at a given time can be used for working capital for months or years before being brought into the United States and, thus, subject to taxes. Of course, the multinational can save on overall taxes by bringing in the income in a year of low domestic income, perhaps even a loss. Second, the U.S. multinational may deduct taxes paid abroad from its U.S. tax under the foreign tax credit.

Companies and Foreign Investment

Advanced technological development of products is not to be confused with technological development of processes for efficient manufacturing. A successful consumer product company should know how to manage and maximize its innovative products. Some products require brand-name packaging and advertising skills. Other industrial products require protective patents or hard-to-copy "know-how" in addition to continuous innovation in the products themselves.

In order for good innovative consumer products to maintain their advantage in the international market, they should be given an individualized brand name and promoted with a unique selling proposition (USP). The level of advertising and promotion should be large enough to make consumers in the country aware of the unique advantages of the product. A dominant position in a foreign market can be obtained by the brand name, making it difficult for other competing products to enter the market successfully.

PLANNING AND IMPLEMENTING AN INTERNATIONAL MARKETING PROGRAM

The key to successfully implementing an international marketing program is to understand the unique characteristics of each market as well as their commonalities. In this planning process, it is often helpful to focus on the following areas in order to analyze data on each country and determine areas of similarity:

Market Characteristics
    a. Size of market, rate of growth
    b. Stage of development
    c. Stage of product life cycle, saturation levels
    d. Buyer behavior characteristics
    e. Social/cultural factors
    f. Physical environment

Marketing Institutions
    a. Distribution systems
    b. Communication media
    c. Marketing services (advertising, research, etc.)

Industry Conditions
    a. Competitive size and practices
    b. Technical development

Legal Environment
    a. Laws
    b. Regulations
    c. Codes
    d. Tariffs
    e. Taxes

Resources
    a. Manpower (availability, skill, potential, cost)
    b. Money (availability, cost)

Financial Environment
    a. Balance of payments
    b. Foreign exchange rate
    c. Regulations

Political Environment
    a. Current government policies and attitudes
    b. Long-range political environment

These aspects of the planning process indicate product strategy for the company. The product planning previously discussed is equally applicable to multinational companies entering international markets. The same steps that a company can use in innovating products in a domestic market can be applied to an international environment as well.

First, the company should study successful products in the United States and in countries with similar cultural characteristics through the use of Nielsen Store Audits, MRCA, and S.A.M.I. It is revealing to identify leading products in the United States and in other countries that have not been produced substantially in the host country. These product ideas can then be adapted to the tastes, customs, and preferences of the target country.

Second, a company should develop a new organization to sell any high-volume ingredient products identified. Ingredient products are those appearing in substantial quantities in other products sold in the country.

Third, a company should analyze all commodity products produced and sold in the country. Any commodity product selling well should be evaluated to determine if a specialty product can be created in this commodity product category.

Many multinationals have used one of these three approaches in their product planning process. The first is the extension philosophy. Based on the assumption that American techniques can work as well and in the same way in the foreign markets as in domestic markets, many companies have extended their marketing programs overseas. In these areas marketing is centralized.

In the delegation or decentralized philosophy, the second philosophy, some foreign markets are viewed as totally different and the responsibility for developing new, or adapting successful, marketing approaches is turned over to foreign subsidiaries.

The third approach, the "interactive" approach, combines the best features of decentralization and centralization. The interactive approach gives the responsibility for adaptation to local conditions to subsidiaries, keeping the strategic planning in centralized headquarters.

Marketing Strategy for Transferring Products

In transferring a product from one country to another, one of the most difficult areas is cross-national advertising. Some companies handle all issues of international advertising at corporate headquarters. For example, a company advertising in Switzerland obtains some advertising coverage in Italy, France, and Germany. In most border areas, consumers understand the neighboring country's language because distances are short and continual interaction occurs between citizens. If this is not understood, waste in advertising and promotion can occur.

You should keep in mind that subsidiaries in various countries usually do not have a worldwide vision. They are not concerned about the advantages of advertising overlap and therefore are not concerned about making their advertising available to affiliated companies in contingent countries. Since it is very difficult to obtain a 100 percent legally safe trade name that is meaningful in many different languages, you should not put forth excessive effort in this area. Instead, you should attempt to develop a nonmeaningful trade name—a new word, really—as Kodak, Zerex, Exxon, and so many others have done. The value in this type of trade name occurs when subsidiaries use it on brands being sold.

Once a name is in use anywhere in the world, it should not be used as a different blanket, category, or product name in another country. If a subsidiary wants to duplicate a product in another country, then the subsidiary should be required not only to use a brand name identical to that used for the product by the originating company, but also to implement an advertising story that is the same as that used by the originating company by having the identical unique selling proposition adapted for each country.

Of course, the copy on the package and the advertising matter (with the exception of the brand name) would be in the language and style of the particular country.

Selecting the Advertising Agency

Just as the basic idea of products can be transferred from one country to another—provided that the product is adjusted to the tastes, lifestyle, and culture of the other country—so can the unique selling proposition and its advertising stories. This transfer of course means that these are adapted to a host country's needs and requirements.

An agency that understands and subscribes to this philosophy should be the one selected. Often agencies want to display their own particular creative and innovative talent in writing copy and do not comprehend the importance of the parent company's copy philosophy. It is better to choose an agency that supports and can adapt the established advertising plan to the culture of the targeted country.

Consumer Research in Underdeveloped Countries

In underdeveloped countries many obstacles are encountered in carrying out product and advertising tests as well as in undertaking other types of marketing research. First, the percentage of the population that have telephones is lower. Second, cultures and lifestyles in some countries cause respondents to be reluctant to respond to surveys. Many times, especially in lower income groups, people are suspicious and afraid that the interviewer is going to report them to government officials. Third, the means of transportation may be very crude or even impossible in some areas. This situation makes proper research difficult or even impossible. Fourth, in some cultures a woman should be accompanied by another woman in doing the work of an interviewer. Fifth, many of the services, such as Nielsen Store Audits, Television Index, or Radio Pulse, do not exist in some countries. Sixth, if a company seeks help from host country research consultants, they may not be acquainted with U.S. research techniques. Finally, data that are readily available in the United States are difficult to obtain or nonexistent in other countries. For example, data similar to U.S. Census data are rarely available.

Given these problems, in order to facilitate the establishment of a strategic marketing plan, it is usually helpful to use all the information available on foreign trade. There are several good sources of information, including the Bureau of the Census, U.S. Bureau of Economic Analysis, Survey of Current Business, and the U.S. Department of Commerce's Overseas Business Reports. Other groups that can also provide good data include state commerce departments and industrial development and international divisions of large banks. The *Statistical Abstract of the United States,* updated annually, is an invaluable source of economic and demographic data. By carefully evaluating all the published information, you can more easily decide which target market and marketing plan are best suited for the particular international market.

CHAPTER PERSPECTIVE

In this chapter we have explained the basics of international marketing. As a domestic market becomes increasingly competitive, many firms look to expand their operations in the international arena. This can be done through exporting a product or service, by direct investment in a foreign country through joint ventures, by establishing foreign subsidiaries, or by granting foreign franchises or licenses. The domestic marketing strategies discussed in this book can also be applied, with adaptations, to international marketing. Understanding the unique characteristics of the culture of the foreign market is essential to achieving successful product sales.

Innovation and Management of Products

INTRODUCTION AND MAIN POINTS

Because new products are being developed that have ever-shortening life spans, organizations need to recognize the importance of good new product review. Although significant rewards can be reaped through innovation, most attempts at the development of new products lead to costly failures. The key to successful innovation begins with better organizational arrangements for screening new product ideas as well as better management of the new development process, which consists of five basic stages: idea, concept, product development, test market, and commercialization. Management must decide at each successive stage whether an idea should be developed further or dropped. Sources of product ideas can come from outside or inside the firm: customer opinion, competitive response, federal regulation, distribution channel needs, research and development, and/or employee suggestions. A firm seeks decision criteria to evaluate these ideas throughout the product life cycle stages to minimize the chances of poor ideas being developed.

After studying the material in this chapter:
━ You will understand and be able to use the product planning and development process for creating successful new products.
━ You will know various sources of new product ideas and how to access these to obtain the best ideas possible.
━ You will understand the adoption process and product life cycle and be able to use them to manage company growth successfully.

The concept of product varies from one manufacturer to another as well as from one consumer to another. In order to innovate and manage products successfully, you must define what is an acceptable product. Is a hospital selling an operation or an entire health care procedure? Is a lawyer selling the writing of a will or the surety that the instrument will do what the person desires after he or she is no longer around to ensure that will happen? Is an automobile manufacturer selling a certain number of nuts and bolts, an engine, and wheels, or a safe, dependable, efficient means of transportation? The answers to these questions provide some insight into the nature of the product—the total offering of the firm that satisfies the needs of the consumer. This concept of product is broad and focuses on the most important aspect, the need to satisfy a customer need. This satisfaction can be derived from such things as the benefits of product use, pride of ownership, or dependable, reliable performance. As the term *product* is defined here, it can mean a physical product or a service. In addition, the product encompasses all those ancillary items that make it what it is, such as the package, the brand, the service, the quality, the options, the breadth and depth of the line, the guarantee, and the warranty.

PRODUCT PLANNING AND THE DEVELOPMENT PROCESS

One of the most useful tools for growing a business is the product planning and development process (see Figure 11-1). Although the actual process and the time and sales involved in each step vary greatly, not only from industry to industry but within a given industry, the overall process still provides a framework for evalu-

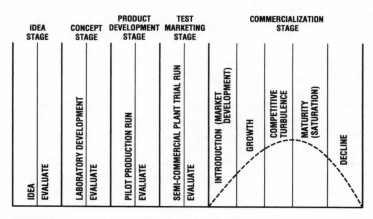

FIG. 11-1. *The product planning and development process.*

Source: Robert D. Hisrich and Michael P. Peters, *Marketing a New Product: Its Planning, Development, and Control.* Menlo Park, CA: The Benjamin/Cummings Co., Inc., 1978.

ating and developing new products as well as formulating basic marketing strategies. In order to implement the product planning and development process, it is essential that an effective method for obtaining new product ideas be established.

Sources of New Ideas

Ideas for new products can emerge from a wide variety of sources—customers, competition, distribution channels, federal government, research and development, and company employees. Many firms ask their customers to submit ideas either informally or through an established process. (These ideas can even be in the form of complaints.) New ideas often emerge from the company's attempt at solving the problem. For example, General Foods developed a new cereal package after determining from customer complaints that their cereal box was too tall for the standard shelf and could tip over.

The competition should also be continuosly monitored by the sales force so that any new developments can be immediately identified. Similarly, members of the channels of distribution close to the market and familiar with market needs are excellent sources for new products or modifications of old ones. For example, Hallmark introduced candles, paper goods, books, and costume jewelry to its product line to take advantage of its existing channel outlets.

The federal government affects new product development in three major ways. First, it provides funds for research and development of new products particularly in high-technology areas of interest such as energy, defense, and the environment. Second, the federal government provides information on patents available for license or purchase. Finally, the government provides opportunities for new products through the passage of legislative acts. All legislation can require new products or services for compliance. For example, many new companies have entered the environment control field, helping corporations comply with the environmental standards set by government. For instance, R & H Safety Sales was formed in order to provide firms with first aid kits in weatherproof containers so that these firms could comply with the Occupational Safety and Health Act (OSHA).

The majority of new product ideas are generated internally. Research can be one of three types: pure research, which is done solely for the sake of knowledge; applied research, which interprets the fundamental research for practical use; and developmental research, which generates new ideas and studies new markets and applications for existing products. Company employees, besides those assigned to research duties, often provide new product or market ideas. Your firm should establish a formal employee suggestion procedure with incentives such as cash awards, bonuses, and contests to encourage participation. Since the sales force is closest to the consumer, they are an especially good source of ideas and feedback on consumer needs and complaints.

Idea Stage

Once a new product idea has evolved, it is very important for the idea to receive a very careful and thorough evaluation. You should screen out as many new product ideas as possible in the early stages, allowing more time and money to be spent on products with a greater probability for market success. For example, if a firm starts with 58 new product ideas, about 80 percent should be eliminated at the end of the idea stage, 40 percent of the remainder eliminated at the end of the concept stage, and 75 percent of the remaining ideas eliminated after the product development stage. How many does that leave for test marketing? About five.

Concept Stage

The new product ideas that successfully make it to the concept stage should be further evaluated, analyzed, and, where appropriate, refined for market success. This often takes the form of determining consumer acceptance by presenting drawings or explanations of the new product to various consumers and members of the distribution channel. Even when there is no actual product prototype, this procedure will obtain valuable information from consumers. The concept test evaluates specific factors in each area of marketing strategy: product (quality, dependability, reliability, warranty, package, and service); price (cost and terms of sale); distribution (channels and physical distribution); and promotion (advertising and sales promotion). This could involve evaluating whether one retail store would do a better job of carrying the product than another or whether one package is preferred over an alternative.

Product Development Stage

Once the new product concept has received a positive evaluation, it is necessary to transform the concept into a physical product or prototype. Whenever possible prior to mass production, the technical and product feasibility of the item should be determined through the development of a prototype that has customer appeal. This stage is very crucial and should involve both marketing and technical research.

Test Marketing Stage

Test marketing is not used for all products prior to commercialization. It is a costly and time-consuming process that gives the competition time to react to your initiatives. It is frequently used for industrial products, regional products, and specialty goods where the information gained is worth the cost of the test. In some highly technical, capital-intensive industrial products, a test market is not even physically possible.

Test marketing has a very broad scope and encompasses many interacting factors. In effect, it is a laboratory where you can evaluate alternative elements of the final national marketing plan. It can provide answers to such questions as: Should Package A or Package B be used? Should the product have a price of 89 cents or 97 cents? Does advertisement A or B have the most impact? In addition to providing answers to these and other questions, the sales achieved in the test market can be used as the base for forecasting national sales. This is particularly important in the case of consumer goods where out-of-stock condition or large inventory buildup should be avoided.

The cost of the test market reflects the size of the region (usually 40 stores within two cities), the number of variables being tested (usually two, such as price and package), the length of the test (usually six to eight weeks), and the repurchase cycle of the product (usually two to four weeks). The length of the test should be weighed against the value of the additional information obtained.

Commercialization

Only a few new products actually reach the market. The capital expenditures for launching the product into the market are extensive and should only take place for those new products that have a high probability of success. In addition to the costs of new equipment and facilities for production, the company has the marketing expenses of training salespeople, extensive introductory advertising, and sales promotion in the trade. These expenses and the best marketing mix can be optimized if the marketing manager understands the diffusion and adoption of new products and the product life cycle.

THE DIFFUSION PROCESS

The process by which an innovation spreads from its conception to its user is called *diffusion*. The diffusion process causes the adoption process, which is the mental process a consumer undergoes upon first hearing about the product until it is used on a regular basis. There are four basic elements in the diffusion process: innovation, communication, social system, and time. The *innovation* is the new product idea as perceived by the firm, the buyer, and the channels of distribution. The newness has two dimensions: technological newness and market newness. Each of these dimensions has various degrees of newness (see Figure 11-2). The greatest problem occurs at the bottom right of the table, where the new product has both technological and market newness. Newness from the consumers' viewpoint should be viewed in terms of the degree of disruption the new product would have on a person's present lifestyle if the product was purchased. Within this framework there are three general types of new products: continuous innovation, dynamically continuous innovation, and discontinuous innovation. You should remember that the more disruption the new product has on a person's lifestyle, the

INCREASING TECHNOLOGICAL NEWNESS

Product Objectives	No Technological Change	Improved Technology	New Technology
No market change		*Reformulation* Change in formula or physical product to optimize costs and quality.	*Replacement* Replace existing product with new one based on improved technology.
Strengthened market	*Remerchandising* Increase sales to existing customers.	*Improved product* Improve product's utility to customers.	*Product life extension* Add new similar products to line; serve more customers based on new technology.
New market	*New use* Add new segments that can use present products.	*Market extension* Add new segments modifying present products.	*Diversification* Add new markets with new products developed from new technology.

FIG. 11-2. *Classifying new products based on product objectives.*

harder it will be for the product to be accepted and the longer time it will take for the product to diffuse. People do not like to radically change their lifestyles.

The second element of the diffusion process—the *communication* of the innovation—is necessary in order for diffusion to occur. Without communication, potential consumers could not learn about the new product and consider its purchase. The more communication in the form of advertising, sales promotion, and publicity, the faster the diffusion process will occur.

The third element in the diffusion process—the *social system*—is all the individuals or firms in a defined area which can use the new product. When all the units (individuals or firms) in a given area have adopted the product, the diffusion process is complete. The social system influences an individual in terms of adopting or not adopting a particular product. The new product must fit within the established norms and values of the individual's society.

The final element—*time*—is the all-encompassing aspect of the diffusion process. Time refers to how long after introduction an individual or firm adopts a new product. The more discontinuous the innovation and the less the communication, the longer time it will take the new product to diffuse.

ADOPTION PROCESS

The adoption process—the mental process an individual undergoes upon first hearing about a product until it is finally adopted—varies greatly by individual, product, and the effectiveness of the diffusion process. Adoption for some products may be in terms of a single purchase whereas for others may be a series of purchases. The underlying feature of what constitutes adoption is commitment. For a larger item such as a refrigerator, adoption is the initial purchase, as an individual is committed to this refrigerator for a period of years. However, for a new brand of coffee, the single purchase of one pound does not represent significant commitment, as the individual can switch brands the next time coffee is purchased.

The adoption process itself is composed of five sequential stages—awareness, interest, evaluation, trial, and adoption. In the awareness stage the consumer is exposed to the new product idea but is not interested enough to seek more information about it. This information seeking occurs in the interest stage. The new product has received an overall favorable response at this point but not specific utility in terms of a usage situation. The individual in the next stage—the evaluation stage—mentally assesses the information about the new product in deciding whether or not to try it. In the trial stage the individual uses or tries the new product on a small scale to determine its suitability. Then the individual decides to continue the use of the new product in the adoption stage.

Since individuals go through this adoption process at different times, there are various categories of adopters over time as indicated in Figure 11-3. The categories range from the individuals who first pass through the stages of the adoption process—the innovators—to those who are the last ones going through this process—the laggards. It is important for you to develop a marketing mix that would be most appealing to those individuals in the innovator and early adopter category, as these would be more likely to adopt the new product in its initial introduction.

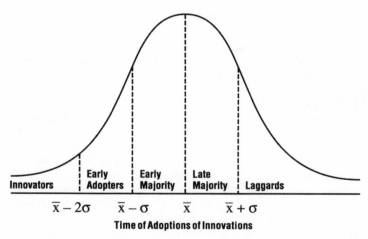

FIG. 11-3. *Categories of adopters over time.*

THE PRODUCT LIFE CYCLE

There is probably no marketing concept more widely known and used than the product life cycle. This is the process a product begins upon commercialization or introduction into the market. The life cycle has five stages. Each stage—introductory (or market development) stage, growth stage, competitive turbulence stage, maturity (or saturation) stage, and decline stage—requires a specific marketing strategy so that sales and profits can be maximized. Some of the key strategies in each stage are indicated in Figure 11-4. You should plan the marketing strategy that will be implemented for the product in each stage before the product is ever introduced. Most new products need some significant recycling after a 1½ to 3 year period if market leadership is to be maintained. Additional flavors, added packs of items, new packaging, new features, and new advertising have all been used to positively affect this needed recycling.

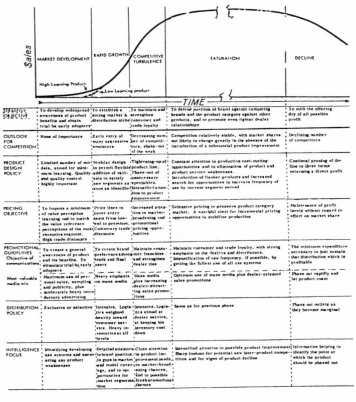

	MARKET DEVELOPMENT	RAPID GROWTH	COMPETITIVE TURBULENCE	SATURATION	DECLINE
STRATEGY OBJECTIVE	To develop widespread awareness of product benefits and obtain trial be early adopters	To establish a strong market & strengthen distribution niche	To maintain and strengthen consumer and trade loyalty	To defend position of brand against competing brands and the product category against other products, and to promote even tighter dealer relationships	To milk the offering dry of all possible profit
OUTLOOK FOR COMPETITION	None of importance	Early entry of many aggressive emulators	Decreasing number of competitors, shake-out of the weak	Competition relatively stable, with market shares not likely to change greatly in the absence of the introduction of a substantial product improvement	Declining number of competitors
PRODUCT DESIGN POLICY	Limited number of models, aimed for minimum learning. Quality and quality control highly important	Modular design to permit flexible addition of variants to satisfy new segments as soon as identified	Tightening-up of product line. Phase-out of unnecessary specialties. Intensification of product improvement	Constant attention to production cost-cutting opportunities and to elimination of product and product service weaknesses. Introduction of flanker products and increased search for opportunities to increase frequency of use by current segment served	Continual pruning of the line to those items returning a direct profit
PRICING OBJECTIVE	To impose a minimum of value perception learning and to match the value reference perceptions of the most receptive segment. High trade discounts	Price lines to cover every taste from low-end to premium. Customary trade discounts	Increased attention to market-broadening and pricing opportunities	Defensive pricing to preserve product category market. A watchful alert for incremental pricing opportunities to stabilize production	Maintenance of profit levels without regard to effect on market share
PROMOTIONAL GUIDELINES Objective of communications	To create a general awareness of product and its benefits. To stimulate trial by early adopters	To create brand preference among trade and final users	Maintain consumer franchise and strengthen dealer ties	Maintain consumer and trade loyalty, with strong emphasis on the dealers and distributors. Intensification of use frequency, if possible, by getting the fullest use of all use systems	The minimum expenditure necessary to just sustain that distribution which is profitable
Most valuable media mix	Maximum use of personal sales, sampling and publicity, plus moderately heavy introductory advertising	Heavy emphasis on mass media	Mass media plus increasing dealer-distracting sales promotions	Optimum use of mass media plus dealer-oriented sales promotions	Phase out rapidly and let product coast
DISTRIBUTION POLICY	Exclusive or selective	Intensive. Logistics weighted heavily toward customer service. Heavy inventories at all levels	Intensive. Logistics aimed at keeping his inventory cost down	Same as for previous phase	Phase out outlets as they become marginal
INTELLIGENCE FOCUS	Identifying developing use systems and uncovering any product weaknesses	Detailed attention to brand position, to gaps in market coverage, and model coverage, and to opportunities for market segmentation	Close attention to product improvement needs, to market-broadening and to possible fresh promotional themes	Intensified attention to possible product improvement. Sharp lookout for potential new inter-product competition and for signs of product decline	Information helping to identify the point at which the product should be phased out

FIG. 11-4. *The product life cycle: a reference chart on managing its constantly changing phases.*

Multiple Size Packages

One way to recycle a product while maintaining its market share and profits is to introduce a second package. A second or even third size package has very little negative impact on the sales of the original package and brings in new customers or more uses for present customers. The problem with new package sizes lies in the ability of channel members to carry them.

Extending a Product Line

Generally you should extend your product line with additional highly acceptable products as long as good market penetration of the original product exists. The extension should involve the same, or a minor variation of, the unique selling proposition established for the first product. Product line extensions generally provide the small company with the opportunity to use the same communication vehicles and distribution channels to fill the needs of the same market. A product line extension could conceivably take two directions. One possibility would be to provide customers with some variations in style, color, quality, or other features. This may increase sales by adding new customers in the same market. Another possible product line extension would be to increase the inventory of the firm's products that any one customer would buy. For example, a company added a new barbecue sauce to its tomato ketchup product so that a consumer loyal to its ketchup would also purchase the company's barbecue sauce.

PRODUCT DIFFERENTIATION

Product differentiation is the process of focusing on the aspects of a product that make it exceptional. Each product can be placed somewhere on a commodity/specialty continuum with commodity products having few, if any, perceived differences and specialty products having many differences to the point of being unique. For a commodity product, profitability will depend on a firm's ability to offer a price lower than the competition's. In order to achieve this, the company needs to be highly skilled in machine design and thereby eliminate costly labor. In addition, the company must have employees with industrial engineering skills who can determine the optimal way to maximize production at the lowest cost. The opposite talents are needed for a specialty product whose profitability depends on the knowledge and application of marketing, an approach centered around the determination and execution of a unique selling proposition.

Differentiating a product or converting a commodity product to a specialty one cannot always be accomplished. To build an image of uniqueness, you need to give the innovation an individualized brand name and advertise the brand and innovative sales message heavily. Two companies that have done this successfully are General Foods with Minute Rice and Quaker Oats with oatmeal. General Foods made its long grain rice a specialty product when there were more than twenty millers of long-grain rice competing on a price basis. There are many manufactured or processed food items that are commodities. One way of converting a commodity product into a specialty one is to process a product in such a way that a specialty item is developed. A second way of converting a commodity product to a specialty one is to add something to the product that is desired by the consumer and is effective in making the product unlike all others in its previous commodity category. Miller, in heavy competition with many other companies making similar beers, eliminated some calories in their product Lite Beer, which was a highly advertisable difference. A third method of changing a commodity product into a specialty one is by "being the firstest with the mostest" and staying there with the "mostest" in advertising. In this strategy, the company determines something unique about its commodity product that is beneficial to the consumer and has not been previously mentioned. Even though competitive products have the same qualities in their product, by being first and consistent in advertising, a company can help the consumer think that its product alone has these qualities. A good example of this is Wonder Bread. When the company started its advertisement—"Wonder Bread Builds Stronger Bodies in 12 Different Ways"—indicating the combination of 12 minerals and vitamins, any competition could have said the same thing. A fourth way of changing a commodity product into a specialty one is through its package, or a combination of package and brand name. Even though salt is salt, Morton's patented spout (the patent rights have now run out), combined with informing the consumer about the uniqueness of "When It Rains, It Pours," moved the company's salt from its commodity category to a specialty position.

An example of combining package and brand name is Janitor in a Drum. The drum, made to look like an industrial drum, combined with the name implies that this floor detergent is stronger than others—perhaps of industrial strength.

A final method of converting a commodity product into a specialty one is by structuring the product differently. This occurred for a quinine-flavored soda pop which was restructured into Schweppes Tonic Water, a product to be mixed with gin. A similar tactic was used by Warner-Lambert upon acquiring Hall's Candy Company in Manchester, England as a minor part of a pharmaceutical merger. Hall's was making forty commodity candy items, none doing well, and was losing money. One of these commodity candy items was restructured into a cough drop, with an advertising story similar to Dristan, namely, "It helps you breathe easier." The item was successfully introduced with this theme in the United States with Hall's Mentho-Lyptus becoming one of the leading-selling cough drops in the United States.

CHAPTER PERSPECTIVE

In this chapter we have examined the introduction of new products. You have seen how to find sources for new ideas and how to evaluate these ideas at each stage of the development process. The next steps—diffusion and adoption—are important for marketing strategy to place the product into use. Once you have launched the product, you need to follow its product life cycle to optimize the marketing strategy for each stage of the product's life. Evaluation of the product over time is crucial to maximizing the growth of the product and your company.

Branding and Packaging

INTRODUCTION AND MAIN POINTS

In this chapter we will expand your understanding of branding and packaging and describe how a well-designed and coordinated brand name and package can add value and uniqueness to the final product. We will discuss the importance of brand loyalty and the procedure for selecting a brand name and package that will enhance the final marketing mix.

After studying the material in this chapter:
- You will be able to identify the reasons for establishing and using an individual brand name.
- You will know when to share a brand name of a new product with a previously used brand name.
- You will be able to develop a good consumer package in terms of size, attention-drawing power, quality impression, and readability.

BRANDING TERMINOLOGY

Before you can effectively incorporate branding into the marketing strategy, you need to be familiar with the various brand terms: manufacturer's brand, family brand name, category brand name, specific product brand name, private label brand, trademark, logo, and patent. A *manufacturer's brand* is one in which the registered name is owned by the company making the product. This name may be an umbrella name, a category name or a specific product name. A *family brand name*—also referred to as a corporate name, umbrella, or family brand—is a brand name placed on all products sold by a firm. Borden is a firm that utilizes a family brand name. A *category brand name* is a brand name used on a common category of products. Firms that use a category name usually have several category brand names. An example is Sears, with "Kenmore" products for household appliances and "Ted Williams" products for outdoor sporting equipment. A *specific product name* is a brand name used on one and only one product. When specific product names are assigned to a second product, it is frequently the start of a category name. An example is the name "Mentho-Lyptus" being put on another flavor in the product line—lemon with the name "Mentho-Lyptus" being applied to an entire line of additional flavors.

A *private label brand* is one in which the company making the product does not own the registered name, but has been contracted to produce the product and put the buyer's registered name on the label. Frequently, the company, in addition to furnishing the product, furnishes the packaging material using the plates, insignia, and artwork specified by the buyer.

A *trademark,* if registered with the federal government, gives the firm the exclusive right of ownership on all goods to which the trademark is applied. The name Kodak, awarded to Eastman Kodak, belongs to the company and cannot be used by anyone else on similar products. Trade names are owned, however, for only a specified category. For example, if the name Keebler has been awarded by the Federal Trade Name Department only in the category of crackers and cookies, this does not prevent another firm from using the Keebler name in other product categories such as automobiles. Keebler owns the name for only the category specified. However, if Keebler also applied and obtained the name in the category of automobiles, then no one else could use the name in this category, as long as the company complied with the legal regulations for maintaining ownership of the name.

A *logo* is a letter, symbol or sign used to represent the entire word or words of the trademark. These can also be registered with the federal government and used on an exclusive basis. While the picture of Aunt Jemima is a logo, the words Aunt Jemima are a trademark.

While *patents* are not granted on brand names, they are granted by the U.S. Patent Office on: (1) unique ideas which contribute something new to the state of the art; or (2) new materials or ingredients which have not been used before, but which can be used as a substitute for the original material or ingredient established in the art. An idea patent has the most value. Frequently material or ingredient patents are easily circumvented by using a slightly different, but similar material or ingredient. Patents are also held on the machinery used in the actual production of the product itself. For example, the spout on Morton Salt was patented and made Morton Salt different from any competitor's salt. Presently, more patents are held on industrial products than consumer products.

BRAND LOYALTY

Brand loyalty—the amount of product satisfaction and unwilling-ness to switch to competing products—affects the type of brand name selected. When the consumer has little product loyalty such as in soups and cake mixes, it is usually better to use a common brand name for the entire product category. Campbell's has over eighty varieties of soups. Similarly, Betty Crocker has a wide variety of cake mixes, such as chocolate, cherry supreme, angel food, or spice. No matter how much you like chocolate cake or chicken noodle soup, you want different soups and cakes on a regular basis.

It is better to use different brand names and advertising sto-ries for follow-up on products when the product category has a high degree of brand loyalty. The laundry detergent product cate-gory, for example, is one with high brand loyalty. A consumer will usually use only one of these products (Tide, Cheer, or Dash) at a time. Frequently, a consumer will also remain with the cho-sen brand for a remarkably long period of time. A similar degree of loyalty occurs in cigarettes, coffee, and toothpaste. In some cases the toothpaste used by the previous generation is used in the new generation's family.

As long as a company maintains quality in a branded line, a satisfied consumer of one of the company's products will proba-bly try another company product. Consumer satisfaction provides the best opportunity for getting a consumer interested in trying other products in the line. Indeed, a new product entering the market under a well-established brand name gains distribution and consumer sales more rapidly than the same product under a new brand name.

Often it is difficult to identify something unique about a product. One company's can of tomatoes looks and tastes very much like another company's can of tomatoes. In addition, few individual canned vegetables or fruits have annual sales that would support a large advertising budget. Once product unique-ness is found, then the product can be extensively advertised. Green Giant, however, felt it had achieved enough product uniqueness that extensive advertising of its entire product line would be supported by increased sales. This could not be done in other product categories such as cigarettes or detergents where the consumer does not stock two or three brands at the same time. When introducing a new brand in a product classification such as cigarettes or detergents, you should assign the new prod-uct a completely different name and let it compete against other products of the company. If the new brand can achieve an established market share and not cannibalize significant sales from other company products, it will be of long-term benefit to the company. It is better that sales be exchanged between products within the same company rather than losing sales to another company's product.

In deciding whether a new product should take its own brand name or be in a category or umbrella name, the product should be viewed in the context of the two forces indicated in Table 12-1.

Table 12-1
Determining a Brand Name Policy

Forces for Individual Brand Name	*Forces for Sharing or Using Previously Used Brand Name*
1. Product either tends to be completely unique in its category or else is located toward unique end of the continuum scale.	1. Product tends to be nearer commodity end of continuum.
2. Product is in a category where the user usually buys a variety of products in the category at the same time.	2. Product is in a field where consumer seeks variety and will stock this and others in category at the same time.
3. Sales potential indicates product will support its own advertising budget.	3. Sales potential indicates that it is doubtful that product can support its own advertising budget.
4. Product acquired through merger or acquisition already has an established brand name that has some market value.	4. Product acquired through acquisition or merger does not have an established brand name and is compatible with previously used category or umbrella products.
5. Product is not compatible with any products in the company's category or umbrella name.	5. The company is marketing an established product with a sound market penetration and selling theme that the new product could effectively align with, thereby starting a category name.
6. Product is in a completely different quality category than are products under any present category or umbrella name.	
7. Product is embarrassing for the consumer to describe.	

The factors in the left column indicate that the product should take an individual brand name. The factors in the right column indicate that the product should probably either share a name with a product, become part of a category name or take the umbrella name of the corporation. Items 1, 2, and 3 in both columns are the key factors affecting the majority of instances of brand name determination. An example of incompatibility (point number 5) occurred when Canada Dry, introducing a medicinal flavored mouthwash to compete with Listerine, used a new brand name (not the previously established umbrella or category names) since the soft drink had a brand image of being sweet and delectable. When Morton's iodized salt was introduced, it was sold with the same pour spout and benefits as the original salt, benefiting from the high advertising penetration of the advertising theme—"When it rains, it pours."

If a product fills most all of the requirements in the right-hand column of Table 12-1, you must then decide on whether to use a category or umbrella name. To the extent that a category name gives a sharper, more distinct advertising theme than an umbrella name, the category name should be used, provided that the product is similar to products in one of the categories. If the product does not fit into any of these categories, then it should be given an umbrella name.

SELECTING A BRAND NAME

In selecting an appropriate brand name, you should recognize that it should be registered and protected via usage. Sometimes, even though a name has been registered, it can be lost through a lack of use.

In selecting a meaningful brand name, all geographic words must be avoided. Many companies have regretted taking the name of a city, a county, a river, or a valley to find out later that others have a right to this name also. One classic example of this is the original "Smithfield Hams," a name based on the town of its location, Smithfield, Virginia. While the original company sold hams to the British navy prior to the Revolutionary War, today, there are three "Smithfield Hams," not all made by the original company because the town name Smithfield could not be protected.

While the law permits usage of a name for one product category that has been registered in a different category, the final product category is decided by the courts. One company had reserved the name "Premium" for use in the candy and confectionery category and decided to market a chocolate wafer under this same name. In the opinion of management and its legal advisors, the product was in the confectionery category and the company could use the name "Premium" on this chocolate wafer bar. However, after spending nearly a million dollars on advertising the bar under the name "Premium," another company registered a complaint that the product was infringing on their trademark "Premium" for the cracker and cookie category. While it may be hard to conceive that the chocolate bar could be considered a cracker, legal advisors of the confectionery company estimated the probability of winning the case was only 50-50. Given the length of time such a case could be in the courts, during which time the company would need to continue advertising the product under the name "Premium," thus building the advertising expenditure into five or six million dollars, the company decided to relinquish the name "Premium" in the new category and write off the million dollars in advertising already spent.

Another category of brand names you need to avoid is one generic in nature. A generic category is one that identifies things or products that are homogeneous in composition and/or use. For example, sodium acetylsalicylic acid is the generic term for aspirin tablets. When a name becomes generic, the public owns that name for its use. Also, all words in the dictionary, as well as all proper names of cities, rivers, and mountains are almost always considered public domain. If any word in the dictionary is commonly used to describe a product in a given category, then any company can use the word to describe a product in that category. It is also risky to use a word whose pronunciation is similar to that of a dictionary word used to describe products in a particular category. Miller beer made this mistake with the name "Lite," which is pronounced like "light," a word in the dictionary commonly used to describe beers. Any beer manufacturer has the right to use the same term, which is exactly what Anheuser-Busch and Schlitz did.

Even though Coca-Cola has fought for years to maintain its name, the courts forced the company to relinquish half of its name, "cola," feeling it was a generic name with others having similar rights to its use. This made a wide variety of colas available such as Pepsi Cola and R.C. Cola.

Often a new product can be effectively linked to a proven brand name, thereby decreasing the odds of failure. By using the recognizable asset of a proven name, many companies have successfully entered new markets and introduced new products.

Examples of this include: Bic Roller pen, Levi's skirts and shoes, Del Monte Mexican Food, Easy-Off window cleaner, and Vaseline Intensive Care skin lotion, bath oil, and baby powder. However, you should take care when using an established brand name on any new product as it does not guarantee success and can even negatively impact the sales of the original product. Such failures as Arm and Hammer Antiperspirant, Certs gum, and Listerine household cleaner illustrate that a strong name in one product category does not necessarily guarantee success in another.

CRITERIA FOR BRAND NAME SELECTION

While there are many criteria that can be used in selecting and establishing a brand name, the most important ones can be classified in three major areas: pronunciation, connotation, and memorability.

Pronunciation

A brand name should be pronounced easily and in only one way in a given market. This aspect can be tested by printing the proposed name in one- to two-inch type on white cardboard and having the name presented for pronouncing to a sample in the market.

Connotation

Although the name selected does not have to be directly related to the product, it should not have an associated use that is incompatible with the product being introduced. Connotations of a name can be determined by adding a question to the pronunciation test: "If this name is the name of one of the products you purchase, what product do you think it is?"

Memorability

A name that can be easily remembered is most desirable. This can be determined by selecting the thirty best possible names and indicating to a sample of consumers that the thirty names are to be used on a "name category of product" (such as a grocery item, pharmaceutical product, or a hardware product). Then each name is presented on a card while being pronounced until each of the thirty names is presented. At this time, each person is asked to write down those names that can be remembered. The name recalled most frequently in each product category is the most memorable.

PRIVATE LABEL MERCHANDISING

Manufacturing private labels is a profitable but risky decision, one which needs to be carefully analyzed from the manufacturer's as well as the retailer's perspective.

Manufacture

A private label name is one in which someone else, usually a wholesaler or a retailer, has its name placed on one of the manufacturer's established products. "Ann Page" has been used on many items that are sold by A & P Food Stores and are manufactured by several different manufacturers. As is the case with A & P, the party requesting the private label usually places a large order with the manufacturer for this packaging change. From the manufacturer's perspective, there are several reasons for not getting involved in any private label business. First, in time a manufacturer can be confronted with both price competition and a profit squeeze. In order to maintain a private label business when this occurs, the manufacturer usually decreases the quality of the product to meet the price competition of others. If the private label has become a substantial part of a manufacturer's business, not meeting price competition and still maintaining volume can result in severe financial problems, even bankruptcy.

Second, a manufacturer has no control over certain key aspects of marketing such as advertising, retailer deals, package design, and brands in the private label business. Third, private label merchandising means tying up additional money as separate inventories must be carried in both packaging materials and finished goods. Separate inventories must often be kept for several private label customers, thereby substantially decreasing money turnover. At the same time, the manufacturer's branded product is being purchased by the consumer at a higher price, a practice that usually results in lower brand name volume.

PACKAGING MIX

The packaging mix is similar to the marketing mix in that the product's final packaging mix represents decisions in a variety of areas. A good packaging mix is one that protects the product; adapts to production line speeds; promotes or sells the product; increases the product density; facilitates the use of the product; provides reusable value to the consumer; satisfies legal requirements (including ecology laws); and keeps the packaging costs as low as possible.

There is no easy formula for successfully meeting all eight requirements for a package. In any packaging strategy, though, at least the conditions of the law need to be satisfied.

PACKAGING CATEGORIES

The consumer package is a package in which the product is purchased and taken home by the consumer. The package can contain a single item or multiple items. Occasionally the consumer package is discarded by the retail store if the product can withstand transportation. This is often true of household appliances such as washing machines, refrigerators, and stoves. At times the consumer package is made so that it can be used as a display to the consumer at the retail level.

The shipping case is the container in which the product is shipped and stored in the warehouse. It is packed either with display boxes, as in the case of Alka-Seltzer retail boxes, with consumer packages such as Pillsbury cake mix boxes, or with bulk products such as kegs of nails.

PROTECTING THE PRODUCT

The first requisite of a good packaging design is that it protect the product. Some products are very hygroscopic (water-retaining) and deteriorate when they absorb water. Others are just the opposite and deteriorate rapidly with the loss of moisture. Still others are fragile and break easily. Each of these types of products must be protected by the proper packaging. If the product is perishable, the manufacturer needs to have temperature and humidity charts for each area in which the product is marketed.

Packaging can also be used to achieve product uniqueness as well as to protect the product. For example, the Morton Salt pour spout, which was a convenience to the consumer, also protected the salt from moisture by sealing the package after usage. Frequently, the packaging innovations are developed by the packing material manufacturers. For example, Procter and Gamble, working with Container Corporation of America, introduced the composite can used today for so many snack items such as Pringles and Cheetos.

A packaging innovation in wines sold to institutions is the Mega-Cask, a bag-in-a-box container. The special container saves money for restaurants, hotels, and clubs by preserving the quality of wine while allowing faster serving in a more efficient manner. The collapsible Mega-Cask has four plys of plastic as a liner in a rectangular, 500-pound corrugated case, holding almost five gallons weighing about 43 pounds.

LEGAL REQUIREMENTS

The Fair Packaging and Labeling Act enacted in 1968 established some strict rules for all packages used in interstate commerce. In order to understand the act and its packaging requirements you need to know several terms. A *label* is composed of all written, printed, or graphic matter included on the container of that article. The *principal display panel* is the part of the label most likely to be shown or seen at the retail level. This panel must contain all mandatory copy. If a package has alternative principal display panels or two primary faces, duplicate mandatory copy must be on each panel. *Mandatory copy* is the information about the contents of the package. The identity of the package must be shown in bold type on the primary display panel with other printed matter parallel to the base of the package as it is displayed. The statement may be either the product name or the common name of the product.

The name and place of the business must be clearly shown on the label, though not necessarily on the principal display panel. This information must include the central corporate name and division, the city, state, zip code, and, if the company is not listed in the telephone book, the street address. The principal display panel and all alternate display panels must show the net quantity in terms of weight, measure, or numerical count. Each panel must also contain a list of ingredients, beginning with the one of greatest predominance and the rest arranged in descending order.

PRODUCTION LINE SPEEDS

Very close in importance to protecting the product and adhering to the legal aspects of package design is a package's adaptability to production line speeds. Often, in trying to have maximum length and width dimensions on a box, the depth of the box is decreased to the point where the product will not easily flow into the box without jamming or clogging. This and other negative aspects of the package must be avoided in order to ensure low-cost, efficient production.

PACKAGE DESIGN FOR PRODUCT SALES

After these three things, the remaining task of the package is to sell the product to the consumer. In terms of this aspect, four general merchandising principles are important: apparent size, attention-drawing power, impression of quality, and brand name readability.

Apparent Size

A package should give an impression of size without being deceptive. The apparent size is often important during the point-of-purchase decision. This is especially true in relatively low-priced, high-consumption items such as rice, flour, and canned fruits and vegetables. In order to achieve apparent size, you should:

1. Decrease the dimension least seen by the consumer when the package is on display.
2. Keep the front panel one solid color, end-to-end, without distorting it with artistic designs, borders, extraneous pictures, or allowing the product to show through transparent film.
3. Print the brand name on the front panel in the largest letters possible.
4. Print horizontally on the package whenever possible.
5. Not put anything on the front panel except the brand name, contents of the package, and any information required by law.

Attention-Drawing Power

Because a product is displayed among a myriad of competing products, a package should have the inherent ability to capture and hold the attention of a consumer. What gives a package this power? The package design—that combination of elements which together produces attractiveness, purity, appetite appeal, and high quality—gives the package attention-drawing power.

Whenever appropriate (such as in the case of food products), a picture of the product should be displayed on the front panel in as appetizing a form as possible. Nothing attracts and holds interest like pictures of a food product. The package should of course be kept current. Since competition may change, you must make sure that you do not have an old-fashioned package which no longer holds and attracts interest.

Quality Impression

A package should convey the feeling of quality. Deftly addressing the other three factors important in successful packaging often results in a very low concept of product quality. However, a low concept of product quality cannot be tolerated. One way to ensure that a package does not denote poor quality is to evaluate the finished package on a scale of several good and bad product qualities. You should always make sure that the package printing does not appear washed-out or faded as this gives an impression of an older product and poor quality. Printing should be bright but not gaudy.

Readability
The brand name on a package should be easily readable. Readability is especially important in the case of packages that are distributed mainly through large self-service outlets since these must compete with numerous items in the same product class in relatively restricted shelf areas. When packaging is tied in closely with advertising efforts, an easily readable brand name tends to reinforce the sales message. To achieve readability, it is important to make the letters as large as possible using the same print as that used in large daily paper headlines.

For a company that does not advertise or whose budget is considerably below average in the product category, the package takes on even more importance. In this case, the package sells the product even more. The brand name space should be shared with advertising space on the package, at least in the product's introduction.

CHAPTER PERSPECTIVE
In this chapter we have looked at branding and packaging as two key elements in the marketing mix. There are various types of brand policies available for use in a marketing strategy: manufacturers' brands, family brand names, category names, specific product names, and private label brands. Besides the brand name, products are also identified by trademarks and logos.

When you are deciding on a specific brand name policy, you can use a new, individual brand name or share a previously used brand name. An individual name is most appropriate when a product is unique; it is incompatible with the company's other products; and it is in a completely different quality category. When you select a brand name, make sure that the name is easily pronounceable, has a specific and directly appropriate connotation, and is easily remembered by the consumer.

Packaging is similarly important for achieving successful sales results, particularly when there is a limited advertising budget. A successful packaging mix is one that protects the product, adapts the product to the production line speeds, promotes the product, increases its density, facilitates the use of the product, and provides reusable value to the consumer.

Pricing

INTRODUCTION AND MAIN POINTS

Even though price may be considered the most important of all the elements in the marketing mix, it is usually the one marketing people know the least about. In fact, in many companies, few executives even know how the price of the product is established. In order to begin to understand pricing, it is important first to have an overall view of the economic dimension underlying price and price theory. In order to understand this economic dimension of pricing, some pricing objectives, and the three Cs of pricing— Cost, Competition, and the Consumer—are discussed. The chapter concludes with a discussion of pricing in practice and the various discounts and allowances that could be offered.

After studying the material in this chapter:

▬ You will understand the various aspects of pricing.

▬ You will be able to establish the correct price for your product or service.

▬ You will be able to change a price with the least negative impact.

ECONOMIC DIMENSION OF PRICING

In a free market system such as the one operating in the United States, price is an important factor in controlling the supply and demand of goods. Although a totally pure economic system of supply and demand rarely exists in the short run, it is important to understand its basis as this will provide the foundation for understanding the economic dimension of pricing.

To have an economic free market system in an industry, several factors need to exist: a large number of manufacturers (sellers); a larger number of buyers; no dominant or very large manufacturer that can control price; manufacturers' ease in entering or leaving the industry; and large differentiating factors between product or producers. While rarely do all these factors exist in a specific industry situation, when they do, a rising price will entice more volume from present manufacturers and attract more manufacturers into the industry. Similarly, a decreasing price will cause sales volume to rise in the industry as the goods will have increasing demand due in part to the lower price. More goods will be sold at the lower price than at a higher price. If the supply of an item is very large in relation to the demand, the price tends to decrease. When market conditions allow the total revenue to increase due to a greater number of units being sold as the price goes down, the price is elastic. If the total revenue does not increase in these conditions, price is inelastic.

While prices frequently fluctuate, they become more stabilized in the industry where supply and demand curves cross. The *supply curve* represents the amount of goods sellers are willing to put on the market at various prices. The *demand curve* represents the amount of goods buyers are willing to purchase at various prices. At the point the two curves intersect, there is no profit incentive to produce more goods or to buy more goods.

Monopoly

When a company has complete control over quantity and price, it is said to be a monopoly. DeBeers Diamonds is an example of a monopoly, as the company has virtual control over the supply of, and therefore to a significant extent the price of, diamonds. Certain associations, such as the American Medical Association and American Dental Association, and certain labor organizations are close to being monopolies as well, at least on the supply side. Monopolistic conditions are more prevalent in other countries, particularly in those that are less developed or largely state-controlled. When you are doing business in any of these countries, the barriers to market entry as well as the problems occurring in supply sources or distribution outlets must be considered.

Oligopolistic Competition

When there are few competitors in an industry, the industry is said to be oligopolistic. Some more oligopolistic industries in the United States are automobiles, tires, oil, and steel. Depending on the nature of the industry, firms often do not have complete control over their pricing practices, which results in a company frequently following an industry leader.

Generally, all the companies in an oligopoly have similar pricing practices to avoid any price competition or price wars.

When products being sold are differentiated in either a real or psychological sense, then a differentiated oligopoly exists, as is the case for automobiles. Firms producing steel ingots, if few in number, would be considered an undifferentiated oligopoly.

Since specialty products have more of an inelastic demand, there can be more use of price as a differentiating marketing variable. This situation is referred to as selling under nonprice competition. Firms producing specialty products are more able to sell at a price that will cover their costs and make a profit than firms having a product that is viewed as having little difference from alternative products available on the market.

When determining the price of a product in either competitive or oligopolistic market conditions, it is necessary for you to understand basic pricing objectives as well as the fundamental factors of pricing: The three Cs of pricing are Cost, Competition, and the Consumer. After investigating the various objectives available, each of these factors will be discussed in terms of its importance and use, therefore enabling you to price your product effectively.

PRICING OBJECTIVES

There are many different pricing objectives that can be used on a single product, a product line, or on all product lines of a company. While some companies use different objectives in different parts of the company's operations, other companies use the same general objectives across all products and operations. The similarity of the pricing objectives used depends on the product and market conditions. Specific pricing objectives can be classified in terms of market penetration, market skimming, early cash recovery, return on investment, and other nonfinancial objectives (product line promotion, market share, meeting competition, and image).

Market Penetration

Some companies establish a relatively low price on a product in order to capture a larger share of the market being entered. This objective is most effective when certain market product conditions exist, such as a highly priced sensitive market where a slightly higher price would cause potential buyers not to purchase the product; mass production of the product that will significantly lower cost; large overhead costs that are best allocated over more units of product; and the product's distinctiveness is short-lived.

Market Skimming

Opposite the market penetration objective is the market skimming objective, where a high price is established to secure initial maximum profits. This high price is lowered at later stages as the market expands. The initial high price "skims the cream off" those market segments that are less price sensitive and therefore do not mind paying a higher price to be one of the first to own the new product. These objectives are most appropriate when there are high research and development costs involved and good protection against competitive products entering the market. Also, there are no economies of scale with few, if any, benefits occurring in production and distribution resulting from a larger production run.

Early Cash Recovery

Frequently, especially for the small firm, long-term sales and profits must give way to the more immediate problem of economic survival. When this occurs, you can establish a lower price on one or more of the firm's products that will result in rapid recovery of cash. Even though this does not take into account the potential for greater sales and profit in the long run, this objective can help a firm strapped for funds gain a foothold and experience in a market which can be expanded later while decreasing the length of time money must be borrowed. This can be very beneficial for a small firm, particularly in periods of high interest rates.

Return on Investment

Many companies, particularly those in relatively high technology areas, price products to achieve a certain percent return on their investment in the product. Using this objective, you would set a target price that would achieve this specified target rate of return. While every company needs to achieve a certain rate of return to remain in business, care should be taken to avoid rigorously using this objective for every product without analyzing the specific product/market conditions. When there is no flexibility in the specific percentage margin used (for example 30 percent margin on every product), then "marginitis" can develop. It is a condition that does not allow a firm to effectively use price in developing an effective marketing strategy. For example, marginitis can prevent a firm from entering relatively lucrative markets because the return does not quite meet the established percent.

Nonfinancial Objectives

There are other price objectives that can also be employed. These include product line promotion, market share, meeting competition, and image. In using the product line promotion objective, one product is priced to stimulate sales of another product or the entire product line without undue concern about the amount of sales or the rate of return on the product itself. Sometimes, particularly in rapid growth markets, a small firm needs to establish a price that effectively meets competition.

Using the guidelines of one or more of these pricing objectives, you must carefully evaluate each of the fundamental three Cs of pricing—Cost, Competition, and the Consumer—in establishing or changing the price of each product in the line.

COST

Cost is of course the floor you must use in determining the price of the product. In the long run, the price of the product cannot be below its cost if the firm expects to achieve a profit. Every product need not provide an established return, but it is rare that a product would be priced below the amount needed to recover its costs. Cost considerations should reflect the historical costs of the product as well as anticipated costs given volume production.

Cost-Plus Pricing

One method for evaluating cost and its impact on price is cost-plus pricing, which can be done in several ways depending on the cost basis used. The cost base most frequently used, particularly by manufacturers, is total cost. In cost-plus pricing, a percent markup is applied to the total cost of the product to determine its selling price. For example, if the percent markup is 100 percent of the cost to produce the product, which is $25, it would be priced at [($25 + 100% ($25)]. The manufacturer is using a 100 percent markup on the $25 cost, yielding a $25 profit margin and a $50 selling price to either the end user or someone in the distribution system.

When using a distribution system, it is important for a small firm to evaluate the effect of a "chain of markups," which occur if certain channels of distribution are used. This chain of markups will be reflected in the final price to the consumer. For example, a firm marketing a cleaning solution for hard contact lenses evaluated the channels available and their impact on price. As indicated in Figure 13-1, the final price to the consumer would vary from $1.75 to $3.71 depending on the channel used. The percent

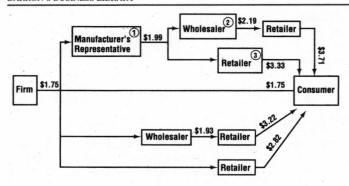

① Manufacturer's Representative has a 12% markup on wholesale or 13.6% markup on cost.
② Wholesaler has a 10% markup on cost.
③ Retailer has a 40% markup on retail or a 66% markup on cost.

FIG. 13-1. *Chain of markups.*

markup taken by each channel member is indicated at the bottom of the figure. The conversion from markup on selling price to markup on cost is achieved through the following formula:

$$\% \text{ mc} = \frac{\% \text{ m sp}}{100\% - \% \text{ m sp}}$$

For the lens cleaning solution in the example, the percentage markup on cost for the manufacturer's representative is:

$$\% \text{ mc} = \frac{12\%}{100\% - 12\%} = 13.6\%$$

Similarly, for the retailer the percentage markup on cost is:

$$\% \text{ mc} = \frac{40\%}{100\% - 40\% \text{ m sp}} = 66.78\%$$

Frequently, a small manufacturing firm will work back from several possible final consumer prices to determine the impact of each price on the firm and the margin. This is particularly important when there is a high degree of price sensitivity in the market or when consumers have a price threshold—a price above which they will not purchase the product. During this determination, it is often necessary to convert markups on cost to selling price or retail using the following formula:

$$\% \text{ m sp} = \frac{\% \text{ markup on cost}}{100\% + \% \text{ mc}}$$

For example, a percentage markup on cost of 50% would be a percent markup on selling price of 33⅓% as is calculated below:

$$\% \text{ m sp} = \frac{50\%}{100\% + 50\%} = 33\frac{1}{3}\%$$

Given the impact on price, you need to carefully evaluate the margins required versus the benefits of each channel member. Even though the cost-plus pricing method, using total cost as the cost base, is simple and is widely used, it does not take into account the fact that total cost has two parts—total fixed costs and total variable costs. *Total fixed costs (TFC)* are those costs that do not vary with the number of units sold. Store rental, salaries, plant, machinery remain the same whether 10 units or 100 units are sold. *Total variable costs (TVC)* are those costs that increase with each additional unit sold. Materials, component parts, labor, heat, light, and electricity are all examples of variable costs. Generally, as long as there is some financial base, the small firm in more volume markets should concentrate more on the variable costs than the fixed costs, as the variable costs are the ones that impact the price the most when the full product is reached. The fixed costs have less impact as more volume is achieved and these costs are spread over more units.

Target-Return Pricing
Many industrial firms establish a price to achieve a target return on investment, such as 20 percent before taxes. Then the marketing strategy is developed to achieve this rate of return using the price that will achieve the target rate of return specified.

Break-Even Analysis
Break-even analysis is an important analytical tool as well as a method for pricing the product. The analysis gives the small firm an idea of the profit potential as well as any safety margin in achieving this profit at alternative prices. Break-even analysis is particularly useful when you are considering a price change. The safety margin is the level of sales in excess of the break-even point, the point at which all costs are covered. As is indicated in the break-even chart in Figure 13-2, the amount of sales needed

for the company to break even varies with alternative prices. You can calculate the break-even point using the following formula:

$$P(x) = FC + VC(x)$$

Where: P = price
x = break-even point (in units)
FC = fixed cost
VC = variable cost

For example, for a small manufacturer of an industrial temperature controlling device that has a fixed cost of $500,000 and the corresponding variable cost for the product is $13.00 per unit, the break-even point at $19.50 per unit is:

$$19.50(x) = 500,000 + 13.00(x)$$
$$x = 76,923 \text{ units}$$

This break-even point will decrease to 52,632 if the price of the product is increased to $22.50:

$$22.50(x) = 500,000 + 13.00(x)$$
$$x = 52,632 \text{ units}$$

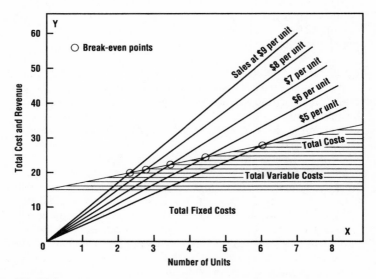

FIG. 13-2. *Graphic display of different break-even points*

The small firm in this example can now compare whether it is better to try to achieve sales of more than 76,923 units at a price of $19.50 or 52,632 units at a price of $22.50 or to calculate the break-even sales at other prices. Two additional factors affecting this decision are competition and the consumer.

COMPETITION

In addition to cost, it is important that the small firm evaluate the competition. The prices of competitive products establish the benchmarks for a pricing decision. You have to decide whether to meet, undersell, or oversell the market prices in existence, knowing that the consumer will compare your price to the prices of these other products, depending to some extent on the amount of product differentiation.

The price of competitive products is also important in evaluating the competitive reaction to a possible price change being considered. You need to determine the most probable competitive reaction and its consequences when your price is changed. Will competition follow your price change? What will be the impact if they do or do not? The small firm should constantly monitor competitive prices so that appropriate timely action can be taken.

CONSUMER

The final C—the consumer and the consumer's reaction to the particular price—is the most important factor in establishing the price, of the product or service. The consumer (whether in the consumer, industrial, or government market) really determines whether the price established is a good one. You should carefully analyze the possible consumer reaction to the product and the price, taking into account the utility of the product and its return to the purchaser. A product having a high utility to the consumer can usually have a higher price than one that does not.

PRICING IN PRACTICE

There are several additional factors a small firm should consider in pricing a product. These include factors that tend to increase a price, the relative importance of the price, the pricing system, and pricing for distribution channels.

Factors Tending to Increase Price

The factors that tend to increase the price of a product can be classified on a micro and macro basis. Some of the micro factors that tend to increase the price include an increase in labor rates without a proportionate increase in productivity; a shortage in the supply of goods relative to demand; a significant increase in the amount of the product desired by buyers; and a postponing of selling by producers due to an expectation that higher prices will prevail later. The macro factors tending to increase price include a monopoly situation or one approaching a monopoly and an increase in the supply of money accompanied by a reduction in interest rates.

Importance of Price

The relative importance of price with respect to the rest of the marketing mix depends in part on the position of the product on the commodity/unique continuum. As the product approaches being a commodity, then price becomes an increasingly important factor in proportion to the other elements in the marketing mix as there is little or no product differentiation. Since there is nothing that differentiates one product from another, the price is often the only factor that leads to the sale of the product.

On the other hand, if the product or some other element of the marketing mix is very unique, then this element becomes more important than the price in affecting product sales. These elements can be in the form of the physical product itself, the package, advertising, sales force, distribution, or location in the store.

Pricing Systems

There are several different pricing systems in operation. One of these is market-determined pricing. This type of pricing occurs in the commodity exchanges for such products as grain, cotton, and cocoa beans. In these cases, the seller does not have control of the price of each separate transaction and instead allows supply and demand to operate freely to determine the price. This situation is an example of pure competition.

Administered pricing occurs when the firm establishes the price and buyers can either buy or not buy at this fixed price. The price established covers costs and a margin of profit.

Government-controlled pricing occurs when the product is subject to regulatory prices established by the federal, state, or local government. This pricing occurs in oligopoly situations (telephone, natural gas, and electricity); in times of national emergency; or when a sudden demand for an important good cannot be supplied and the price rapidly increases. Occasionally, particularly in international markets, government-controlled pricing, which is frequently accompanied by rationing, creates a "black market," a situation in which goods are bought and sold illegally outside the established government controls.

Pricing for the Channels of Distribution

The small firm needs to always be attentive to its channel members and the resulting chain of markups. Channel members such as retailers and wholesalers use markups based on their selling price, not based on their costs as manufacturers do. This is sometimes called off-list pricing. Since the denominator is the selling price, which is larger than the cost, the percentage markup on the selling price is always smaller than the percentage markup on the cost. For example, if in a supermarket chain the standard markup in a category is 25 percent of the selling price, the chain would take 25 percent off the selling price in order to determine the cost basis it would be willing to pay for the merchandise and still keep the 25 percent markup desired. In the case of a snack item shipped to a store packed 24 to the case and priced at $8.82 a case, if the store wants to sell the item at 49 cents a box, it would take 25 percent off 49 cents to arrive at 36.75 cents. The case price of $8.82 divided by 24 packs in the case yields the same unit price to the store—36.75 cents. Therefore, the store would stock and sell the item for 49 cents as it would be making the margin desired. If the price paid was higher than 36.75 cents, the store would not stock the product unless a lower price was offered.

You should know the standard retail markup for the product category as well as any favored unit price at which the retailers prefer to sell. For example, chain grocery stores prefer prices ending in nines, such as 29 cents, 39 cents, 49 cents. Their second preference is usually prices ending in threes, such as 43 cents, 53 cents, 63 cents.

Most companies price to enable the retailers to sell at their preferred price while giving their store their standard markup. A few manufacturers, such as those introducing a new product or those having difficulty selling an item, will price the product to give retailers a slightly higher markup than the standard one for the category in order to stimulate sales.

DISCOUNTS AND ALLOWANCES

A variety of discounts and allowances are frequently offered by small manufacturing firms to secure favorable shelf space, promotion, or quicker payment from the trade. The discount or allowance for a specific service is usually included in the price. Each price reduction must be offered to all buyers of like grade and quality to avoid being in violation of the Robinson-Patman Act, which was passed in 1936. This act makes it illegal for any person or company engaged in commerce to knowingly induce or receive a discriminatory practice between different buyers of goods or services of similar types of quality sold under similar conditions. The act banned any discriminatory practices that would injure, destroy, prevent, or lessen competition.

Quantity Discounts

Quantity discounts are those discounts given on the basis of units or dollars of the product purchased. These discounts may be on the immediate order or on cumulative orders over the year. They are usually offered by the manufacturer to make volume buying more attractive by channel members. In a sense, the savings from the efficiency of processing one order rather than several orders are passed on to the buyer in terms of the discount. Cumulative discounts encourage the buyer to stay with one company over the period of time covered by the discount and can be an effective strategy for a small firm attempting to establish channel reactions.

Trade Discounts

Trade discounts are offered to channel members for their assistance in getting the product to the retailer and then to the ultimate consumer. The manufacturer of wristwatches might have a list price of $50−30%−5% with the price to the consumer being $50. The price to the retailer is $35 ($50−(.30 × $50)), and the price to the wholesaler is $33.25. Thus, the wholesaler would get 5 percent off the price to the retailer, and the retailer would get 30 percent off the list price.

Cash Discounts

Cash discounts are given to encourage prompt payment, thereby increasing money turnover and, to some extent, decreasing bad debts. There are various types and rates for different time periods. Two percent/10/net/30 is one type, which means 2 percent is taken off if the bill is paid within 10 days and none is taken off thereafter; if the bill is not paid in 30 days, future goods may not be shipped and a finance charge may be added. A small firm should establish a policy for dealing with companies that take discounts even though they have not followed the terms of the discount. This frequently happens in terms of cash discounts where a store will deduct the 2 percent offered for payment in 30 days and still pay in 60 days. One company has the policy that if more than three unearned discounts are taken, goods will not be shipped until the last illegitimately taken discount is repaid.

Forward-dating is used by some small firms, allowing extra time before payment is due even though the goods are received. This method is advantageous on seasonal items such as suntan lotion as it allows the manufacturer to ship the product in the winter (off season) forward-dating the invoice to the beginning of the sunbathing season, allowing the retailer to store the goods and yet not pay until the time the product is sold during the season.

Seasonal Discounts

Seasonal discounts are given by the manufacturer to avoid carrying inventory of products in the manufacturer's warehouse by having the channel members carry the inventory instead. Seasonal discounts help maintain an even flow of production without the accompanying increase in inventory. This practice differs from forward-dating in that the manufacturer receives its money less the discount more quickly instead of waiting until the season begins, as would be the case under forward-dating.

Promotion Allowances

A variety of promotional allowances can be given. These allowances are paid by the manufacturer to obtain some promotional service from the channel member, such as appearing in the channel member's weekly advertisement or having a display in the store. For example, Procter and Gamble will give a $.50/case display allowance for a store displaying 10 cases of 3-pound containers of Crisco shortening for a week.

Cash Rebates

Cash rebates are used by the manufacturer to stimulate retail sales. The rebates are given by the manufacturer through the retailer to the consumer who buys the products. For example, rebates are used periodically throughout the year and particularly at model year end in August to stimulate sluggish retail automobile sales.

Trade-in Allowances

When the product has a high unit value, trade-in allowances on old equipment are used by the manufacturer to encourage the purchase of a new unit. In the earth-moving equipment business, for example, companies are encouraged to trade in for new models more frequently because of the lucrative trade-in allowances offered. The old equipment traded in can then be refurbished and resold to buyers interested in used equipment.

LEGAL ASPECTS OF PRICING

Collusive price fixing occurs when a group of competitors agree to sell a product or products at a given price. There is probably no more strictly enforced part of the antitrust laws than the prohibition against price fixing.

A violation occurs when a manufacturer does not treat all channel members alike. While the price charged is determined by the company, this price must be the same for all customers for products of like grade and quality. Again, the law includes not only the sales price but also all terms of sale, such as the amount that is required as a down payment and any discounts or allowances given. Most of the charges of price fixing and price discrimination are prosecuted under the Clayton Act and the Robinson-Patman Act.

Customer promotional programs are considered illegal unless such promotions are made available to all channel members and the promotion is practical for each category of customer. For example, many manufacturers selling to the grocery trade are often concerned about their cooperative advertising contracts where they share in the cost of the advertising done by the retailer on the firm's products. The problem of treating all customers equally is particularly acute since their customers are very diverse: chain grocery stores, independent supermarkets, small retail grocers, delicatessens, and wholesalers. Most advertising contracts are designed for the chain stores, giving a discount of 2–3 percent on the goods purchased, with the discount being used in advertising the manufacturer's products. Although the manufacturer might prefer advertising only in the major papers in the area, some of the retail outlets might only advertise in suburban district papers while others only pass out handbills. A manufacturer's advertising contract must provide money for carrying out each of these types of promotion.

CHAPTER PERSPECTIVE

In this chapter we have examined the factors affecting the pricing of a product. You have learned about various pricing objectives. Once you have chosen an objective, you can use one of the methods described in this chapter to determine a pricing policy based upon costs, competition, and the consumer. You have also learned various aspects of pricing in practice and how various discounts can be employed.

Physical Distribution

INTRODUCTION AND MAIN POINTS

In this chapter we expand your understanding of physical distribution—the movement or flow of the product from the firm to the consumer—which primarily involves the transportation and storage of the product. Physical distribution was not considered a critical issue in the marketing mix, but its importance has continued to grow as controlling the costs of doing business has become more and more critical to a firm's survival. These concerns become more important in times of fluctuating energy costs, raw material shortages, high interest rates, rapidly changing consumer tastes, and significant (almost hyper) competition. We will mainly focus on the two components of physical distribution—transportation and storage. We will analyze the actual functions of physical distribution by looking at four areas: the determination of location of distribution centers; the establishment of an order-processing system; the development of a customer service department; and the determination of the best mode of transportation.

After studying the material in this chapter:

■ You will be able to evaluate the alternative transportation services being considered in terms of cost, speed, and lost and damaged merchandise.

■ You will understand the importance of and cost problems of inventory.

■ You will have a better appreciation for the importance of physical distribution.

IMPORTANCE OF DISTRIBUTION

Physical distribution was at one time an overlooked part of the marketing mix. Getting the right goods to buyers at the right time and at the lowest possible cost is an important aspect of every good marketing program. It is particularly critical for selling seasonal goods.

The functions of physical distribution can be classified in four major areas:

1. Location of distribution centers; these may be company-owned centers, public warehouses, or centralized distribution centers where products are stored for longer periods.
2. Development and maintenance of an inventory control system.
3. Development and maintenance of an order-processing system and a customer service department.
4. Determination of the best transportation method.

Physical distribution involves the cost of moving goods to consumers from a variety of facilities such as factories, sub-assembly plants, company-owned warehouses, public warehouses, or trucker-owned warehouses, as well as the additional costs involved in storing and handling the inventory in each of these locations. The mode of transportation used can vary between oceangoing vessels, barge, railroad, piggyback on rail, trucks, airplanes, or combinations of these modes.

Physical distribution is directly related to customer service, the lack of which can result in several costs. First, when the warehouse is out of a product, in-store shelves will not receive the needed stock, causing initial lost sales that can be permanent if the customer switches to a competitive product. Second, there may be a lack of inventory to handle periodic demand generated by such things as customer-initiated promotion. This out of stock will result in customer irritation. Third, goods damaged in transit or while stored in the warehouse can result in non-salable merchandise or damaged merchandise that can also cause negative customer reaction.

The importance of physical distribution is due to several factors. Warehouse costs have increased significantly due to increases in labor and material costs. Transportation in a world of variable energy costs has become more expensive. Also, money for financing inventory is more costly and often difficult to obtain. A company "inventory" sheet covering most variables of physical distribution for use in your firm is indicated in Figure 14-1.

Before discussing these and other factors involved in physical distribution, its terminology needs to be clearly understood. The key terms of particular importance are of rates and routing, transport regulation, modes of transportation, and transport services.

TRANSPORTATION COSTS

Total costs by company, operating division, or major product group
- Boat
- Plane
- Rail
- Truck—common carrier
- Truck—company-operated
- Comparison of above costs to sales this year versus last year

Total plant to warehouse costs
- To individual warehouses
- Each as percent of sales, this year versus last

Total warehouse to customer costs
- By areas
- Each as percent of sales, this year versus last

Inbound freight costs
- Major material categories
- Cost per dollar of material

Penalty costs
- For partial shipments
- For other than lowest method of transportation

WAREHOUSING COSTS

Public warehouse costs
- Per square foot
- Per dollar of product handled

Company-operated warehouse costs
- Total operating cost
- Per square foot
- Per dollar of product handled

INVENTORY PERFORMANCE

Actual versus planned inventory
- By major category
- By location

Inventory versus sales
- By major item
- As a group for low-volume items

Cost of carrying inventories

QUALITY OF SERVICE COSTS

On-time order performance
- Percent of orders shipped on time

Severity of late orders
- Customer problems resulting

Comparison with competitive services offered
- Reliability
- Speed
- Timely delivery

FIG. 14-1. *Company inventory sheet on various aspects of physical distribution.*

RATES AND ROUTING

There are several unique terms used in the area of rates and routing.

Ton-Mile: A ton-mile is the movement of one ton of goods one mile. Most freight is measured in this unit.

Mixed Cars: Mixed cars are used when various commodities are shipped in a car and when one or more of the items are not in the same freight classification. The rate of the entire car is at the rate of the highest-class commodity in the car.

L.C.L.: Less than carload (L.C.L.) is an abbreviation originating with the railroads that indicates less than a full rail car and, later, truck load is being used. Because it is less than a full load, the rate per item is considerably higher than that occurring with a full rail car or truck basis.

Class Rates: The railroads have many different rates for different classes of products. The rates assigned to each class depend on the cost and value of the service, the size of the shipment, and the distance shipped.

Commodity Rates: Commodity rates usually result from negotiations on such low-value bulk items as wheat, coal, and lumber. Since these products are of substantial volume and are shipped regularly, commodity rates generally cover a broad area regardless of the specific distance, resulting in their being frequently called "blanket rates."

Exception Rates: If the originator of the freight needs certain rates in order to compete in certain markets, special lower rates can be negotiated. These are called "exception rates." These rates can also be offered by the carrier in order to compete.

Traffic-Manager-Bargained Rates: Often, rates are set by competition between carriers. A good traffic manager of a company, in addition to auditing the traffic bill to ensure that the correct freight was charged, can often negotiate between carriers and secure a lower rate. This is particularly important in light of the over 150 changes in rates that can occur in a year. Traffic managers frequently have initiated changes in the actual truck or railway car to bring about lower freight charges. For example, a chocolate plant on the East Coast had always received cocoa butter and chocolate liquor (from ground and cleaned roasted cocoa beans) in 10- or 20-pound blocks wrapped in heavy brown paper in 100-pound burlap bags. Since the company wanted to use these materials within the plant in liquid form, it encouraged a truck company to try transporting the materials in 52-gallon drums. This encouragement eventually led to the development of large jacketed tank trucks with agitators at a substantial cost savings.

TRANSPORT REGULATION

The amount and type of transport regulation centers around the type of carrier being used—private, common, or contract.

Private carriers are those owned by the manufacturer and are usually trucks. These private carriers are not controlled by law and can operate anywhere and in any manner desired by the manufacturer.

Common carriers such as railroads, major truck lines, airlines, and pipelines are sometimes given a franchise by the government with the stipulation that they must accept merchandise from anyone who wants to transport through them. Usually each of these common carriers must obtain permission to discontinue a service or change rates.

Contract carriers (usually trucks) are not required to maintain a service and are given freedom to establish their own rates. While they can carry freight for anyone for any specified period of time, the rates charged each customer must be made public.

MODES OF TRANSPORTATION

Five basic modes of transportation are available to the small firm to move the goods forward to the consumer: trucks, railroads, airlines, oceangoing vessels and vessels on inland waterways, and pipelines.

Trucks

Trucks are considered the most flexible carrier and the most suitable for moving small quantities relatively short distances. Since trucks eliminate much of the in-transit unloading and loading, they provide a fast service without the handling costs. While truck rates are usually reasonable for the service rendered, for some higher-valued commodities, truck rates are sometimes equal to or lower than rail rates.

Railroads

Railroads are generally used to move products long distances. Their rates, where water is not accessible, are almost always lower than truck rates.

Airlines

The airlines are, of course, the fastest but also the most expensive means of transportation. Air freight requires little capital, inventory, and warehouses. In some cases, transporting products by air is comparable in cost due to other factors in physical distribution, such as the need to develop and manage a warehouse or maintain a significant amount of a wide variety of inventory to ensure no out of stocks occur.

Ships and Barges
Ships are usually the least expensive carriers. Their rates are often one third of those of rail, but they are slow and tie up money in "floating" inventory. In addition, the amount of product necessary to fill a ship is considerably more than the amount necessary to fill a rail car. Oceangoing vessels are of course used extensively in international marketing.

Pipelines
Pipelines are used primarily to transport crude oil or oil products and natural gas and to move coal slurry (a liquid coal product) from mines to points of processing.

It is important to evaluate each possible type of transportation in terms of its cost, speed, absolute and percent delivery time variability, and the amount of loss or damaged products in order to make sure the product is always available at the lowest possible cost.

TRANSPORT SERVICES
There are a variety of transport services available which you should evaluate in establishing an optimal distribution system. These include freight forwarders, pool car, diversion in transit, transloading privilege, in-transit privilege, fast freight, piggyback service, fishback service, and trucker-owned, public, or company-owned warehouses.

Freight Forwarders
Freight forwarders are brokers of air, ship, rail, and truck transportation who make their living on the differences between full car—or truckload, which they obtain from the less than carload (L.C.L.) or less than truckload (L.T.L.) rate paid by each shipper. Occasionally they charge an additional small fee. Although paying the higher L.C.L. or L.T.L. rate, freight forwarders have the advantage of faster service and less handling than what occurs in full car and truckload lots. For a small firm, the freight forwarder actually becomes the firm's traffic manager, determining the best way to ship the product. For small manufacturers or retailers who are shipping numerous small quantities to many different places, freight forwarders are extremely valuable. Even in large companies, their services are often used in overseas shipments.

Pool Car

When a company ships L.C.L. with other companies, the extra handling and stops can cause considerable delay in receiving goods, in addition to the extra cost incurred. These extra costs and delays can be avoided by the company developing a full car load with one or more manufacturers (preferably in the same industry) with goods going to a specified city. This arrangement is called a "pool car." There is almost no delay if all the companies have the same type of goods going to the same distributing center. The products move at the same lower rate until the point the pool car is broken up and then at the higher L.C.L. rates. Retailers buying in quantity from a large city often use a pool car, using local truckers to deliver the products from the point of arrival.

Diversion in Transit

By paying a slightly higher fee, a rail car can actually start even before its final destination is determined, with the determination being done in transit. As long as there is no change in the forward movement of the car (no backtracking), the fee is from the point of origin to the point of destination with a small charge for the diversion privilege. Diversion in transit is often used when a large agricultural crop such as potatoes is being harvested, and salespeople are securing orders in each of several large cities as the car moves forward. The car can be diverted to wherever necessary, depending on the location at the first city sold or where the highest price is offered.

Transloading Privilege

Shippers who want their L.C.L. shipment to move quickly to its final destination after a pool car is broken up can obtain this special service—having trucks available for transloading upon arrival—at an extra fee. The railroad arranges for the trucks to be ready upon arrival at the destination.

In-Transit Privilege

In-transit privilege is used when a manufacturer processes or partially processes goods along the way from the point of origin to the final user. This is common for such commodities as wheat used for flour.

Fast Freight

When perishable products are shipped, they can be shipped on continuously moving trains in either refrigerated or nonrefrigerated cars. Fast freight is used for the movement of much of the fruits, produce, and meats in the United States.

Piggyback Service

Piggyback service is a service in which specially designed railroad flat cars are used to haul trailer trucks. The tractors then deliver the products to their final destination. Piggyback service uses less personnel and fuel costs since rail fuel costs on long hauls is less than that of trucks. This is a very common procedure in the automobile industry.

Fishback Service

In this service, barges or intercoastal canal boats are equipped to haul trailer trucks on board using tractors on either end. One Eastern Seaboard consumer product manufacturer shipped goods from Port Newark, New Jersey, to the entire Gulf Coast by this method, including such cities as New Orleans, Houston, and Dallas/Fort Worth. This procedure is frequently used in times of high fuel costs.

Warehouses

In most large cities, there is usually more than one trucker-owned warehouse. As the name implies, each of these warehouses is owned by a trucking company that usually specializes in local delivery within the metropolitan area. For many companies, these can be used to develop the most economical method of delivery—a combined trucking and warehousing service. The company can transport in either carload or truckload lots directly to the trucking company's warehouse, where the trucker's fleet of trucks distribute to local customers. This provides the company with cheaper rates for local delivery. Often, these warehouses can furnish full services such as billing and collection as well.

Public warehouses are warehouses providing almost any kind of space (refrigerated or nonrefrigerated) or service needed by the manufacturer. Warehouse receipts can be obtained from public warehouses and used for financing inventories.

Many companies prefer to own their own warehouses. These warehouses are operated by the firm's personnel.

MANAGERIAL PRACTICES IN PHYSICAL DISTRIBUTION

There are several practices in physical distribution which you should understand in order to develop the best physical distribution system for your firm.

Directing and Billing Orders

When the manufacturer's plant is located a long distance from the warehouse, some manufacturers have orders processed directly at the warehouse for shipment instead of at the home office first. These orders are then wired to the home office for billing, saving the time lost when the order goes first to the home office. While some companies prefer to have orders sent, shipped, and billed from the warehouse, other companies prefer to never lose contact with an order and have orders sent to the home office.

Company-Owned Warehouses and Transportation Facilities

Many companies prefer to own their own warehouses in order to have greater control in processing and billing orders locally as well as to maintain proper rotation and quality of their inventories. Other companies own their own freight carriers. However, you should consider three things before having your firm get involved in the warehousing or transportation field.

First, you should consider the management abilities of your firm in operating a warehouse and transportation system. Just because your firm is good at manufacturing does not mean that it is good at physical distribution—particularly warehousing and transportation. Frequently, these specialized areas are more cost-effectively handled outside the firm, particularly if the firm is small and growing. Second, the firm needs to have the funds available to invest in the needed personnel, warehouse facilities, and transportation vehicles.

Finally, the firm needs to feel that by building a carrier system or a warehouse especially adapted to the company's needs, considerable savings will result. Additionally, an analysis should determine whether there is a similar facility already available. Often when each of these items is carefully evaluated, a firm finds out that there is no reason to enter the warehousing or trucking business. Frequently, warehousing and transportation tie up so much capital and decrease a company's money turnover with such little additional profit that the return on the investment is not equal to what the company is making in other areas.

Establishing a Target Level of Customer Service

In terms of customer service, the major factors that are affected by physical distribution are (1) the length of time from the placement of an order to the delivery date; (2) the percent of "out-of-stock" orders; (3) the quantities of merchandise stocked to cover special promotions or emergency needs of the customer; (4) the availability of parts and/or installation services of the manufacturer; (5) the condition and care with which merchandise is delivered to the customer; and (6) the manufacturer's willingness and promptness in replacing defective merchandise.

Each of these factors should be evaluated to determine the cost of imperfect customer service. This figure can then be used to evaluate the many issues involved in speed and size of inventories.

F.O.B.
F.O.B. (Freight on Board) shipping point means the customer pays the freight costs in addition to the costs of goods. F.O.B. destination means the company will include the average freight cost per point for all customers in the invoice of the cost of goods. Here, customers pay the cost of the freight without knowing the exact amount being charged for transportation and the exact amount being charged for the product itself. Most retailers prefer this latter arrangement.

Inventory Control
While accurate forecasting is the key to managing a business efficiently and controlling all the marketing factors, it is also certainly the key to maintaining a minimum level of inventory and the established target level of customer service. There is probably no other factor more important for minimizing costs in physical distribution than accurate forecasting. Accurate forecasting can avoid excess rental of warehouse space as well as unnecessary inventory. A decrease in both factors helps increase money turnover.

While too much inventory can result in significantly higher holding costs, too little inventory can result in lost sales. Some factors that need to be considered in developing an inventory model include the repetitiveness of the inventory decision (are most orders being processed on time or are they repeat orders); whether the source of supply is inside or outside the company; the amount of knowledge available about future demand (variable or constant); knowledge of the amount of lead time needed (variable or constant); and the type of inventory system in use (perpetual or periodic).

Economic Order Quantity
The economic order quantity (E.O.Q.) system of controlling inventory is widely used. E.O.Q. operates on a formula basis:

$$E.O.Q. = \sqrt{\frac{2ab}{i}}$$

Where:

a = order cost per order
b = total units sold per year
i = the interest charge per unit per year

The E.O.Q. provides an indication of the inventory needed for average stock requirements, meaning that the warehouse will be out of inventory half the time. If this is not desirable, then more inventory—a safety stock—will need to be carried. The E.O.Q. formula is based on an average and takes into account seasonal demands or inventory needs resulting from company promotions.

Total Cost Concept

Some large multiple-product organizations such as Procter and Gamble and General Motors consider physical distribution a separate important area of the company headed by a senior manager who is as important as the head of manufacturing or brands. This reflects the fact that, all too often in an organization, no one seems to be responsible for physical distribution. A sales department may want to have excessive inventories to ensure no out of stocks ever exist; the financial department might like to decrease the cost of warehouse space and the dollars tied up in inventory even though out of stocks might periodically occur.

Generally, transportation costs and order processing costs should be parallel and allocated to most products on a unit basis. Similarly, inventory financing costs and warehouse space costs should parallel each other by being allocated on a unit basis. The smaller the shipment, the greater the cost per pound; the larger the shipment, the greater the cost of financing inventories and warehouse space per pound. In fact, sometimes airlines can be used to deliver frequent small shipments due to the lower inventory financing and warehousing space costs incurred with trucks.

MANAGERIAL TOOLS

Managerial tools, techniques, and systems have positively impacted every aspect of physical distribution management, particularly in the areas of order processing, transportation, warehousing, and inventory. Marketing managers are trying to shorten the time it takes from receipt of the order to delivery of the order to payment for the order (the order-to-remittance cycle). The longer this cycle takes, the lower the customer's satisfaction and the lower the company's profits. The cycle can be shortened by creating an information and goods flow system in which customer requirements and demand determine the mechanics and momentum of order fulfillment. This requires obtaining quality information relating to customer demand, which requires cooperation in the supply chain to openly share information, and a company information system, which reprioritizes information toward customer demand. To succeed in the marketplace today, marketing managers need to develop deep and detailed customer profiles, handle customer orders expediently, and provide a flexible replenishment system that matches customer consumption and expectations. There is probably no market where this is more essential than the hypercompetitive international passenger airline business. In response to market conditions and pressures, British Airways developed a system for centralizing the order fulfillment process for its entire fleet of aircraft. By overhauling the entire airlines catering supply software system, British Airways has integrated and streamlined the supply of several hundred million items each year to its flights, helping the airline increase its control of supplier relations and product quality, which increases the level of customer satisfaction.

A strong customer-oriented information system allows marketing managers to make better transportation decisions by being able to make the best trade-off between the various transportation modes available and the impact on the other physical distribution elements—warehousing and inventory. This requires the development of the optimal market-logistics system for customer satisfaction.

Finally, marketing managers need a good system and tools to optimize warehousing and inventory decisions. Decisions regarding the level of inventory needed and where to store this inventory significantly impact customer satisfaction and company profits. Costs of inventory and warehousing increase at an increasing rate as the level of customer satisfaction approaches 100 percent. One company, Dade Bearing Inc., a manufacturer and supplier of world-renowned medical equipment, developed a flexible, highly customized inventory and warehouse management system that improved inventory accuracy and productivity by automatically processing orders when received; storing high-activity products in the most accessible areas; directing the order fulfillment process, logically eliminating backtracking; and driving the entire process through RF terminals, bar code label data, and electronic data exchange between systems. The new system allows the warehouse to ship and track over 500 orders and 1,400 line items each day with an inventory accuracy of over 99 percent and a shipping error rate of less than .05 percent. The new system, which cost $250,000, provided a return on investment within nine months.

CHAPTER PERSPECTIVE

Physical distribution is the movement or flow of the product from the firm to the consumer. This usually occurs through a network of channel members. Physical distribution can be effectively divided into two basic components: transportation and storage. Storage can be best managed by further division into warehousing and inventory. Both storage and transportation have two elements—demand and cost. Although a major emphasis has been placed on the cost element, you must also keep in mind the demand aspect of distribution, since no sale can be completed unless the product is physically available.

Channels of Distribution: The Retail System

INTRODUCTION AND MAIN POINTS

In this chapter we will expand your understanding of retailing—that is, any transaction made by a seller with a final consumer. It also includes all direct sales to the consumer from the producer, whether through the producer's own stores, door-to-door calls, or direct mail, as well as the more traditional retail store establishments. We will focus on the numerous types of retail store establishments, from single-line stores to superstores, that sell virtually everything. Methods of operations vary from an extensive use of computerized systems such as automotive inventory and ordering systems to a simple cash drawer. It is important for you to understand that the retailer can enhance retail profits through innovation. You should keep in mind that new products, new methods of distribution, new types of competitors, and new sales approaches can make existing marketing relationships untenable, altering existing patterns of competition and cost-price relationships. A continuous stream of new items has significantly shortened the retailing life cycle.

After studying the material in this chapter:

▬ You will understand the basics of retailing and its role in the distribution system.

▬ You will be able to distinguish and choose among the various types of retail establishments available.

▬ You will understand the role of nonstore retailing.

▬ You will be able to establish a channel-of-distribution system.

OVERVIEW OF RETAILING

Definition

In general, retailing involves any transaction made by a seller with a final consumer. The Standard Industrial Classification defines retail establishments as those engaged in selling merchandise for personal or household consumption and rendering services incidental to the sale of goods. Retailing thus includes all direct sales to the consumer from the producer, whether through the producer's own stores, independent stores, vending machines, door-to-door calls, or direct mail. Establishments, on the other hand, that sell exclusively to business establishments, institutional and industrial users, or contractors are viewed as wholesale establishments.

The national income originating in retailing and wholesaling as well as services has increased over the years (see Figure 15-1). As indicated, retail sales has had more growth than its wholesale counterpart.

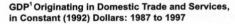

Domestic Trade and Services

GDP[1] Originating in Domestic Trade and Services, in Constant (1992) Dollars: 1987 to 1997

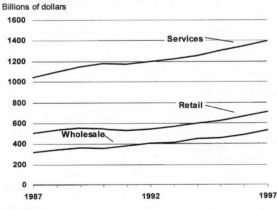

[1]Gross National Product

FIG. 15-1. *National income originating by domestic trade and services.*

Source: U.S. Bureau of Economic Analysis, *Industry and Wealth Data.* http://www.bea.doc.gov/bea/dn2/gpox.htm.

Types of Retailing

Retailing also has more variability within its parameters than almost any other category of business or industrial activity. The number of employees may vary from 1, in the case of a sole-proprietor store, to more than 324,000 employed by Sears Roebuck and 910,000 employed by Wal-Mart . The number of items in the store may vary from 1 to 8,000 grocery store items or 10,000 department store items. The variety of items may be either single line, limited line, or broad line. Retail sales are largest for food stores, followed by automotive dealers, general merchandise, gasoline stations, and eating and drinking establishments (see Figure 15-2). The demographic aspects of retailing vary from a general store carrying almost every conceivable item in the country with no other stores nearby to a specialty store carrying only men's ties in a metropolitan center in a mall along with numerous other store types.

Methods of retail operations vary from a wide use of computerized systems to nothing more than a cigar box used to collect the cash. The amount of the markup (price charged consumer less cost of merchandise) varies from the chain grocery stores with an average of 17 percent to vending machines with an average of 55 percent.

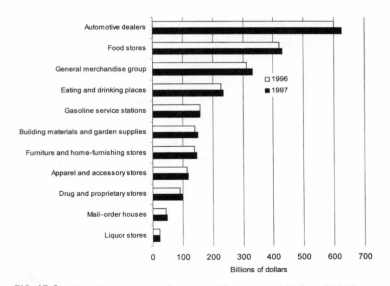

FIG. 15-2. *Retail store sales by type of business: 1996 and 1997.*
Source: Bureau of the Census, U.S. Department of Commerce, *Statistical Abstract of the United States,* 1998.

Methods of selling vary from door-to-door sales calls to a "superstore," which sells everything from lumber to eggs without divisions in the store. The volume of these stores can be so great that the merchandise is handled by forklift trucks stacking merchandise for display in wide aisles.

Common Problems in Retailing

In spite of the variations that exist within retailing, there are five types of problems each retailer encounters to some degree:

1. Shoplifting (pilferage). Petty theft may not seem like a serious crime to the person who pockets a ball point pen, but to the small business trying to survive it can be a significant problem. Retail theft loss estimates vary depending on the type of store and management efficiency. It can range from 1.3 percent of sales for a well-managed department store to 7 percent for a loosely controlled operation. Dishonest employees account for about one half of the retail theft.

2. Risk. While every business has some risks, there is the basic risk in retailing of not being able to sell the inventory profitably, as well as the risk that the capital investment in fixtures or buildings may depreciate, particularly if the area deteriorates.

3. Low productivity. The nature of retailing does not easily lend itself to significant human or machine efficiencies as does manufacturing.

4. Stock turnover problems. Since a large investment is committed to inventory due to the rather low profit-to-sales ratio, turnover of inventory is necessary for success.

5. Perishable and damaged merchandise. Vegetables, meats, dairy and frozen products, and confectionery items are subject to a certain amount of spoilage. In addition, canned goods, eggs, and other items may be damaged in handling.

Creating Specialty Differentiation

Some elements of developing creative ideas in order to obtain uniqueness in retailing are indicated in Table 15-1 along with past successes and the use of the particular elements in the retailing mix. For example, McDonald's overwhelming success in marketing fast food, primarily hamburgers, was achieved through an emphasis on:

3b. Merchandising quality products.

2a. Training employees to give consistently fast, polite, friendly service.

3e. Orderly and clean premises with prescribed procedures for mopping floors at regular intervals and regular cleanup of the parking lot.

2b. Codes of discipline for personal appearance of employees such as uniforms and caps.

4a. Locations near main arteries and population centers.

Other elements such as advertising, promotion, and product development contributed to the success of McDonald's.

Table 15-1a
Elements from Which Unique Products or Services are Molded

Search for uniqueness through:

1. Business policies
   a. More convenient hours
   b. Extending credit
   c. Accepting credit cards
   d. Cashing checks
   e. Giving warranties
   f. Accepting returned goods willingly
2. Store personnel
   a. Training employees in skills and attitudes in order to provide consistently fast, polite, friendly service
   b. Codes of discipline for personal appearance of employees
   c. Selection of personnel to match customers' desires
3. The image portrayed
   a. Furnishings and fixtures
   b. Merchandising prestigious quality products
   c. Quality of stores nearby
   d. Engaging in community activities
   e. Orderly and clean premises
4. Stores' geographic location
   a. Near main arteries and population centers
   b. Not congested area
   c. Parking lots available
   d. Within walking distance
   e. Near other shops
5. Price
   a. An outstanding purchasing department
   b. By operating efficiencies through use of quality personnel and machines

Table 15-1b
Examples of Success Built on Uniqueness

Merchandising		
Merchandising Processor	*Wholesaling*	*Retailing*
McDonald's Hamburgers, Salads, and Breakfast	Monette Military Sales, all Products in line	Sears, Inc. Ted Williams line

Elements Stressed in Obtaining Uniqueness
(Indicated below by reference to number
and letter in Table 15-1a)

2a	2a	1c
2b	3b	1e
3b		1f
3e		2b
4a		4a
		4b
		4c
		4e
		5a
		5b

The Retailing Life Cycle

One way of increasing retail profits is through understanding the retailing life cycle indicated in Figure 15-3. While in 1860 it took department stores a century to move from the early growth stage to the maturity stage, catalog showrooms in the late 1960s took only 10 years to move through these same stages. This market acceleration will continue to shorten the differential advantage of each new innovation. If this pattern continues, innovations in retailing, such as the supermarkets of the 1930s or the hypermarkets of the 1970s, will have an early growth followed by an accelerated development of profit and sales moving quickly through the various stages of the retail life cycle. The advent and movement of the Home Shopping Network exemplifies this extremely fast retailing cycle.

You can often increase profits in retailing by adjusting the retailing mix according to the store's stage in its life cycle. In the retail growth and accelerated development stages, for example, a strong store image can be established by advertising and promoting the different elements in the store's retailing mix making it unique.

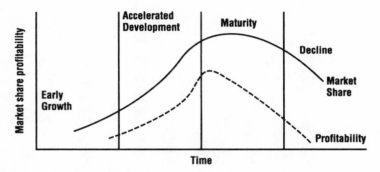

FIG. 15-3. *The life cycle in retailing.*

RETAIL STORE CLASSIFICATION

In order to understand the wide variety of retail establishments, two major classification systems are useful: type of products and type of ownership. There are a variety of different retail classifications possible when considering the types of products carried: durable-goods stores, nondurable-goods stores, food stores, dealers, general merchandise stores, discount stores, department stores, and service stations. The percent retail sales by type of product is indicated in Figure 15-4 (see page 218). As is indicated, automotive, food, and general merchandise have the largest percent of sales. Less variety occurs when looking at retail stores by type of ownership: individual proprietorships, small chains (two to ten stores), medium and large chains (eleven establishments or more), and company-owned stores.

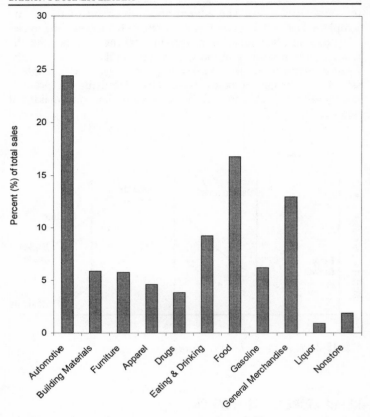

FIG. 15-4. *Percent retail sales of different merchandise lines.*
Source: Bureau of the Census, U.S. Department of Commerce, *Statistical Abstract of the United States,* 1998.

From Small Independent Stores to Giant Chains

The dominant era of the independent store was prior to 1920, when chain stores first began to appear. In this independent era, still operational in many international economies, consumers shopped at various stores—the butcher shop, the bakery, the grocery, and the hardware store—to complete each day's shopping needs. Also, shopping had to be done more frequently in order to avoid spoilage. In the 1920s, changes in lifestyles, improved standards of living, and a better transportation infrastructure established an environment advantageous to the chain store. Of course, modern chains did not appear suddenly but, instead, their growth went through several stages. First, there was an accumulation of several store outlets under one enterprise. Then, the concept of cash and carry occurred, providing better value for the consumer. Then, self-service in retailing started, which decreased costs even more. Costs were further decreased by an increase in national brand names accompanied by advertising and promotion and the resultant increase in sales volume. This eventually led to the closing of smaller units and the opening of larger ones having more parking and display space—the advent of the supermarket. These supermarkets soon took the form of the chain of supermarkets present today. The concept of chain stores spread from the grocery field to other fields such as hardware, drugs, variety store items, and discount merchandise. Now there are chain general merchandise discount stores such as Sam's Wholesale Outlets that require a membership card for purchasing.

The Independent Grocer

The advent of chains forced changes in the independent grocers' method of operation. The independents responded by forming cooperatives that obtained the efficiencies of volume buying while still providing friendly, personal service. These organizations, or what are often referred to as buying cooperatives or, in some cases, wholesale/retail franchises, include True Value (hardware) and IGA (groceries).

The Convenience Store

A convenience store (C-store) typically has a building of 1,000 to 3,200 square feet with parking for five to fifteen automobiles; extended hours beyond those of other stores in the area; self-service with the purpose of offering the customer complete convenience in shopping; a balanced inventory of daily needs such as dairy products, baked goods, beverages, tobacco, frozen foods, deli items, grocery items, nonfoods, and gasoline. Increases in disposable income, an increasing number of women in the workforce, and dual-career families have significantly increased the growth in convenience stores. Typically, the profit before taxes for convenience stores averages twice that of supermarkets, reflecting the 20 percent margin of convenience stores versus the supermarkets' 17 percent. The main advantage these stores offer is convenience in time and place. Because of their small size, they are in many locations that are neither available nor desirable for supermarkets. 7-Eleven and Quik-Trip are two examples of successful C-stores.

Franchising

Franchising has become an increasingly prevalent form of retail operation. A franchise agreement is a right to do or use something granted to a franchisee by a franchiser. The item can be an intangible such as a trademark or a business technique or the tangible product of the franchiser. Generally the agreement restricts the use of the franchised item or process to a specified geographical area or to one category of business, guaranteeing the franchisee that no other franchisees will be given a franchise in the same area. Franchise agreements that restrict the franchisee to a geographical area are McDonald's, Burger King, Thrifty Car Rental, and U-Haul. The franchiser usually requires the franchisee to purchase certain materials or equipment from the franchiser. The franchiser establishes standards which if not met would result in the withdrawal of the franchise. Franchising should continue to grow in importance in the changing environment of the future.

There are many advantages in franchising. The franchisees can get into business with less capital and less risk and make a profit in far less time than if they initiated the business themselves. Promotional and management help are usually provided along with assistance in selecting a site. In turn, the franchiser obtains a motivated partner, one who has far more at stake than someone without the investment commitment. This enables the franchiser to grow more quickly than would be possible using only its own capital. The franchising system is of course not without its problems, such as supply and service restrictions in the franchise agreement and "capricious termination" terms allowing franchisers to terminate a franchise for an insufficient reason.

Discount Stores

Although discount stores exist in many different forms and types, most have such characteristics as a percentage of store space occupied by leased departments; high volume; limited assortment; fast inventory turnover; limited customer service; usually a suburban location; and extended store hours.

The average markup (the difference between selling price and price of goods to the store divided by the selling price) for discount stores is usually about 25 percent. By encouraging fast turnover of inventory and money as well as limiting invested capital through leasing and long payment terms to suppliers of merchandise (usually 60–90 days), a good return on investment can be achieved. Discount stores spread rapidly from 1950 to 1970. Because of their limited lines and efficiency in operation, these stores significantly impacted the sales of department stores. Discount stores achieved in sales in 15 years what the department stores took 100 years to build, with sales of the two being equal by 1965.

Department Stores

A department store serves a wide target market with the principal products being home furnishings, appliances, yard goods, and apparel for men, women, and children. Usually department stores are characterized by good personal attention. The average markup of a department store is about 42 percent. Department stores can be placed on a continuum—those catering to a more upscale customer (Neiman-Marcus and Bloomingdale's) and those catering mainly to middle-income groups (Filenes and Shillitoes). To continue to be effective in light of the intense competition between department stores themselves as well as from discount and specialty stores, department stores must be innovative in their merchandise and merchandising techniques while developing effective cost-control measures.

Superstores

Unlike the chain, the supermarket, and the discount store, all of which were American innovations, the "hypermarche" (Hypermarket) or superstore originated in France. A hypermarket generally has a complete food and nonfood selection and a broad mix of services obtained through self-service in most departments. There is usually a minimum of 2,500 square meters of selling space, with parking space being four to six times larger. A hypermarket can be the largest tenant in a small shopping center.

Shopping Mall

Shopping malls developed to meet the consumer needs not being met by the available central city shopping. A shopping mall generally has the following characteristics: single ownership under one roof; sometimes built underground in congested areas forming a small enclosed underground "city"; many different stores; and a wide range of products offered.

NONSTORE RETAILING

There are several forms of nonstore retailing which continue to have an increasing share of the total retail sales.

Truck Jobber Operations

Truck jobbers are nonstore retailers that pick up merchandise from the wholesaler (or the factory if nearby), pay for it, and deliver it to either the small retailer or the consumer. Due to the high operational costs and the increasing use of the automobile, the number of truck jobbers has significantly decreased.

Vending Machines

Vending machines occur in a variety of places such as schools, retail establishments, hospitals, and plane, rail and bus stations. A vending machine operation usually needs about a 55 percent markup and dispenses a slightly smaller product, allowing this markup to be obtained. Vending machine sales have been steadily increasing and should continue to do so in the future with more and more products being offered.

Door-to-Door Selling

This nonstore retail method was first popularized by Fuller Brush but has since been widely employed by Avon, Tupperware, and Amway. Door-to-door selling continues to expand rapidly and will be even more prominent in the future with a wider variety of products being offered.

Catalog Stores and Mail-Order Sales

In a catalog store operation, the catalog is sent to consumers who select the items and pick up the merchandise at the warehouse or store. In some cases, such as Sears, an order is mailed in after the selection and the merchandise is mailed or shipped back to the store for pickup if the item is not in stock. Some catalog stores include showrooms where customers select merchandise directly from the catalog or from store merchandise. In many cases the merchandise can be taken without waiting. This latter operation so closely resembles a retail store operation that it actually should not be categorized under nonstore retailing.

KEY FACTORS IN DECIDING ON YOUR MARKETING CHANNEL

Why does Goodyear use multiple marketing channels to sell tires? Why does Tupperware sell through home parties and demonstrations? Why does Burger King use franchising? The answers to these questions are important in order for you to understand the role of the retailer in establishing your channel of distribution. Certain critical factors need to be taken into account in making this decision. These are particularly important in regard to consumer products for the grocery or discount store, as there is limited shelf space, a situation which makes it very difficult for the single-line small firm to achieve retail distribution.

Company Characteristics

Being aware of the strengths and weaknesses and goals and objectives of the company is important in deciding on a channel of distribution strategy and the retail stores that should be involved. For example, a small firm with limited financial resources may need to use only a few retailers who pay more promptly in order to have enough money to finance the needed inventory.

Market Characteristics

The frequency of purchase, use of the product, service required, and the profit margin all affect the distribution strategy and retail store decision. Perhaps the most important factor of these is the replacement rate—the rate at which the product is purchased and consumed. For example, bread has a high replacement rate. The higher the replacement rate (the more frequently the product is purchased) the more indirect routes of distribution are required. In other words, product exposure and availability in many retail stores will positively impact sales for high replacement items.

Product Characteristics

The replacement rate is tied to the characteristics of the product also. A particularly important product characteristic in addition to its overall price, value, bulk, and perishability is the patronage motives involved in its purchase. In other words, how much evaluation and comparison shopping does the consumer do before purchasing? The more the comparison-shopping gains, such as occurs in shopping goods (clothing, furniture, and appliances) and specialty goods (tennis rackets, stereo systems, and cameras), the more important the retail store becomes. In fact the retail store influences the purchase decision in some instances more than the product itself.

ELECTRONIC COMMERCE

One of the events that will continue to affect firms radically in the new millennium is electronic commerce, which is buying and selling of information, services, and/or products via the computer and computer networks that make up the information superhighway. The marketing, promotion, buying, and selling of goods and services electronically, particularly via the Internet, is experiencing unprecedented growth. It appears that there were 1.3 billion online shopping visits during the 1999 holiday season, up 71 percent from 1998, but only 11 percent of the shoppers actually bought online. Over $9 billion sales of consumer goods and over $90 billion sales of industrial products took place in 1999, which increased in the next year to $10 billion and $171 billion, respectively, for each of the categories. In the year 2000, over 1 billion people will be connected to the Internet, over 1.5 billion people will use the World Wide Web, and over 1.5 million companies will have home pages.

A growing number of small businesses are tapping into the Internet to conduct business and to reach new prospective customers. Even though online sales are booming, such electronic commerce is a small part of the use of the Internet. Small businesses are more likely to be online to identify customers and promote products and services before the point of sale. Access to the Internet includes telephone networks, computer bulletin boards, commercial online services, satellite and broadcast television, cable networks, cellular networks, and established corporate proprietary and open networks.

The two catalysts that transformed the Internet into a system of universal usage were the Web (WWW) and the browser software that provides a low-cost, user-friendly interface to the Web. To successfully market on the Web, two things are essential: a good web site and a mechanism to easily lead web users to the site rather than to the site of a competitor. Although web site design is both an art and a science that requires significant expertise, a successful business web site has several characteristics. First, for a business to go online successfully, there must be a good business reason and a sound business strategy. A firm needs to recognize that the site may lose money or not even generate any direct income; however, it is good public relations, useful in generating interest in the rest of the business. Second, a business should do a thorough market analysis, making sure that their customers or potential customers like to use computers and enjoy surfing the Web. Third, a firm needs a very appealing, professional web page design that is user-friendly. Finally, successful marketing via the Web requires the firm to have a secure method to conduct any commercial transactions. This means establishing a secure server that will encrypt the customers' personal and credit card information. This security is absolutely essential; the biggest reason cited for not using the Internet is the lack of data and message security.

The second element is having the web site listed where people are searching. It is necessary to make the company's site more findable and actively market this site to customers and potential customers. Two strategies that need to be employed are optimizing the search engine and partnering with other sites. Search engine optimization involves coding the site so that it rises to the top of the list of search results. This is a difficult task because not only does every search engine have different criteria for what makes a good search result, but most search engines also frequently change their algorithms so that a company's site will come up one week and not surface the next. A company needs to register its site with key search engines and then carefully monitor the results making any changes necessary.

Initiating a partnering (a reciprocal-linking) relationship is also key and can be as simple as sending an e-mail to the selected sites and, where appropriate, swapping links to signing affiliate agreements. Affiliate programs generally involve tracking programs and are much more extensive than reciprocal-linking agreements in both the technology used and the depth of the relationship.

Given the extremely rapid growth of e-commerce, which will continue in the next decade, it is essential that your firm develop a strategy and have at least a presence on the Internet. Every marketing manager should be prepared to put forth the necessary time, effort, and money to overcome the barriers in successfully doing business on the Internet and the World Wide Web.

TYPES OF DISTRIBUTION

Regardless of the type of retail store, a manufacturer must carefully evaluate the overall nature of the distribution channel system in terms of the product exposure achieved. Basically, there are three types of distribution: intensive distribution, selective distribution, and exclusive distribution.

Intensive Distribution

Intensive distribution involves merchandising and selling the product through every suitable retailer that will handle the product. While this method maximizes product exposure and coverage, thereby enabling the consumer to conveniently purchase the item, it gives the smallest amount of control to the manufacturer since every possible retailer is carrying the product.

Selective Distribution

As the name implies, selective distribution involves selecting only retailers who will provide a certain image or who will sell only certain merchandise. By establishing selection criteria, a manufacturer can avoid selling to stores that are poor credit risks, make too many returns, request too much service, place orders too small to be cost-effective, or do not do a good job marketing the company's product. Unless it is clearly evident that the situation warrants a different distribution policy, selective distribution usually produces better results than intensive or exclusive distribution.

Exclusive Distribution

On the other end of the continuum is exclusive distribution, where a retailer is granted exclusive rights to distribute the product in a defined geographic area. The retailer will in turn provide the services stipulated in handling the company's product line. The exact conditions of the contract depend to a large extent on the marketability of the company's line and the eagerness of channel members to be the exclusive dealer. Sometimes channel members are so anxious to be the sole source of the product in a geographic area that they will agree to almost any condition. The channel member can actually become a part of the manufacturer's organization by supplying capital and local management under the guidelines of the marketing plans and policies established by the company.

Exclusive distribution is generally more suited for some shopping goods, more expensive specialty goods, and such industrial products as raw materials, installations, and large accessory equipment. In each of these cases, the market volume does not warrant more intensive distribution efforts, allowing better sales results to be achieved through having one channel member aggressively market the item in the defined geographic area. In addition to market volume, an exclusive distribution system can be advantageous when there is a need to carry larger inventories of the final product or parts of it; to service the product; or to establish a solid product image.

SUPPLY CHAIN MANAGEMENT

One of the marketing tasks that is receiving significant attention is supply chain management, which is due in part to the increasing pressures to maximize sales and profits, the hypercompetition occurring, the increasing level of customer sophistication, and the high level of sophistication of information technology. To cope with these changes, marketing managers need to use a supply chain design framework such as the one depicted in Figure 15-5.

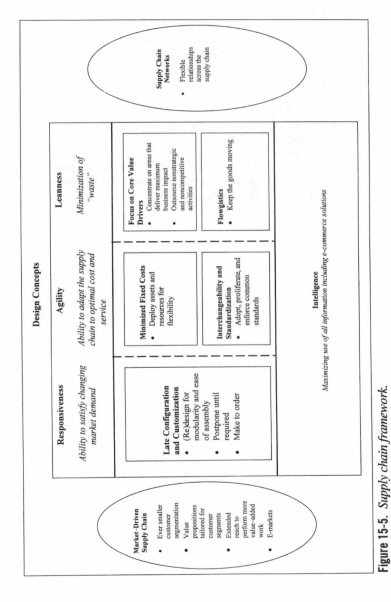

Figure 15-5. *Supply chain framework.*

Source: Dr. Hans-Christian Pfohl, *Insight to Impact* (Brussels: A.T. Kearney/ELA European Logistics Association), 1999, p. 33.

At the center of this supply chain design are responsiveness, agility, leanness, and intelligence that relate to the design concept. A design concept is needed because of imperatives for change: market driven supply chain (focusing the supply chain on ever smaller customers and offering increased value-added services) and supply chain networks (developing flexible relationships with other supply chains).

CHAPTER PERSPECTIVE

Retailing is constantly changing and continues to play a very important role in getting the products from the firm to the consumer. Even though it is just one of the various channel options available, the retail distribution system is indeed an important element in the firm's marketing activities and has its own retailing mix and retailing life cycle.

Channels of Distribution: The Wholesale System

INTRODUCTION AND MAIN POINTS

In this chapter we will expand your understanding of wholesaling, a process that generally involves the activities of selling products (and/or services) to others who intend to resell them as is or as a part of another product. Wholesalers can be grouped into several principal categories: merchant wholesalers who take title of the goods they sell; sales offices maintained by manufacturing or mining enterprises as separate entities apart from other operations for marketing their products; and merchant agents and brokers as well as commission merchants who do not take title to the goods.

You will learn that one of the most important factors distinguishing wholesale operations is whether title to the goods is taken by the wholesalers. Wholesaler-controlled voluntaries, rack jobbers, wagon jobbers, cash-and-carry wholesalers, and drop shippers all take title of the goods they handle. Manufacturers' representatives and selling agents do not.

After studying the material in this chapter:
- You will understand various aspects of using merchant wholesalers, manufacturers' representatives, and sales offices.
- You will be able to explain the characteristics of each of the wholesale alternatives.
- You will understand the trends occurring in wholesaling.

OVERVIEW OF WHOLESALING

While wholesaling is an important component in many channels of distribution, it is probably one of the least understood aspects of marketing. This is due in part to the trade's loose usage of the term, which implies to customers that low wholesale prices are offered. Wholesale trade includes establishments or places of business primarily engaged in selling merchandise to retailers, to industrial, commercial, institutional, or professional business users, or to other wholesalers. Any sale made to anyone except the final consumer constitutes a wholesaling transaction. Wholesalers vary greatly in terms of size, product lines carried, and services offered. For example, information on sales of merchant wholesalers by product type is indicated in Figure 16-1.

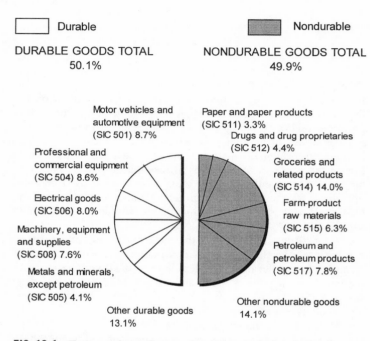

FIG. 16-1. *Estimated purchases of merchant wholesalers.*

Source: *Current Business Reports, BW/97 Annual Benchmark Report for Wholesale Trade,* U.S. Department of Commerce. http://www.census. gov/prod/1/bus/whsle/bw_month.html.

THE NEED FOR WHOLESALERS

Do intermediaries, particularly wholesalers, cause higher product prices? Can they be eliminated? These questions address the added costs indicated in the chain of markup phenomena (see Chapter 13). While in some cases it may be possible to eliminate middlemen, particularly wholesalers, their cost needs to be evaluated in terms of the functions performed.

Just what marketing functions do the wholesalers perform? The answer depends on the type of wholesaler. Small full-service wholesalers perform almost all the following functions, while other limited-service wholesalers perform very few. Wholesale functions can include:

- Maintaining inventory
- Reducing the number of transactions needed for exchange
- Breaking the goods down into the size needed
- Transporting goods to the retail outlets
- Providing market information
- Providing financing for retail outlets by granting credit
- Providing capital
- Providing a sales force to call on retail outlets
- Communicating the manufacturer's promotions to retail outlets

MERCHANT WHOLESALERS
Merchant wholesale establishments are independent businesses holding ownership of the goods they market and are primarily engaged in buying and selling merchandise on their own. They include: wholesale merchants or jobbers, industrial distributors, voluntary group wholesalers, exporters, importers, cash-and-carry wholesalers, wagon distributors, retailer cooperative warehouses, terminal and country grain elevators, farm-product assemblers, wholesale cooperative associations, and petroleum bulk plants and terminals operated by nonrefining companies.

Wholesale Merchants and Distributors
These establishments are primarily engaged in buying and selling merchandise in the domestic market and performing the principal wholesale functions. Included in this category are wholesalers primarily engaged in the purchasing, assembling, and marketing of wholesale farm products.

Import-Export Wholesalers
Import wholesalers principally buy and sell foreign goods at wholesale on their own account in the United States. Export wholesalers are primarily involved in purchasing goods in the United States and selling them in foreign countries.

Grain Elevators
Grain elevators consist generally of two types: terminal and counting. Terminal grain elevators are mainly engaged in buying

and selling grain received from country grain elevators and grain-marketing establishments usually by rail or barge rather than by truck. Counting grain elevators, cooperative or otherwise, buy and receive grain directly from farmers by truck and sell at wholesale.

Wholesaler-Controlled Voluntary

The jobber or wholesaler-controlled voluntary is composed of a group of large-volume, independently owned stores, each buying the majority of their merchandise from this common wholesaler who has organized the group. The stores involved agree to assume a common name such as IGA (Independent Grocers Association) or True-Value and to purchase most if not all their merchandise from the wholesaler. The merchandise is offered by the wholesaler at a lower markup than normal. In addition, the wholesaler advertises the common name (i.e., True-Value).

Wholly Owned Cooperative

A wholly owned cooperative is a group of large-volume retail stores who establish a warehouse facility, hire a manager or buyer, and stock specified items, with each store sharing the costs and profit in proportion to the size of withdrawals from the warehouse. In addition, the stores agree on a common name for all the stores and proceed to advertise products under that common name.

Both the wholesaler-controlled voluntary and the wholly owned cooperative make it possible for the independent retailer to compete with chain stores. Due to the intense competition, independent retailers will continue to be forced out of business unless they belong to a wholesale group such as these or else are large enough to buy direct from manufacturers at the same low prices of the chain stores or wholly owned cooperatives.

Repacker

Repackers are wholesalers that buy goods in bulk from the manufacturer, package these goods under their own brand name, then sell and deliver these at the retail level. The repackers often compete with the manufacturer of the products, who could take the time and effort and realize even more cost savings in packing due to the larger volume and less handling. Indeed, there are fewer repackers today and they should continue to decrease in the present rapidly changing environment.

Rack Jobber

The rack jobber is a wholesaler that displays merchandise in racks in the retail store. There are two types of rack jobbers: one that has its own retail racks for display of the merchandise of a company or one that handles manufacturer's brands by merchandising and servicing their products on racks at the retail level. Rack jobbers either sell goods to the retailer and service the rack or rent space for the rack from the retailer, usually on a percentage-of-sales basis. In both instances, the rack jobber is responsible for the products in the racks which almost constitute a separate retail business within the store. A wide variety of products are rack jobbed: records, toys in the supermarket, snack food, and milk.

Concessionaire

A concessionaire is basically a rack jobber who either rents the concession in a theater, sports arena, or park or sells goods to the operator in these areas. Concessionaires usually obtain the accounts in one or more of these areas in a geographic area. They differ from the rack jobber in that they sometimes supply company personnel to operate the business, often paying rental on a percentage-of-sales basis to the owner of a theater, arena, or park. Concessionaires usually have a warehouse and trucks to deliver the goods to the specific outlets.

Cash-and-Carry Wholesalers

As the name implies, cash-and-carry wholesalers do not extend credit or deliver any products. Rather, these wholesalers take lower markups because of the fewer services offered and usually break down the case allotments to small retailers. A small retailer is usually not called on by the large wholesalers and needs a smaller amount than a case allotment of 12 packages per case.

Drop Shipper

A drop shipper sells the product and arranges for the manufacturer to ship directly to the customer. They usually take title to the merchandise and assume the risk of collecting from the customers sold. These wholesalers are common in many commodity categories such as stone, lumber, coal, or potatoes.

MANUFACTURERS' SALES BRANCHES AND OFFICES

Sales branches or sales offices are frequently maintained by manufacturing, refining, and mining companies separately from their plants or mines for the purpose of marketing their products at the wholesale level. Sales offices differ from sales branches in that they normally do not carry stocks of merchandise for delivery to customers.

MERCHANT AGENTS AND BROKERS

Agents and brokers are private business establishments primarily engaged in selling or buying goods for different companies. There are a wide variety of operations such as auction companies, commission merchants, export agents, import agents, selling agents, and merchandise brokers. Establishments in this category rarely ever take title to the merchandise.

Auction Companies

Auction companies are wholesale establishments primarily engaged in selling merchandise by auction. Various types of merchandise can be auctioned, such as used and new cars, used farm equipment, or appliances. For example, if a used traded-in car is not being successfully resold in a period of time, a dealer may want it sold by an auction company rather than have the costs of maintaining it in inventory.

Merchant Brokers

Merchant brokers are wholesale establishments that do not take title to the goods and are predominantly involved in the selling or buying of merchandise in the domestic market on a brokerage basis. They are paid on a commission basis and never physically handle the actual products.

Commission Merchants

Commission merchants are wholesale establishments operating in the domestic market that handle goods for sale on a consignment basis. Antiques are often sold in this manner since it is difficult to put an exact value on an antique until the transaction is complete.

Import and Export Agents

Import agents are a type of merchant agent or broker in the domestic market who buys or sells merchandise with foreign firms. An example would be an import agent who specialized in selling Irish woolens to clothing manufacturers.

Export agents are merchant agents or brokers in the domestic market who sells or buys goods for foreign customers. Export agents often act as the international department for many non-competing small companies.

Manufacturers' Agents or Representatives

These wholesale establishments in the domestic market sell for a limited number of manufacturers on a contractual basis that usually can be terminated by either the manufacturer or wholesaler within 60 days upon receipt of written notification. Manufacturers' agents (or representatives) are used extensively by industrial, institutional, and government product manufacturers. They operate when the sales volume for a product, or a small number of products in a particular geographic area, does not warrant a company salesperson. As such, they are an excellent source for penetrating new markets.

Selling Agents

Selling agents are wholesale establishments primarily engaged in selling in the domestic market all or most of the products of client companies. Occasionally, these agents perform all marketing functions, including advertising and promotion in addition to personal selling. They are very similar in operation to a manufacturer's agent except on an expanded product and functional basis.

Since certain retail outlets such as grocery stores sell as many as 8,000 items produced by about 6,000 different manufacturers, wholesalers create transactional efficiencies in the buying process, and the selling system as well, by reducing the number of sales contacts needed. This allows the manufacturer to obtain complete coverage of specified SIC customers or broad geographical representation.

Wholesalers also assemble and break down or divide goods from several manufacturers. Packaging and shipping in small quantities directly from the factory to retailers would significantly increase the cost of some products. A wholesaler can take large quantities, break down the bulk, and distribute in smaller units for the retailer.

Many wholesalers provide warehousing and delivery services. Because inventory is closer, delivery time is shortened with wholesalers being much more efficient in these operations. Also, by partly financing these inventories and taking some of the credit risk for their customers, the capital needs of the manufacturer are significantly reduced.

ESTABLISHING A CHANNEL

Considerable problems or benefits can occur with the wholesale members of an established channel of distribution. Since a manufacturing company's greatest asset is its brand name and image, care must be taken to ensure that a poor brand image is not created by an incompetent agent or industrial representative.

Company Salespeople vs. Representatives

A firm needs to evaluate several factors in deciding whether to use company salespeople or representatives in distributing the product. When a product is widely consumed geographically but has long intervals between purchases, the cost to the manufacturer of company salespeople given the likely small territorial sales volumes may be too high. Also with an underfinanced company and a new product or a small firm, even though the product may eventually be heavily consumed, the company may find it cannot afford its own salesforce while sales volume is being built. When a sales representative is being used, a company should periodically compare the costs of having its own salesperson with the commissions being paid to indicate when (if ever) the sales representative should be replaced. A company salesperson will of course do a better job of selling and representing the company.

Sales Agents

The use of sales agents who work exclusively for one company occurs rather infrequently. When it does, the agent acts as the entire marketing department, handling advertising and promotion as well as selling. For this, the agent receives a higher commission and usually receives a contract that is longer than the typical two-month contract.

Evaluating an Agent, Broker, or Representative

The usual method of evaluating a potential agent or broker involves two steps. First, you should obtain all the information in advance on all potential candidates in the territory being considered. Information on each prospect is usually available from trade associations and retail stores on the products they presently distribute, length of time with each company, SIC Code numbers for each type of customer called on, the amount of other advertising and promotional support service provided, the number of personnel employed, the availability of any specialized selling departments, and the exact territory covered with present products.

For each of the best candidates, you should call on some customers they are presently servicing. The buyers should be asked several questions. Is the agent an aggressive worker? Does he or she call on a regular basis or are there sometimes long lapses between calls? Is the agent cooperative and forceful in getting manufacturer cooperation on servicing when needed? Does the agent have an excellent reputation particularly with the large volume buyers?

Advantages of Company Salespeople

There are rarely any outside representatives who will give the manufacturer's line more attention than company salespeople. They should be used whenever the product is used heavily enough to support them. Many companies start with agents, brokers, or representatives in their early low-volume years and then use their own salespeople when larger sales volume warrants. Since outside agents or representatives are also aware that when sales volume reaches a certain size in a territory they are often replaced by company salespeople, you should carefully track the company sales to make sure the outside agency is not keeping sales just below this needed volume.

TRENDS IN WHOLESALING

The trends taking place in wholesaling in the changing environment can be classified into four areas: elimination of the small wholesaler, the legality of territorial restriction, wholesaling services, and symbiotic marketing organizational structures.

Elimination of the Small Wholesaler

The trend of eliminating some small wholesale outlets is going to continue. An indication of the sales by business type for merchant wholesalers is indicated in Figure 16-2 (see page 238). Particularly in jeopardy is the wholesaler servicing the small retailer. Food chains, cooperatives, and voluntaries are much too competitive for the small retailer to continue to survive. Wholesalers servicing these small retailers will of course simultaneously disappear unless they have begun a voluntary wholesaler cooperative.

Legality of Territorial Restrictions

Until 1963, a manufacturer had little concern about defining the territory of each wholesaler's operation. However, beginning with the *White Motor* case decision, manufacturers not only have been limited in their authority to define territories but have also been left somewhat confused. In the *White Motor* case, the Supreme Court ruled that the use of reason would be employed to determine an antitrust violation in defining wholesale territories. In other words, depending on how this vague general rule of rea-

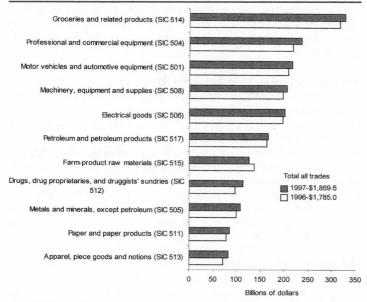

FIG. 16-2. *Estimated sales of merchant wholesalers by selected kinds of business.*

Source: *Current Business Reports, BW/97 Annual Benchmark Report for Wholesale Trade,* U.S. Department of Commerce. http://www.census. gov/prod/1/bus/whsle/bw_month.html.

son is defined, restricting a wholesaler's territory might constitute an antitrust violation.

This decision was followed in 1967 by the *Schwinn* case, in which the Supreme Court ruled that all control devices exercised to restrict a wholesaler were a violation of antitrust if title had passed to the wholesaler. However, the courts then proceeded to develop a series of exceptions to this ruling. Since there are still some areas of confusion, you should carefully, under legal counsel, establish the company's territories and operations.

Wholesaling Services

Only recently has attention been paid to the wholesaling of services, even though there have always been present many marketing intermediaries in their distribution. In the health care industry, one organization that has assumed increasing importance in the delivery of health services is the health maintenance organization (HMO). HMOs create health care clinics that hire teams of professionals to provide health services for a specific membership.

The insurance industry has used many different kinds of intermediaries. Group insurance available through intermediaries, such as employment and labor unions, has achieved a great deal of success.

Symbiotic Marketing Organizational Structures

Symbiotic marketing occurs when two or more independent organizations combine in a joint venture that provides benefits to the parties involved. This arrangement is becoming increasingly prevalent, though it is not always easily recognizable.

While many different types of marketing agreements are possible, they generally fall into two categories: a company brokers its product through another company on either a long- or short-term basis without making any major organizational changes or two companies create a third organization, which may be a temporary group or a separate corporation. Most symbiotic marketing ventures involve the creation of new entities, even though many brokering relationships are quite sophisticated operations.

One interesting symbiotic venture involved Pillsbury and its line of refrigerated doughs that had received wide acceptance in stores. Pillsbury's marketing problem centered around the fact that the items required special refrigerated display cases. Since Kraft Foods had extensive experience in this area with its cheese products, a symbiotic arrangement was established whereby Kraft initially sold and distributed these Pillsbury products.

Another beneficial opportunity for a symbiotic organizational structure occurs when an existing sales force is unavailable or inappropriate. When this occurs, several noncompeting companies can establish a sales staff that is independent but jointly owned. For example, five newspapers—the *St. Louis Post Dispatch*, the *Washington Star*, the *Boston Globe*, the *Philadelphia Bulletin*, and the *Milwaukee Journal-Sentinel*—established and jointly owned Million Market Newspapers, Inc., a sales/advertising company. This symbiotic arrangement gave each of the newspapers marketing impact far beyond its individual capability.

In these and other instances, symbiotic marketing allowed companies to take advantage of new opportunities. As costs soar and competition intensifies, more symbiotic arrangements will be established.

CHAPTER PERSPECTIVE

In this chapter we have explained the various types of wholesalers and merchandise agents that are available for setting up a distribution channel. The primary difference between wholesalers and agents is that wholesalers take title to the merchandise whereas agents rarely take title. Although the wholesaler adds costs to the price for the final consumer, the wholesaler is often a necessary step in efficient distribution. By evaluating the services and costs of each type of wholesaler, you can establish an effective channel that will benefit your company. You should frequently reevaluate the use of outside agents and replace them with company salespeople whenever it becomes cost effective.

The Promotion Program and Sales Promotion and Publicity

CHAPTER 17

INTRODUCTION AND MAIN POINTS

In this chapter you will learn how promotion and the promotion mix can be used to communicate the positive facts about a product to prospective consumers. Promotion and the promotion mix generally involve a forward communication flow, as in the case of manufacturers promoting to channel members and ultimate consumers, or retailers promoting to ultimate consumers. Promotion and its mix can be divided into four categories—publicity, sales promotion, advertising, and personal selling. Each of these categories in turn has its own mix of elements, which a small firm can blend together to create their own promotion mix. In this material, we will focus especially on sales promotion and publicity, with sales promotion defined as a nonpersonal, periodically, or one-time occurring promotional activity, and publicity described as a nonpersonal promotional activity not directly paid for by the company.

After studying the material in this chapter:

- You will understand the elements in the promotion mix.
- You will know how to use various types of store promotions.
- You will understand the importance of, and how to use, samples and coupons.
- You will understand the various types of publicity and how to use them effectively.

OVERALL PROMOTIONAL CONSIDERATIONS

In considering promotion and the promotion mix, it is important to first understand several overall promotional considerations. There are four general areas of issues that a small firm needs to consider in developing its promotional campaign: the external environment, internal company considerations, its marketing department, and the promotional strategy. The areas of the external environment affecting the promotion decision also impact all the marketing activities of the firm: consumer demand, competition, and the regulatory/legal requirements. The buying influences and the buying process in the consumer demand area are particularly important in developing an effective promotion mix. The buying influences include the cultural and social environment and the attitudes of the target group. For example, if the target market has a negative attitude toward foreign-made products, no reference of this should be made in the communication. The buying process should be looked at in terms of the decision process of the target group and how this can be positively influenced by the message. You can evaluate the competitive environment by looking at the innovative efforts that have recently taken place in the industry.

One final important area in the external environment—the regulatory/legal requirements—significantly affects promotion decisions. These requirements have had, and will continue to have, a significant impact on all aspects of the promotion process. Currently, the Federal Trade Commission (FTC) is concentrating on ensuring that advertising claims are accurate and truthful. Advertisers' claims need to be supported by reasonable proof, which can be in the form of authoritative opinions, market tests, or independent scientific tests. When a claim is challenged, the FTC can request the firm to provide the needed support. When a claim cannot be substantiated, the FTC can require a firm to place corrective advertisements correcting the false claims. Recently, industry self-regulation has become almost as important as the FTC in ensuring accurate claims in some industries.

These external factors impact the internal company considerations in establishing the corporate objectives and policies, as well as the total promotion budget. Company policies affecting the promotion decision are personnel, distribution, and the methods used for the creation of the actual promotional campaign. The promotion decision needs to be integrated with the goals and constraints of other functional areas in the company. For example, there is nothing worse than having an effective promotion program stimulating sales demand and not having the product available for purchase. This occurred when Kodak introduced their first instamatic camera and when Gillette introduced the Atra razor. Not only can initial sales be lost, but loyalty to a competitive product may also be established because a customer likes the competitive product purchased and does not switch back. Besides other functional areas, the promotion decision needs to be coordinated with other areas of the marketing mix—product, price, and place. For example, some merchandising allowances and cooperative advertising monies can be used to establish distribution in a new chain. Or, coupons giving 25¢ off the next product purchased can be used to offset the negative impact of a price increase.

The fourth area in the promotion decision—the promotion strategy—involves determining the correct promotion mix from the four areas available—personal selling, public relations, sales promotion, and advertising.

The Promotion Mix

While promotion must be carefully coordinated with all the other elements of the marketing mix, promotion itself has its own mix consisting of advertising, personal selling, sales promotion, and publicity, each of which includes various elements (see Figure 17-1).

Advertising is a paid nonpersonal presentation and perhaps the most visible component of the promotion mix. Many firms

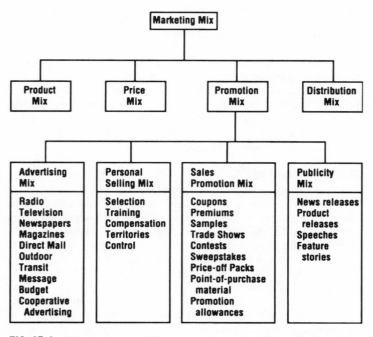

FIG. 17-1. *The elements of the promotion mix and marketing mix.*

rely heavily on advertising as the primary element in their promotion strategy. The primary components of advertising are media and message. Such media as radio, television, magazine, newspaper, direct mail, outdoor, and transit are selected in light of the message to be communicated, the budget, and the target audience.

Unlike advertising, which is nonpersonal in nature, personal selling involves a personal presentation on an individual or group basis. While personal selling is frequently done face-to-face, it also occurs via telephone. Personal selling involves such activities as selection, training, compensation, territories, and control.

Sales promotion is perhaps the most diverse area in the promotion mix, consisting of all those nonrecurring activities that are not considered advertising or personal selling. Its mix consists of such things as coupons, samples, trade contests, sweepstakes, price-off-packs, point-of-purchase material, and retail promotion allowances. The use of these activities as part of the promotion strategy has significantly increased in the past several years. As the cost of advertising and personal selling continues to escalate and more creative attention is devoted to this area, sales promotion will continue to have an increasing share of the promotion budget.

Publicity is a nonpersonal form of promotion that is not paid for by the sponsoring organization. Publicity generally involves the favorable presentation of the sponsoring organization in a print or broadcast medium. Specifically, this is generated through news releases, product releases, or company events covered in feature stories. Speeches by employees of the organization are also an effective form of publicity.

The Promotion Budget

Of all the areas of marketing, none is both more glamorized or criticized than promotion. It is held in awe and vehemently criticized in terms of its negative influence on society, usually through causing excessive purchasing behavior. One of the most important and yet difficult questions is determining how much to spend on promotion. Total promotion spending varies greatly from 40 percent of total sales in the cosmetic industry to about 15 percent in the industrial machinery industry.

You should consider several key factors in determining the size of your firm's budget: the nature of the market, the nature of the product and its stage in the life cycle, the channels of distribution, and the objectives.

Characteristics of the market affect the intensity of the promotional effort needed. When an organization is marketing its product or service in a concentrated geographic area to a very homogeneous customer group, or in an established market with existing favorable consumer attitudes, less promotional effort is needed. More promotional effort is needed when an organization is trying to obtain a market position in an area dominated by a strong competitor. Such was the case when Procter and Gamble expended significant promotion dollars to introduce Folger's Coffee in the New England area which was then dominated by General Foods' Maxwell House Coffee.

The nature of the product and its stage in the life cycle also affect the size of the promotion budget. Different kinds of products require different kinds and amounts of promotion. Whereas convenience goods purchased frequently at the most convenient location must be supported by a great deal of advertising, industrial pallets used in transporting goods or carrying a product along a conveyor system in the manufacturing process require very little.

Consumers need to be aware that the convenience goods are available and will fulfill a need, whereas pallets are ordered on a regular basis usually from the same two or three suppliers. A given product's promotion needs also vary with the stage in its life cycle. During the introduction and growth stages of the product, more promotional effort is needed to inform the target market about the existence and benefits of the product. As was discussed in the product life cycle section of the product chapter 11, significant promotional expenditures are often needed as well in the maturity stage when competition becomes intense. In the decline stage, of course, promotion becomes less effective and should be used sparingly.

The channel of distribution also affects the size of the promotion budget. The elements of the channel of distribution that most affect the promotion decision are the number of outlets and the number of channel members between the firm and the final consumer—the length of the channel. A manufacturer who uses more members in the channel usually needs more promotional effort than one who uses a shorter channel as it takes different types of promotion to reach each of the channel members involved. A wholesaler, for example, may be effectively reached by personal selling, which could not be used cost effectively to reach all of the small retailers served by the wholesaler. These can be better reached through a direct mail piece. Similarly the greater the number of retailers in the channel system, the more intense the distribution strategy, the more promotion needed.

The final factor affecting the size of the promotion budget—the promotion objectives—is usually the most important. Objectives not only help determine the size of the budget but also provide a basis for evaluating the results of the promotion effort. For example, if a college wants to attract 10 percent more students with higher SAT scores, then a promotion budget needs to be established to achieve this objective. An evaluation of the applicants will indicate whether or not the promotion campaign achieved the results.

Given these factors, how can you determine the budget for your firm? There are five methods for determining a promotion budget: arbitary determination method, competitive parity method, objective and task method, percent of sales method, and various quantitative methods.

In the arbitrary determination method, the promotion budget is determined in a seemingly arbitrary manner. When using this method, company executives rely on their intuition and past experience in establishing the budget. This is a very unsophisticated method, but more firms use this method than any other. A common benchmark used more frequently than others is 10 percent of last year's sales.

In the competitive parity method, a company uses the promotion expenditures of competitors to establish their own budget. This information on the competitor's budget is also useful in evaluating the overall competitive environment, and can be obtained through carefully analyzing a company's financial statements or through a service that monitors all the advertisements in a given product/market area for a fee. The competitive parity method has some drawbacks as it employs historical data of competitive expenditures and assumes that all have very similar marketing situations.

Probably the best method for establishing a promotion budget is the third method—the objective and task method. When using this method, you establish definitive promotion objectives and then determine the amount and cost of the promotion to reach these objectives by costing each element of the promotion mix needed. Not only does this method allow for each element in the promotion mix to be effectively used, but it also makes sure that the amount of money to be spent on promotion is commensurate with the task at hand. A clearer basis for evaluation of the promotion expenditures also results.

The fourth method—the percent-of-sales method—is also widely used mainly because it is easy to use. This method involves applying a fixed percentage to either past or future sales figures. If last year's sales were $200 million and the percentage used is 3 percent, the promotion budget for this coming year would be $6 million. The sales figure used can be the sales for the last year or an average of sales achieved over the past several years. By using an average sales figure, the impact of any erratic sales fluctuations on promotion expenditures are eliminated. You can also use a percentage of future sales, basing the promotions budget on future conditions, not on past events. When you use the percent-of-sales method for determining the promotion budget, you should compare it to the percents of leading competitors as well as industry norms.

The final method for establishing the size of the promotion budget—the quantitative method—involves implementing one or several mathematical models or more sophisticated quantitative techniques. While these add a more vigorous dimension to the budgeting process, their use requires a significant amount of data and expertise. As the costs of promotion continue to increase, quantitative methods will continue to have increasing use, usually in conjunction with one of the other four methods.

Regardless of the size of the promotion budget, the expenditures need to be carefully evaluated to determine if the target audience is being effectively reached, the objectives accomplished, and the desired sales achieved. Promotion is generally organized on a functional, geographic, product, or matrix basis. Recently, there has been increasing use of the matrix organization in which there are equal influences by different lines of authority on promotion expenditures. Such firms as Citicorp, Dow Chemical, Corning Glass, General Electric, and Shell Oil have effectively implemented this organizational structure and actually combine elements in both the functional and product manager structures.

SALES PROMOTION OBJECTIVES

In order to optimize the company's efforts in the area of sales promotion, it is important for you to understand the overall general objectives that can be achieved. These objectives can be grouped into four major categories.

One objective of sales promotion is to maintain the lowest price possible in a product category or to keep channel members from taking too high a markup. A second objective is to maintain the number of shelf facings (the number of times the product is exposed on the shelf) in the store. This can be very important in increasing product sales since sales often double with two shelf facings versus one. A third objective of sales promotion is to increase the frequency of use of the product by present users through offering recipes or companion products. Finally, sales promotion can be used to attract new users to the product. Regardless of the objective, there are two broad classifications of sales promotion: store promotions and consumer promotions.

STORE PROMOTIONS

Except for those companies having their own totally integrated direct marketing channel such as Avon, World Book Encyclopedia, and Amway, most consumer goods manufacturers need some retail help and support to successfully market their products. When the retailer is an independent business entity, as is usually the case, this help is often hard to obtain. The retailer is not concerned about the exact product purchased, only that a product in the category is purchased in their store. If an out-of-stock condition exists or if the particular product is not carried, a substitute product will be suggested by store personnel. The retailer will not help promote your particular product unless there is some direct benefit involved, as described in the following store promotions.

Feature Payment Offer

A feature payment offer is a manufacturer payment offer to the retailer passed on by the wholesaler and not used by the wholesaler as a price reduction. One example is a display allowance where a reduction in price per case is given to the retailer for displaying the product for a period of time, usually from three days to one week.

Another type of feature payment offer is offering the retailer a reduced price for each unit of the product ordered and moved out of the warehouse in a six-week period, based on the inventory count before and after the promotion period. This promotion is designed to encourage the salespeople of the wholesaler to obtain new retail accounts for the product as well as to get present customers to stock greater quantities of the product, possibly using an in-store display.

Cooperative Advertising

Cooperative advertising is probably the most important store promotion, particularly for a small firm. A cooperative advertising offer allows the retailer to advertise the product, sharing the cost of that part of the advertisement featuring the manufacturer's product with the manufacturer.

Many cooperative advertising agreements are on a "proof of advertising basis," with the retail store submitting a copy of the retail advertisement in order to receive payment. Cooperative advertising agreements can take a wide variety of forms, such as the retailer receiving 2 percent off on all purchases as long as the brand is featured in an advertisement a specified number of times per year. Cooperative advertising allowances can also be used to help control markups in the channel. For example, if grocery store chains ordinarily take a 25 percent markup on the product category, and in one geographic area all chains increased this markup to 33 percent on the company's product, then cooperative advertising can sometimes reduce the higher markup. If a company's product, having a retail selling price of 39 cents, ordinarily has a 25 percent markup for the retailer, but in the Chicago area the retail selling price increases to 43 cents (higher than the regular 25 percent markup) and competitive products remain at a 25 percent markup, sales will then be lost. If a large number of retail accounts in the area feature the product in cooperative advertisements at a retail price of 39 cents (with the standard 25 percent markup), after a period of time the retailers will be forced to reduce the markup to the standard 25 percent and a price of 39 cents in order to compete effectively. Often a manufacturer provides print advertising mats for use by the retailer in the cooperative advertisement in a newspaper or handbill.

Trade Deal

Another type of store promotion is a trade deal. Under this arrangement, the manufacturer offers goods to the wholesaler at a reduced price, hoping to stimulate a reduction in price at the retail level.

CONSUMER PROMOTIONS

In addition to store promotions, you need to offer some consumer promotions as these usually obtain more immediate consumer response and sales than advertising. Consumer promotions are particularly beneficial in introducing a new product as they help consumers overcome their hesitancy about trying something new. In addition, consumer promotions can be used to encourage the consumer to purchase more of the product at a time. More product on hand will tend to increase total usage of the product as, for example, a consumer will tend to discard a small bar of soap if another is on hand and easily accessible for use. The two major types of consumer promotions are sampling and coupons.

Sampling

Probably one of the most effective yet expensive ways to introduce a new product is sampling, wherein a consumer is given a free trial size of the product being introduced. Sampling is particularly important when the product is extremely new and different and has high product resistance. Sampling can be done with or without an accompanying coupon to further stimulate the first purchase. The cents-off coupon aids in establishing familiarity with the actual location and purchase of the product in a retail store, thereby helping to establish a purchasing pattern. In-store sampling can also be done with or without a coupon. In this case a company representative distributes samples to customers in the retail store itself.

Coupons

Offering cents-off coupons in newspapers or through direct mail is a less expensive, and usually less effective, method of getting the customer to try a new product. However, coupons can be very effective in getting a consumer to buy the product for a second, third, or fourth time, thereby establishing repeat purchasing behavior and helping to establish brand loyalty. At the very least this reinforces a positive shopping pattern and eventually can establish brand loyalty and shopping behavior. Other consumer promotions giving similar results include: an extra amount of product in a package for the same price; a premium placed in the package (a product gift of some type similar to the Cracker Jack promotion); or a bonus pack giving the customer another package of the same size free.

Another use of coupons is a self-liquidating offer where a coupon from the package and a certain dollar amount allows the consumer to purchase some item of merchandise. The dollar amount is usually large enough to cover the cost of the merchandise and handling. Sometimes merchandise is given for several proofs of purchase. This was used successfully in Gillette's introduction of the Atra razor where the purchaser received a men's travel toilet kit upon sending a portion of the package to a redemption center. In premium-redemption plans, coupons are cut off the package and saved until a customer accumulates enough to redeem a more valuable item of merchandise.

"Cents-off-the-label coupon" is a practice in which the price of a product is reduced and the reduction noted, as illustrated in Figure 17-2. Although many feel that cents-off-the-label coupon promotions attract more consumers to sample and then purchase the product, this is frequently not the case. Instead, cents-off-the-label promotions are more likely to give the present buyers of the product a lower price and therefore reinforce the purchasing process, rewarding loyalty and returning less profit to the company.

FIG. 17-2. *Coupon to stimulate purchase.*

An example of a premium that can attract many new users is shown in Figure 17-3 where another product is offered as a bonus with a well-established item. This allows the new item to be sampled at a reasonable cost and without the risk associated with an outright purchase.

FIG. 17-3. *Coupon to attract new users.*

An example of a promotion that should increase the frequency of use of a product with present users is shown in Figure 17-4. These promotions can feature companion products as well as menus and recipes.

FIG.17-4. *Coupon to increase frequency of use.*

Misredemption

Sometimes errors in coupon redemption occur. One type of misredemption is when retailers give numerous coupons to one of their better customers or friends. Another form of misredemption occurs for coupons printed in newspapers or magazines. Groups collect these coupons and receive all or part of the value of the coupon from retailers who receive at least the handling fee without any product being purchased. You need to periodically monitor redemption by retail stores to make sure that the coupon redemption occurring is commensurate with the amount of product being sold. While it is impossible to determine the extent of misredemption, some estimates place it between 15 and 33 percent.

Use of a clearinghouse is an excellent method by which a manufacturer can distribute and redeem coupons. Once the coupons are sent to the clearinghouse by the retailer, the clearinghouse mails the check to the retailer collecting the amount plus a handling fee from the manufacturer. Since about 25 percent of the coupons valued at 10, 15, or 25 cents are redeemed, the cost per redeemed coupon can be relatively high. A method for computing total coupon costs is indicated in Table 17-1. The cost of couponing which includes the estimated redemption rate and misredemption rate needs to be carefully checked before a coupon promotion is undertaken. Usually the total costs of a coupon promotion are highest in magazines and then in supplements.

OTHER TYPES OF SALES PROMOTION

One type of sales promotion—specialty advertising—is printing the trade name and sometimes the advertising slogan on a match book, pen, calendar, T-shirt, or other lower-priced articles which

Table 17-1
Method of Computing Coupon Costs

Type of Program	Circulation	Cost of Distributing and Printing	Estimated Redemption	Quantity Redeemed[b]	Cost of Handling and Clearance	Cost of Face Value of 10¢ Coupon	Cost of Misredemption	Total Cost
Co-op direct mail	12,000,000	$192,000[a]	11.7%	1,404,000	$96,876[c]	$140,400[d]	$35,100[e]	$464,676

[a] @$16/M
[b] 11.7% of 12,000,000 = 1,404,000
[c] 1,404,000 × 6.9¢ = $96,876
[d] 1,404,000 × 10¢ = $140,400
[e] $140,400 × 25¢ = $35,100

are then given away, or sold, if possible, to customers. For example, Coca-Cola T-shirts are actually sold. Another form of specialty advertising is sponsoring sporting events, musical activities, or other social and cultural events. For example, L'eggs Mini Marathon and the Dinah Shore Golf Tournament are sponsored by Colgate. These types of specialty promotions are getting more and more common and sophisticated.

Contests are also a useful promotion vehicle for rejuvenating interest in the retail trade for a product. Contests usually result in a large supply of the product being purchased by the retail stores in preparation for the contest. Forms or entry blanks for the contest are usually carried in the store to attract the customer. Since being barred from television advertising, cigarette manufacturers have used contests extensively. Also contests are used for seasonal products, such as suntan lotion, to obtain heavy retail stocking of the item at the start of a new season. Contests can also be used to encourage distribution as well as salespeople.

TRADE SHOWS

Another very effective sales promotion device is exhibiting at a trade show. This is particularly important (and in some cases imperative) in certain categories of products, particularly industrial and consumer electronics, in order to achieve any degree of sales success. The trade show allows the manufacturer to obtain buyer reaction to new or regular products on a face-to-face basis. When a product demonstration is important for success, a trade show may be the only means of economically accomplishing this. During the trade show, buyer interests can be monitored and any questions or problems addressed.

Since there are more than 8,000 trade shows a year in the United States, you must carefully select the show or shows that will maximize the product's exposure with the best target audience. One method for evaluating a show is to analyze the list of exhibitors at the show the previous year. A sample of these exhibitors should be queried regarding the usefulness of the show, the cost of displaying at the show, any problems encountered, and benefits gained.

Once a trade show has been selected, you must determine the size and type of display. The most common display space is a 10 foot by 10 foot booth, although some trade shows offer both larger and smaller areas. Also, there is often a price difference depending on the location of the booth with some more higher priced areas having more exposure and traffic. Generally, two company personnel can effectively work a standard 10 × 10 booth.

In designing the actual booth, you should remember that the booth should attract the attention of prospects attending the trade show and display the product in the best way possible. The real effectiveness of the booth depends to a large extent on the effectiveness of the people manning it. Booth personnel must be: friendly; able to differentiate prospects from curiosity-seekers; able to present the product effectively and knowledgeably; and able to close the sale.

PUBLICITY

There is often confusion about publicity and public relations. Public relations is more broad in scope, referring to all of the company's efforts in positively impacting the society in which it operates. While public relations, and simultaneously is affected by all of the company's promotional activity, it is much broader than promotion itself. Ideally, all the activities and functions of a company should take place under a public relations umbrella that maximizes the firm's image internally and externally.

Publicity, on the other hand, is one of the tools in the promotion mix. Publicity is concerned with disseminating positive information about the company to the public at no cost to the company. The items of interest for coverage through publicity usually deal with: the company's products or services; any ideas, activities, or events identified with the company; or people in the company's organization. Primarily, publicity is used as part of the promotion mix in publicizing new products and new product ideas. When good publicity is combined with the rest of the elements in the promotion mix—sales promotion, advertising, and personnel selling—a synergistic effect occurs. The important aspects of publicity include its characteristics, forms, and implementation.

Characteristics

One of the major characteristics of publicity is that there is no charge for the space or time in which the message appears. However, the actual costs associated with all the activities that generate good publicity may be quite extensive. It can be costly to prepare appropriate publicity releases and costly to properly present these to the appropriate people.

Another characteristic of publicity is that it always involves a third party who determines whether to use the item and its format as well as the timing of the release. This, in effect, puts the control of publicity outside the company but gives the message source credibility as the company does not control the release or pay for it.

Recipients of the publicity message view the media as the source of the message and not the sponsoring company. Since publicity items are perceived as news and not as advertisements, people tend to read them more and perceive the message favorably and as being more accurate.

Forms of Publicity

Given these characteristics of publicity, it is important for each company to generate as much publicity as possible. The four most common forms of publicity are: news releases, news conferences, speeches, and feature articles.

Of these four forms, the most widely used is news releases. A typical news release is about 200 to 300 words describing a newsworthy event about the company. A news release should always include a name and telephone number of a person in the company to contact for further information. When appropriate for the printed media, a glossy photograph should also be included. The key to a successful news release is writing it in the style and format desired by the media which might carry the item.

News conferences are used much more infrequently. These involve inviting representatives of the press to a meeting where company representatives discuss the publicity item. These not only involve the time of members of the company, but are usually poorly attended by the news media as well.

When a news release is increased to 1,000 to 3,000 words, it becomes a feature article. Feature articles often deal with stories, philosophies, or some other feature of the company that may not be considered news per se. Even more than news releases, a feature article must be specifically tailored to a specified medium in order for it to be more effectively used.

Speeches by company executives are becoming a more frequently used publicity method. Unique features of a product or a unique production process often are noteworthy topics for presentation at various types of meetings. Company executives should not only accept invitations to speak whenever possible but should solicit opportunities whenever the occasion occurs as well.

Implementation

While publicity is a very useful and cost-effective element of the promotion mix, it is probably the most difficult to implement and manage. For example, because it is new, publicity must be very carefully planned. If an item appears in a promotion, it frequently is perceived as no longer being newsworthy and will probably not be carried by any media. Sometimes, however, a very unique innovative promotion can be newsworthy.

In order to be successfully implemented, a publicity item needs to be expertly written and tailored to the specific medium. Best results occur when appropriate media are selected which are compatible with the company's particular publicity item. Properly implemented and controlled publicity can effectively augment the promotion program by helping consumers view the company and its products and services more favorably.

CHAPTER PERSPECTIVE

In this chapter we have discussed the promotion mix and learned about establishing and coordinating the promotional budget. Successful management and evaluation of the promotion process will yield achievement of your marketing goals. We have also experienced how to implement various methods of sales promotion publicity. To optimize your efforts in this area, you must first determine your exact objectives, which will probably include either customer loyalty, attracting new customers, or establishing and enhancing the company's image. Store promotions are essential in enlisting the support of retailers in promoting your product. Additionally, you can attract consumers through coupons and sampling. You should take advantage of any publicity to increase consumer awareness and reception of your product.

Advertising

INTRODUCTION AND MAIN POINTS

In this chapter we introduce the concept of advertising—the impersonal selling or mass communication component of a company's promotion mix—and describe the overall position of corporate advertising. We will review the functions and aspects of advertising in order to describe the effect advertising has on the marketing and promotional mixes. Budgeting, media, and message decisions need to be made in light of environmental, corporate, legal, and consumer practices. We will discuss advertising, advertising research, agency selection, and in-house review with respect to historical trends and their importance in establishing and maintaining the unique selling proposition (USP). Finally, we introduce several models for measuring the effectiveness of advertising copy.

After studying the material in this chapter:

━━ You will know what it takes to create and write newspaper, radio, and television advertisements.

━━ You will be able to develop your own unique selling proposition.

━━ You will be able to select an advertising agency.

FUNCTIONS OF ADVERTISING

There is no aspect of the promotion mix that affects an individual more than advertising. From the morning newspaper to the evening news, each individual is constantly exposed to advertising. Advertising is a nonpersonal, paid-for communication device. From the vantage point of the company, advertising is a very important yet expensive part of the marketing effort.

Advertising is best understood in terms of its functions and its three basic aspects: budget, media, and message. After these have been developed, the chapter will deal with advertising institutions, selecting an advertising agency, advertising research, local advertising, and selected advertising topics.

There are several major functions of an advertising campaign. Some advertising campaigns are designed to make the complete sale of the product by having such an impact that the consumer will purchase the product without any additional stimulus. This is generally the case with the advertising campaigns of such lower priced consumer goods as Maxwell House Coffee, Imperial Margarine, and Total Cereal. Other advertising campaigns assist in the sale of the product via the physical display of the merchandise, point-of-sale materials, and the salesperson. This function of advertising generally occurs in the sale of such items as personal computers, golf clubs, and color televisions. A third function of an advertising campaign is to obtain leads for follow-up promotional efforts such as company sales calls or the sending of additional materials. This function of advertising frequently occurs in industrial advertising as well as in some consumer advertisements for specialized products occurring in specialized magazines such as *Golf Digest* and *Better Homes and Gardens.* This type of advertisement can be easily identified when it contains information and often a bingo card for the reader to return for more information. Finally, some advertising campaigns are designed to reinforce the purchase decision of the consumer or their positive feelings about the product or the company. This type of advertisement is primarily aimed at such groups as stockholders, financial analysts, employees, voters, or purchasers. The campaign is trying to positively affect sales in the long run by producing a positive company and brand image.

Regardless of the function of the advertisement and the advertising campaign, each advertisement has three major components—the budget, the media, and the message—each of which we will discuss in turn.

THE ADVERTISING BUDGET

The function of the advertisement is one of the key variables in establishing the advertising budget, one of the most difficult decisions in marketing. This is particularly important since the amount of advertising impacts sales while its cost affects profitability. This decision cannot be made simply by developing and using an advertising-to-sales ratio since this ratio reflects the low sales of a new product and the high sales of an established mature product. Also, two different advertising-to-sales ratios could actually produce the same advertising dollar expenditure. For example, a high ratio on a low sales base could equal that of a low ratio on a high sales base. In addition, the advertising-to-sales ratio does not take into account competitive activities or future company plans. The advertising-to-sales ratio should only be used as a guideline in establishing the advertising budget.

In establishing an advertising budget, you should consider the rate of corporate expenditures in relation to the total advertising expenditures in the product category, or in relation to expenditures of the leading selling products in the category. With respect to this process, it is important to consider two things.

First, if you are entering a new field, you should spend, if financially possible, more in advertising than the average of the top two or three leaders for the first two or three years of the market entrance. Second, if your company has already obtained a share of the market and wants to maintain that share, then it should spend slightly above its percent share of the market in advertising in that particular product category. In other words, if a company has 20 percent share of the market, it should spend 22 percent to 25 percent of the total advertising dollars in the product category to maintain its market share.

The total amount of advertising dollars being spent in a product category is data that can usually be ascertained by an advertising agency. It can also be determined through using information in several journals. For example, the *Standard Directory of Advertisers*, a yearly publication, indicates the type of media a company is using. *Advertising Age*, a weekly publication, publishes data on the amount being spent in product categories and by individual companies.

Advertising budgets are usually reported for all of a company's products as opposed to individual products. The method for obtaining individual product budgets, therefore, is to use a clipping service to obtain data on competitive product advertising in any media and then to determine each advertisement's cost through the use of standard rate and data service.

Commercial Length and Advertisement Size

A commercial should be as long and an advertisement as large as necessary to communicate the unique selling proposition while positively impacting the brand image. The USP is the description of the unique benefits of the product that the company wants the consumer to remember as it will help in the decision to purchase the particular product. With new products, this requires at least 30-second or often one-minute commercials or half-page advertisements. Once the unique selling proposition has been sufficiently exposed to a large percent of the market, shorter commercials and eighth- or quarter-page advertisements can be used.

Surveys should be regularly conducted to determine the degree to which the unique selling proposition is being remembered, using questions such as: "The ____ Generation" or "What beer is made from Rocky Mountain sky-blue water?" The percentage of correct answers indicates the degree to which the unique selling proposition is being remembered for that particular product.

Dispersion Theory
Some consumer goods companies have the objective of the advertisement reaching the maximum number of unduplicated units such as households in a particular interval of time. This is the dispersion theory, which has its best application when the media department develops a plan for the lowest possible cost per *unduplicated* home in the target market. The coverage is achieved by randomly buying the best spots locally available along several dimensions: across stations (all stations in the city); across different types of programs; across days of the week; and across hours of the day. Using this method, a company would first determine the time of day that produced the lowest cost per 1,000 homes across all stations in one city in reaching the target market. With an advertisement being aired on each of the stations for that time, every home tuned to any station would be an unduplicated home because the home could be tuned only to one station at a time unless, of course, several televisions were in simultaneous operation.

Media Characteristics
One of the most important factors in establishing the advertising budget is analyzing the characteristics and costs of the various alternative media involved in accomplishing the advertising objectives. This can be achieved by calculating for each media the rate comparison index indicated in Table 18-1 and comparing the rates to determine the appropriate budget and media plan needed to accomplish the objectives (see page 264).

THE MEDIA
In selecting media for an advertising campaign, it is important to consider the characteristics and costs of each media alternative.

Magazines

There are several types of magazines: trade journals, specific consumer magazines, and more general consumer magazines. Magazines are specialized so they offer an efficient means of reaching specific target markets. For example, *Design News* can effectively reach design engineers; *House Beautiful*—upper-income women; and *Shape*—individuals concerned with how they look.

Direct Mail

When target markets are widely dispersed and very heterogeneous, direct mail, even with its high cost per individual reached, may be the most efficient media. For example, direct mail is very effective for reaching electronic design engineers when utilizing a purchased mailing list such as the list of subscribers of *Design News* magazine. Direct mail is also a very effective medium when no printed media is regularly read by the target market and sales people are needed to follow up on the advertisement in order to ensure a sale.

Television

When the average dollar amount of the product or service purchased is substantial, or the product needs good visual display to be understood, there is no better media than television. Since a large number of people watch television, the cost per thousand viewers in television is lower than in any other media for broad markets. However, even though this is the case, the real issue is again one of targeting—how much of the television audience reached is in the target market. You must assess how much of the product is bought, or might be bought, by the television audience reached in light of the high expense of the television advertisement.

Newspapers

A large part of newspaper advertising is cooperative, which is defined as advertising jointly paid for by manufacturers and retailers to feature the product and the store. This advertising is important in increasing sales, building good channel relations, and helping to keep channel distributors from either discounting the price, raising the price, or taking a higher mark-up. Stores tend not to raise prices when advertisements featuring the product at a standard mark-up are occurring. Newspapers are also effective in informing consumers about retail store promotions such as the store's spring linen sale or winter furniture sale.

Table 18-1
Characteristics and Costs of Various Advertising Media

Media	Example	Rate Comparison Index	Factors Affecting Rate	Rate Base
Radio	AM FM	$CPM = \dfrac{\text{cost per minute} \times 1000}{\text{audience size}}$	• Time of day • Size of audience • Length of advertisement • Volume discounts	• Program • 5, 10, 15, 30, or 60 second spots
Television	Network Local CATV	$CPM = \dfrac{\text{cost per minute} \times 1000}{\text{audience size}}$	• Time of day • Length of advertisement • Size of audience • Volume discounts • Frequency discounts	• Program • 5, 10, 20, 30 or 60 second spots
Direct	Letters Catalogs Brochures Coupons Price lists	Cost per contact	• Postage • Production • Handling • Mailing list	
Newspaper	Daily (morning or evening) Sunday Weekly supplement	Milliline rate = cost per agate × 1,000,000 circulation	• Number of readers • Number of colors in advertisement • Position • Guaranteed charges • Size of advertisement • Volume discounts • Frequency discounts	• Agate lines • Column inch

Magazine	Consumer General business Trade Form	$$CPP = \frac{\text{Cost per page} \times 10{,}000}{\text{Circulation}}$$	• Number of readers • Number of colors in advertisement • Position of advertisement • Type of audience • Size of advertisement • Volume discounts • Frequency discounts	• Page • Part of page
Transit	Buses Subway Taxicabs	Cost per thousand exposures on riders	• Number • Position • Frequency discounts	• Size of advertisement
Outdoor	Posters Painted displays Signs		• Length of time • Cost of production • Frequency of audience counts • Volume discounts • Frequency discounts	

Radio

Radio is useful for advertisers who encounter wasted exposure in television, or who do not need the video part of television to sell their product. Radio is particularly good when the point of efficiency is reached in the television budget, as it can be used to reach new homes more efficiently. Radio is also good in obtaining wide exposure during commuting hours and reinforcing print or television advertisements in a cost-effective way. Radio advertisements are especially effective when a catchy jingle or slogan can be developed.

Outdoor

Outdoor advertising is a very effective method in which advertising maintains the association between the product, package, and brand name. Familiarity advertising is a good follow-up advertisement after the major advertising has been accomplished through other media. The problem is, of course, the limited time period available to read the copy of an outdoor advertisement. Sometimes, the available time is hundredths of a second compared to the 30-second average for a television and radio advertisement or two to four minutes for a one-page magazine advertisement.

Media Buying

In buying media, there are three general theories that can be used: frequency, pressure, and dispersion. When using frequency, you want the maximum number of impressions per 1,000 homes, with an impression being a copy message that a viewer or listener is exposed to. Usually, when a commercial appears two or three times on the same hour television show, the advertiser is employing the frequency theory.

When using the pressure theory, you are not concerned whether your advertisement is in the same or different homes as long as you are achieving maximum efficiency. To determine this, you plot the cost-per-commercial-minute per thousand listeners of the advertisement against a norm or average of the three lowest cost-per-commercial-minute advertisers on the same type of show such as a family show, children's show, or adult comedy show.

When using dispersion theory, you want the maximum number of different unduplicated homes to be reached in an interval of time. Obtaining maximum exposure using the dispersion theory requires different techniques for television and radio than for the print media. To increase dispersion on television or radio, you should first purchase another commercial on a second show as different from the first show as possible, rather than a second commercial on the same show. Also, as many different stations as possible reaching the same market should be used. Since there is often high station loyalty, each station—even those with low ratings—can generate an exclusive audience. Finally, instead of buying commercial time at the same time each day (if advertisements appear more than once a week), you should buy commercial time (using peak listening times as much as possible) at different times of the day.

In applying the dispersion theory to print media, every dollar possible for reaching new homes should be spent before a dollar is used for reaching the same home twice. A subscriber profile is needed on the magazine—the age of the family members and their socioeconomic groups.

You can also use dispersion theory to reach very specialized markets effectively. For example, in the case of electronic engineers, there are over 15 engineering magazines possible. Using dispersion theory, you should place an advertisement in each magazine relative to the proportion of the size of the circulation with the largest circulation getting the largest allocation.

MESSAGE

There are many principles you should follow in developing advertising copy. The most important of these can be combined into the unique selling proposition. Even for well-financed companies that have a strong market share, using the unique selling proposition can significantly increase sales. For example, Viceroy cigarettes was an unknown brand until the USP campaign generated $200 million in sales, making Viceroy the first successful filter cigarette. Similarly, Tums dominated the antacid market until the principles of USP gave Rolaids the dominant market share position. Principles of USP were used in developing a commercial for M&M Candies which did not change for years.

The USP concept offers the public something desirable and different from that offered by competitors. To qualify as a USP, the offering needs to be unique in being the sole source of the promised benefit. The offering should have to "sell" to the extent that consumers will desire the product and should present a benefit based on a specified reason, with this reason being so dramatically presented that consumers believe that the benefit will be obtained upon product purchase. There are three general principles behind USP—*u*nique, *s*elling, and *p*roposition.

Uniqueness

Optimally, a product should achieve uniqueness by being the sole provider of a benefit not offered by the competition. If the product itself is not unique, then the package, message, or perhaps the informed benefits need to be unique. There are two categories of uniqueness, either a checkable (ascertainable) benefit or an uncheckable one. Whether the uniqueness is checkable or uncheckable depends on whether the consumer can check the product's claims for the promised benefit. You can build checkable qualities into the product to ensure uniqueness by making the product different from competition in terms of ingredients, processing, packaging, odor, taste, performance, convenience, economy, speed, or effect. An example of a product with a unique checkable benefit is Woolite. Its USP, "Washes Sweaters Clean in Cold Water in Just Four Minutes," can be checked immediately by the consumer upon washing a sweater. You can also develop a unique benefit claim that is not checkable. This type of uniqueness is developed by claiming something about the product or its benefits that has not been claimed through any real advertising expenditure by competition. An example of an uncheckable USP was Wonder Bread's "Helps Grow Healthier Bodies." Consumers could not possibly check this benefit. Lower advertising expenditures are required to establish checkable USPs than uncheckable ones. While it is indeed more effective to maintain and defend a good USP than to switch to a new one, whenever a competitor is increasing their sales volume at a faster rate than the originator of the USP, the originator should discontinue its use of the USP and develop a new one.

There are other ways to obtain the uniqueness portion of the USP. One way is to combine the brand name with the product package, as in the case of "Black Magic," a chocolate candy originally sold in England. The product is packaged in a solid black box with an advertising message conveying that a certain type of magic starts when a box is given to a member of the opposite sex. Another way is adding or deleting an ingredient that removes the product from the general commodity category. For example, Crest toothpaste added fluoride, thereby removing Crest from the commodity toothpaste category. Crest became the market leader in the toothpaste market and still retains a strong market position in spite of fluoride being added to many competitive toothpastes.

Selling

To qualify as a unique selling proposition, an attribute should be presented so persuasively that it helps the consumer decide on purchasing—the selling aspect of the USP. The copy or message delivering this selling aspect should be aimed at the basic needs of the consumer. A good copy story is rarely derived from what consumers say they desire in a product but is rather based on deeper motivations. Many good copy stories aim at solving basic concerns of the consumer that often stem from threatened or implied frustration as well as learned and unlearned needs. Learned needs are such things as appearance, weight, and social prestige. Unlearned needs are basic physiological needs such as health, shelter, hunger, and thirst.

Whenever possible the copy should try to simultaneously appeal to several needs without indicating any need hierarchy. Wherever possible, the basic need selected should be specific rather than general as solutions to specific needs provide more effective advertising copy than do solutions to more general ones. For example, a solution to the problem of decaying teeth would be much more effective than one aimed at "general well-being." Once a basic need has been determined to be the basis of the unique selling proposition, it should be used in all markets unless there are different reasons for buying the product.

In order to use basic needs in USP copy, it is necessary to identify the needs that can be uniquely fulfilled by the particular product. For example Carter's Little Liver Pills identified and filled a need using the theme "Break the Laxative Habit." Prior to the use of this advertisement few consumers could articulate a need for their product purchase—the purchase of Liver Pills.

Proposition

To satisfy the proposition part of the USP, the message should clearly indicate that the promised benefit will be obtained upon product purchase. In order to accomplish this, the USP needs to be believable and credible. To ensure credibility, the USP needs to specifically emphasize the source that provides that benefit. Credibility is the most important aspect of the USP, without which there cannot be a unique selling proposition. Credibility in a USP derives from the specific source that is believable and that provides the benefit.

Since people generally tend to believe and to retain information that they see more than information that they only hear, the USP needs to lend itself to demonstration as much as possible.

Demonstration is so important that it may be necessary to accept a USP with a lesser impact in order to achieve the increased believability derived from demonstration.

Even though illustration and demonstration are the most widely used auxiliary aids for obtaining credibility, these do not always lend themselves to the situation. Another aid often employed is prestige through association of a product with either a person or an institution. In case of a person, he or she should be considered an acknowledged authority on the subject and not just a sports figure or celebrity. Another auxiliary aid for establishing credibility is testimony by ordinary individuals who describe the good qualities of the product.

Developing and Using USPs

Learning theory indicates that the more separate the ideas consumers are asked to recall, the less they can recall any of them. Since the dollars available for advertising are limited, it is better to concentrate the dollar impact on one rather than several ideas.

Once established, a USP should not be dropped quickly. Substituting one USP for another can result in the loss of the impact of previous dollars spent on the old USP, and can in some cases actually cause confusion on the part of some consumers. USPs should only be dropped when: (1) the USP has been adopted by competition and thoroughly identified with their products as well; (2) several competitors have taken advantage of a USP by product imitation and have increased their sales volume at a faster rate than the original advertiser; (3) a shifting of consumer needs has eliminated the impact of the present USP; (4) a superior USP is devised and tested; or (5) the current USP is not adaptable to the advertising media selected.

Few good commercials come about solely by inspiration. Most are a result of significant research, testing, and modification. This process frequently starts with interviewing consumers in depth to identify any hidden needs. Often 40 to 50 possible storyboards (the blueprints or plans of commercials developed by the copywriter) are developed into four to six commercials and tested. Then the good parts of one commercial are combined with the good parts of another, retested with the composite commercial being used in sales test territories. For example, for a one-minute television commercial, a storyboard usually consists of 16 artists' drawings to portray photography needed for each frame, which is accompanied by the words to be spoken in that frame. Since most consumers cannot follow the sequence of artists' drawings in a typical storyboard, an animation made from the storyboard is usually better for testing the commercial. An animation is a series of 16 to 32 colored still frames on a strip of film which can be projected with a slide projector with the words recorded and synchronized with the showing of the still slides.

Copy for Radio

The copy for radio should not only be related to the unique selling proposition but should also perform the most difficult task of obtaining the listener's attention. There are generally three different attention-getting devices: voice (call for Philip Morris or the Tarzan yell); sound effects (razor scraping over sand paper, sirens, or airplanes taking-off); and jingles (McDonald's hamburger). Generally, more impact occurs when the unique selling proposition is mentioned several times in the commercial, such as at the beginning, in the middle, and at the end.

Copy for Print Media

Application of the unique selling proposition to print copy has been done effectively in print advertisements using the "split screen," or the "Xout" technique. In these cases, the benefit and the reason are presented side by side along with something generally representing competition with an X drawn through it for consumers' acceptance.

Besides the split screen, there are two other effective methods: the before and after and the involvement. The before and after technique is effective in a campaign such as: before I started Weight Watchers and after I completed just three weeks. Since about five times as many people read the headline as read the copy, the headline is the most important part of the advertisement and needs to promise a benefit to the reader. Whenever possible, the brand name should be in the heading just in case the rest of the advertisement is not read.

The copy of the advertisement should begin with something interesting enough to get the reader to continue reading. It should be direct and give facts about the product without using superlatives, generalizations, or platitudes. Testimonials and helpful advice should be included whenever possible.

Finally, the illustration is important in clearly indicating the nature of the product. While photographs are much more vivid and effective than drawings, any good illustration can arouse the reader's curiosity, as is the case in the advertisement indicated in Figure 18-1 (see page 272).

Thursday, 6:05 pm

Friday, 9:10 am

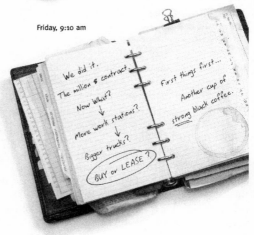

FIG. 18-1. *Example of industrial service advertisement.*

Source: *U.S. News and World Report*, October 4, 1999, p. 6a.

THE ADVERTISING AGENCY

There are three basic types of advertising agencies: full service, specialty service, and in-house.

Full-Service Agency

A full-service advertising agency provides a client with services in copy, media, promotion advice, research, consumer packaging design, public relations, and publicity. The agency usually obtains a 15 percent rebate from all media purchases made on behalf of the client. For large accounts, this 15 percent is the total fee with no extra charges for other services performed, except for public relations and publicity. These are provided on a dollar fee basis since there are no billings involved.

Specialty Service Agency

A specialty service agency is one that makes no attempt to provide all the services of a full-service agency, but specializes in only one or two. There are many agencies that provide services on only copy, media, or research. There also are wholesale media brokers who provide a more efficient method of buying time in television and radio by using representatives in the network cities that have at least one of the three major networks (CBS, NBC, and ABC). The more companies that use these network brokers in the future, the more full-service agencies will become specialty service agencies.

In-House Agencies

An advertising agency that is a part of a particular firm is an in-house agency. Such an agency may perform all or some advertising services. Even firms with an in-house agency may still use outside agencies for certain products or services.

SELECTING THE ADVERTISING AGENCY

Selecting the agency or agencies is a very difficult task. Unfortunately, a company is often selected by the agency rather than the company selecting the agency.

The following procedure should be implemented to properly select an advertising agency: (1) determine the major services needing to be provided by an agency; (2) review current advertising agencies for good performance in the services needed; (3) meet the individuals at the agencies responsible for this work; (4) select two or three agencies to present their ideas about your advertising campaign with the understanding that if selected the individual identified would be assigned to your account; and (5) select the agency making the most cost-effective creative presentation.

LOCAL ADVERTISING

Similar principles apply to local as well as national advertising. The unique selling proposition philosophy can be successfully employed in all advertising—radio, TV, and print—regardless of the size of the budget. A one-minute spot on a local radio show should be developed and evaluated in the same manner that a national spot on a network would be developed. This is also true for local versus national television advertising or the local weekly newspaper advertisement versus a larger daily newspaper ad.

A dispersion media philosophy can also be applied in local advertising in a smaller community. Take for example, a midwestern city with a population of 30,000, without a television station, but with access to television spots in a city 35 miles away. In this city, television, because of its high cost, is not possible for most single establishment businesses. However, possible media include: two daily newspapers, one local radio station, a shoppers' guide, and the yellow pages in the telephone directory. To get the most effective dispersion, any combination of or all four of these media can be used. If advertising dollars were allocated to each in proportion to the circulation or listenership, the number of media needed for the appropriate penetration could be determined.

CHAPTER PERSPECTIVE

In this chapter you have learned how to develop an advertising plan as a part of your promotion mix. Your plan should include a budget established to provide the amount of advertising your product needs. You will need to choose among several available media while considering costs and characteristics of each. In developing your message, you can obtain the best results by creating a unique selling proposition. The advertising can be done in-house or by selecting an advertising agency to implement your strategy.

Personal Selling and Sales Management

INTRODUCTION AND MAIN POINTS

Salespeople are one of the most important aspects of a company. Regardless of the level of advertising, sales promotion, or publicity, the personal selling aspect of the promotion mix is often needed for the sale to be made. In this chapter we will describe all the aspects of personal selling as well as managing the sales force. We will demonstrate that regardless of whether a firm employs 10 or 800 salespeople, one of the keys to success for any sales organization is the quality of the selection, training, and management of its salespeople.

After studying the material in this chapter:

■ You will understand what it takes to make a successful sales call.

■ You will be able to present the proper motivations to a prospect.

■ You will know how to handle objections raised.

■ You will understand the general principles of sales management and the basis for selecting, training, motivating, and managing a sales force.

SELECTION OF SALESPEOPLE

Regardless of the size of the firm, there are two important aspects of proper salespeople selection. First, an appropriate job description of the sales job needs to be developed. Secondly, a plan for comprehensive recruiting should be formulated to achieve the best results possible. The other aspects of the selection procedure—employee specifications, preliminary interview, personal history, principal interview, work reference investigation, and aptitude and ability tests—may vary somewhat, depending on whether the sales force is large (50 or more) or small. If you are in a company with 50 or more salespeople, you should identify the best and worst salespeople from the company's present force and examine their characteristics and background. Based on this profile, you can then establish the best sources of good salespeople and develop a procedure for their recruitment. This procedure is difficult to implement for companies with a small sales force since there are not enough salespeople available to create a baseline for what constitutes a good and bad salesperson. A smaller company can use a standard salesperson selection approach and form such as the ones produced by the Dartnell Corporation or Stevens, Thurow and Associates, Inc.

Salesperson Qualities

Selling positions differ greatly in terms of technical product knowledge a salesperson must have. For example, there is a significant difference between a salesperson selling ethical drugs, calling on M.D.s and pharmacists, and a beer salesperson calling on restaurants and bars. Little technical product knowledge or education is needed to sell beer. This large variation makes it difficult to identify some common sales qualities. There are, however, several qualities that are essential in a successful salesperson regardless of the position. A successful salesperson is: persuasive; more intuitive than analytical; outgoing; motivated by prestige and power; in possession of a high energy level; dominant but not domineering; empathetic (has the ability to put one's self in the other person's shoes); and driven by a high ego. Of these, if there is any common thread in selling, it is probably a balance between empathy and ego. In interviewing or hiring salespeople, it is important for you to attempt to evaluate the person in terms of the existence and balance of these two traits in particular. This can be accomplished by having the candidates describe their actions in previous experiences or elicit their response to the presence of the two traits.

TRAINING SALESPEOPLE

Salespeople generally need training on company procedures and policies, the company's products, and human relations. Most salespeople, even those with years of successful selling experience, can be more effective through formal training in selling principles. This training should occur within the first three months of employment. Salespeople who have been selling the longest and are the most successful are generally the ones who appreciate the sales training the most. Even though a good sales course may introduce little that experienced salespeople have not used before, such a course can introduce a system and provide understanding that will enable each individual to be even more effective and knowledgeable about the company and its products and policies.

While the sales training program reflects the particular company's products and markets and should be modified to meet the needs of individuals involved, there are certain basic activities needed in any good training program:

1. Establishing the basis for making the sales with proper customer rapport
   a. the disposition agent
   b. the common-interest agent
   c. the complimentary agent
   d. the personal-favor agent
2. Planning and making the sales presentation using proper sequence of reasons and motives
3. Handling a sales objection or obstacle
   a. listening to the buyer
   b. returning to the reasoning level
      (1) questions that require no answers
      (2) assurance statements
      (3) time
   c. beginning proper sequence of reasons and motives
      (1) price
      (2) financing
      (3) poor quality product
      (4) lack of confidence
      (5) time

Establishing Customer Rapport

One very important part of the sales job is establishing good customer relations. This will help the customer give attention and consideration to what is being proposed. Good relationships can be established through the use of certain emotional agents.

Everything a salesperson says and does that emotionally affects and influences the listener is an emotional agent. Emotional agents can also influence feelings, causing the buyer to be more favorably disposed and willing to listen, which can result in a more favorable reaction to the sales proposal. There are four major emotional agents: the disposition agent, the common-interest agent, the complimentary agent, and the personal-favor agent. These sales agents are most effective when there is no immediate sale being sought.

When a salesperson's physical bearing, facial expressions, and tone of voice impact people to feel more favorably inclined, the *disposition* agent is being used. To use this agent effectively, you must do three things. First, you must analyze your good characteristics. Second, you must determine the disposition that the person responds to best. Finally, you must plan the use of this sales disposition agent accordingly. Using the disposition agent can be particularly difficult when the buyer is personally disagreeable and appears to have few positive qualities. However, a sale is more likely to be consummated if a positive attitude is maintained even with a negative buyer.

It is also important for the salesperson to determine the disposition agent that will achieve the best buyer response. For example, customers who are generally serious and businesslike usually react more favorably to a salesperson's disposition that is straightforward and businesslike.

In using this disposition agent, a salesperson should recognize their two-sided personality—a good side (one that people like and respond to) and a bad side (one that antagonizes people and loses friends). A salesperson can learn to exhibit their better side through a more conscious use of the disposition agent.

When a salesperson and a customer discuss a mutual interest and liking of something and this draws the two closer together, the *common-interest* agent is occurring. A salesperson can build harmonious relationships with customers by maintaining and discussing common interests. This requires that you get to know each customer's background, sports interest, hobbies, or activities which are in any way similar to your own. Once these points of common interest are known, they can be used in day-to-day contacts with each customer. When two people discover that they are from the same city, are ex-baseball players, or have the same hobby, they are drawn together through the common interest they share. If this common interest is maintained, a basis is developed for eliciting a favorable response on a proposal being made.

The *complimentary* agent is using words or expressions that affirm and show approval for a job well done while instilling a feeling of self-satisfaction. Four factors are important in effectively using this agent. First, as with all emotional issues, you must be sincere and honest in using the complimentary agent. If an individual is praised, and the salesperson is insincere or the praise is not deserved, the recipient will resent the insincere comment and mistrust will start to develop. Second, in order to use the complimentary agent effectively, you need to be continually looking for extra effort or unusual performance by the other individual. Third, you should always give credit where credit is due.

A deserving individual should be praised as strongly as the occasion merits. Finally, you should pay the compliment while the occasion is recent. On-the-spot compliments are much more effective than delayed ones.

When a salesperson goes out of the way to do a personal favor, or offer to do one, the *personal-favor* agent is being employed. There are of course a number of ways a salesperson can do favors for customers. You should remember that using this agent as well as the other three will not bring about a sale by themselves—a good proposal is needed.

Using the Proper Sequence

In order to obtain a good sequence for a sales presentation, it is helpful to follow a more standard format, such as the one indicated in Table 19-1. First, you should analyze the good and bad characteristics of the prospect. What are the customer's good qualities? What type of mood and manner will be used—jovial, serious, businesslike? Next, you should introduce the sales presentations in an objective manner that does not overwhelm the customer. If there are any unique qualities of the product that produce unique benefits which competitors cannot produce, these should be stressed.

It is beneficial to use auxiliary aids such as story, illustration, testimony, or prestige. Story is relating an experience of a mutual acquaintance of the customer and salesperson in order to prove a point. An illustration can be a drawing or a diagram, showing a picture, or actually demonstrating the product itself. A Heinz salesperson once demonstrated the "less water" quality of Heinz ketchup by pouring the ketchup on a paper towel along with competing ketchups, demonstrating that there was more water absorbed from the other ketchups. Testimony is usually describing the good experience of several customers, whose testimony, in total, helps finalize the sale.

Prestige is using a prestigious institution or person who is an expert on the subject. For example, Crest Toothpaste used the American Dental Association. Usually a movie star or sports figure is not enough, as the individual needs to be a recognized expert in the product area.

In the actual sales presentation, a salesperson should determine the appropriate mood and manner and proceed through the sales format. Take for example the sales presentation of a new type of wood golf club just developed. Most golf club heads on the market have steel shafts with weighting in the toe, heel, and soleplate of the club. The numbers at the top of Table 19-2 indi-

Table 19-1
Sales Closing Form

Client _____

Product(s) _____

Analyze Person		Decide on mood to be used	Introduce subject	Benefits	Right way or sources of benefits; characteristics of product or service	Auxilliary aids: 1. Story 2. Illustration 3. Testimony 4. Prestige
Characteristics						
Bad	*Good*					
1	*2*	*3*	*4*	*6*	*5*	*7*

Table 19-2
Sales Presentation Sequence

CLIENT: Bill, a golfer in golf shop
PRODUCT: Golf club with weighting behind sweet spot

Thinking Sequence: 4, 5, 2, 1, 3
Speaking Sequence: 1, 2, 3, 4, 5 and either 2, 1 or 1, 2

1 Benefits or Portrayal of Desired Brand Image to User	2 Source of Benefits: Right Way or Product Qualities	3 Auxiliary Aids: Prestige Illus., & Demonstration, Testimony	4 Wrong Way or Poor Qualities of Competitor's Product	5 Losses from Use of Competitor's Product or Lack of Use of Your Product.
Increase the distance of drives and all wood shots. Fewer slices and hooks. Begin immediately to bring down that handicap.	Buy Acradista woods; they put all possible weight behind sweet spot. $2\frac{1}{2}$ oz. extra lead directly behind the point of impact. Weighting behind sweet spot decreases torque. So give me a check for $125 for one of these new Acradista drivers now and get the other three woods later.	Ten members of a university golf team hit five balls with an Acradista driver and five with a driver twice as expensive. Acradista-hit balls averaged 28 yards greater distance with greater accuracy.	Buy a club with heel, toe, and plate weighting. Continue with present improperly weighted clubs.	Others' products do not deliver the goods on drives and other woods. Shots are just not as long. You will need to learn to live with your slice because you are going to continue to have it.

cate both the thinking and speaking sequences in the sales presentation. One should avoid the natural tendency to start thinking about the poor qualities of competitive products. Note how the thinking sequence, which is the proper sequence for filling out the form, differs from the speaking sequence used in the actual sales presentation (see Table 19-2). The actual sales presentation presented to a golf pro in a golf shop might take the following format.

"Bill, you could increase the distance of your drives, as well as the distances of all your wood shots, if you would invest in a new set of Acradista woods. The company has put all weight possible behind the sweet spot. Two and one-half ounces of extra lead is placed directly behind the point of impact. Recently ten players on a university golf team each hit five balls with a leading $140 graphite-shafted driver and five balls with an Acradista driver. Acradista averaged 28 yards farther, and 20 percent more shots stayed in the fairway. If you buy any other brand of club, you will get weighting in the heel, toe, and plate of the club, which will not give you the long shots. You will also have fewer slices and hooks with the weighting behind the sweet spot because this decreases torque. With the weight in the heel and toe, there is more tendency for the club to twist as you come through with your swing like this (swing pro demonstrated at this point). If you decide to stay with your present clubs, you will need to learn to compensate for them. You will need to learn to compensate for your slice because you are going to continue to have it. Why don't you give me a check for $125 for a new Acradista driver? You can pick up the other three fairway woods later. This way you can begin to start bringing down that handicap of yours right now."

In this presentation, the salesperson's first auxiliary aid was testimony and the second was illustration and demonstration. When the salesperson indicated both the right way and the wrong way, the customer had the opportunity to weigh both and choose between them. In a difficult selling area, it is usually better to present both sides.

In order to successfully employ this system of sales presentation, a form similar to the one just used should be developed. However, the actual sales presentation should be made from memory. After significant usage you will be able to fill out the forms mentally and make the presentation without even writing down the sales presentation facts.

Table 19-3

Steps and Points in Handling Sales Objections

Steps	Key Points
1. Listen to their story.	A. Stay calm and cool. B. Put them at ease. C. Give them all the time they need. D. Show them that you are interested in their story.
2. Calm them and utilize time to think.	A. Use questions that require no answers. B. Assure them you see their viewpoint. C. Speak slowly.
3. Do something about overcoming the obstacle.	A. If necessary, starting with benefits, question them to get more facts. B. Starting with benefits, continue with sequence you had planned for sales presentation.

Handling Objections

It is an important part of every salesperson's job to handle objections raised by the consumer. When potential customers believe they are right and the salesperson is wrong, obstacles that may not allow the sale to be made occur. Complaints and objections are a normal part of human behavior and likely to be made by every potential customer. Four of the most frequently encountered objections are price, financing, time, and lack of confidence.

People may resist buying when they feel the price is either higher than it should be or is higher than a competitor's price. Also, people resist buying something when they are uncertain about the operation or maintenance of the product being sold.

When people raise objections, they are often somewhat emotional. Before they can react calmly and clearly, the salesperson needs to return the customer's emotions to normal. This can be accomplished by following the steps indicated in Table 19-3.

Assurance statements are important in successfully handling objections and closing the sale. Some good assurance statements include: (1) "I understand your viewpoint"; (2) "That is a natural way to look at things"; (3) "No doubt you have good reason for feeling that way"; (4) "I understand what you mean"; (5) "I can see why at first glance"; (6) "That is an important point"; (7) "You may have a point there."

When using these, it is very important that you watch tonal inflections. If you are not extremely careful, these statements can sound like a challenge to the authenticity of the customers' statements. None of the assurance statements indicates to the customer that they are right about the objections raised. These statements only assure the customer that you understand their viewpoint. You never want to totally agree with a customer's objection but rather demonstrate empathy, a tactic illustrated in the following scenario:

> *Prospect to salesperson:* "Your price on this dust collector is about five hundred dollars higher than that of the XYZ Company. I can't afford to throw the company's money away like that."
>
> *Salesperson:* "It is? I am sorry to hear that, but I can understand why you would want to save the company money and that is exactly what I thought I was helping you do in presenting this model. You see, studies that have run for large users of dust-collecting equipment, testing ours and the XYZ Company's model, indicate that our model operates at a cost of fifty dollars per month less than theirs. This gives you six hundred dollars back in a year and you continue getting the fifty-dollars-a-month-savings for the balance of the life of the collector, which should be at least ten years."

In this example, the salesperson used both a question that required no answer and an assurance statement. When the salesperson felt the customer could again be reasoned with logically, a strong and strategic benefit was presented.

The following example involved the time obstacle and a salesperson entering a customer's office after the customer had just had an argument with another executive in the company:

> *Prospect:* "Oh you're back again. I told you I was going to need at least six months to decide this issue. You might think I have nothing to do except hold your hand."
>
> *Salesperson:* "No, I fully appreciate that you are a very busy person indeed, much too busy to have anyone waste even one minute of your time. And I do not intend to do that, but I just thought you would like to get in on some of the tremendous savings that will be made possible by the installation of this inventory control system, particularly at

a time of the year when your inventories are going to be at their highest levels. You see, if we wait three months, you are going to miss out on substantial savings."

In this example, the salesperson used only the assurance statement in the presentation and then continued with the sales presentation, by presenting both the right way and wrong way (delay until after large inventory build-up).

SALES MANAGEMENT

One of the questions faced by a young company developing its first sales force is how much of the distribution job should be done by the company itself. While in large firms with multiple product lines and their own sales force, each product line can bear its share of the costs involved. In a small company with limited resources where it is necessary to keep selling expense a variable rather than a fixed cost, manufacturers' representatives are often used. When internal salespeople are hired on a salary or a salary with a draw, a certain fixed expense that cannot be avoided is incurred. Even though there are no fixed costs, it is not always advantageous to hire salespeople on a straight commission basis. Also, there are some products with such low sales volumes that it is not ever cost effective to use internal salespeople. A broker or manufacturers' representative with 10 to 15 other noncompeting lines can more effectively handle the product.

The consumption of the product also affects the type of selling organization employed, as is illustrated in the following figures of three food companies. Two of the food companies produced products in the high-consumption area (Companies A and B) and one company produced products in the low-consumption area (Company C).

	Company A	Company B	Company C
Costs of goods sold . . .	70%	70%	40%
Profit (except factory overhead)	16%	16%	16%
Sales personnel	2%	14%	22%
Advertising	12%	0%	22%

Company A uses only wholesale salespeople and keeps the rest of its promotion expenditures in advertising. Company A was servicing 18,000 customers throughout the United States with 50 people in its sales force calling only at the wholesale level.

Company B decided to have wholesale salespeople and a somewhat limited retail sales force, putting little, if any money in advertising. Both companies A and B were high-consumption product companies.

Company C, with mostly low-consumption food products, could not only have 22 percent of the net-sales-dollar allocated in the retail sales force but 22 percent in its advertising budget as well. It is usually possible for a low-consumption product company to have a higher percent profit to sales ratio because of reduced overhead expenditures. If a high-consumption product company wants to achieve a high return on its invested capital, then the company must have a high sales volume per item.

Which sales system is better—the one used by company A or company B? Both can be successful in spite of the entirely different approaches used. The approach utilized often depends largely on the direction and strength of management skills in the company. Usually, a company with good advertising can achieve success faster than a company using comparably good skills and money in managing sales personnel.

When a company has its own sales force, it is imperative that good sales management exists. Not only is the selling process very costly, but it also requires a large amount of managerial guidance and coordination. The costs and guidance needed depend on the type of salesperson. Generally there are five categories of salespeople: detail salespeople (missionary representatives of a company); service salespeople (who sell such intangibles as advertising and insurance); industrial salespeople (who sell products to industrial or commercial purchasers); account representatives (who sell to a large number of established accounts); and sales engineers (who sell products requiring a high level of technical know-how).

The job of managing the sales force requires more than learning and following the steps in the selling process. That is why a highly successful salesperson often does not make a good sales manager. The core of the sales manager's job is to plan, staff, organize, control, and direct the sales efforts of the individual salespeople and to build these individual salespeople into a team that achieves sales objectives that are linked to the overall marketing strategy of the firm and particularly to the promotion strategy.

STRUCTURING THE SALES TERRITORIES

Establishing the structure of the sales force is another key responsibility of the sales manager. Ideally, the sales effort needed in each territory is about equal. When sales grow large enough, you can approach this situation by first obtaining information on the population by country and the per capita consumption. Using these figures, consumer potential should be determined by county. Second, sales territories should be developed using the data from step one with the understanding that these territories will eventually have roads as boundaries. The efforts needed in each territory should be such that a salesperson can cover each account and potential account on a regular basis through an organized route.

Third, a salesperson should be hired, trained, and then trained in the field. The careful selection and training of a sales force is probably the most important job of the sales manager. Care in this makes the rest of the job much easier.

Finally, any differences between the types of customers in territories should be evaluated in order to balance territories more accurately on the basis of the sales effort needed. For instance, a product selling to grocery stores in some territories may be sold 98 percent through chain groceries where one sale achieves distribution in 30 to 200 stores. In another territory, the same product may be sold through several supermarkets where one sale achieves distribution in only one or two stores. The selling effort needed in this second territory to achieve the same level of sales is much greater.

Sometimes a different sales structure is used, such as structuring by products, structuring by customers, and multiple sales force structuring. These sales structures allow more focus on products or customers depending on the need of the company.

In developing the territories and balancing the sales effort needed, you should follow one of the following two principles:

1. Call on every customer in the territory, regardless of size, the same number of times a year. In other words, follow a route until the route is covered (perhaps in six weeks) and then repeat the route.

2. Call on the customers in relation to the volume or potential volume of each customer. The larger-volume customer will get called upon more frequently than the smaller-volume customers.

Principle number 2 is more frequently employed as it allows more time to be spent with larger accounts. Procter and Gamble, for example, has its sales force call on the small "Mom and Pop" food stores every eight weeks, the large food stores every four weeks, and the very large food stores every two weeks.

Compensation

The various types of sales remuneration can be broadly categorized into: (1) salary, (2) salary and commission, and (3) straight commission. If the company is distributing a perishable product, one with a short shelf life, or one with a significant amount of existing recognition and advertising support, it is usually better to have a straight salary system. The company does not want any customer to have any excess merchandise that cannot be sold before it reaches an unsaleable condition.

Whether a straight commission should be used with nonperishable products depends to a large degree on the accuracy of the forecasts of the sales and sales potential and the amount of support marketing efforts. A good commission system uses this potential in determining the commission. If the potentials are not reasonably accurate between territories, then poor morale results from a straight commission remuneration system. Probably the biggest overall benefit of straight commission is that it turns selling costs into direct costs with no overhead. Also, it provides maximum incentive for extra effort.

The salary plus commission arrangement provides a compromise between straight salary and straight commission. While a salary plus commission remuneration system does not solve the problem of inaccurate sales potentials and the resulting bad morale, it does reduce the severity of the problem.

The Salesperson's Car

One of the biggest expenses in selling, and therefore one of the biggest concerns, particularly for the small firm, is the salesperson's car. Basically three options exist: (1) buying a car for each salesperson; (2) having each salesperson furnish his or her own car and remunerate on a cents-per-mile basis; or (3) using a service that provides the appropriate reimbursements. For a small firm with limited resources, option 2 is usually the most cost-effective alternative.

Supervisory Relationships and Job Duties

A sales manager should make sure salespeople call on all possible customers in their territory. Salespeople should immediately add the name of a new customer to their route in order of priority. At the wholesale level, it is better for a sales manager to supervise no more than eight salespeople, spending time with the salespeople making calls. The sales manager should always have an up-to-date route list so that a salesperson can be easily located.

When an entirely new advertising program is to be implemented, training should be accompanied by a refresher course on general selling principles. During the sales meeting, some salespeople should role-play making sales presentations to the group.

An efficient customer service department in the home office should be established and be responsible for the liaison between the customers and salespeople handling any problems that occur. The same department should also handle all liaisons between the sales manager and customers, minimizing the amount of time needed in the home office.

CHAPTER PERSPECTIVE

In this chapter we have learned how to recruit and select a sales force. This involves developing ideal personnel profiles for a larger sales force and using published techniques or those developed by consulting firms for a smaller sales force. The importance of training was discussed. This training should review topics ranging from customer rapport to sales presentation techniques. Finally, you learned the fundamentals of sales management, particularly the aspects of organizing sales territories, determining compensation, authorizing travel reimbursements, supervising sales-customer relationships, and evaluating the job being done.

Index